International
Bartender's
Guide

International Bartender's Guide

BALLANTINE BOOKS • NEW YORK

Copyright © 1996, 1984 by Random House, Inc.

All rights reserved under International and Pan-American Copyright Conventions. No part of this publication may be reproduced in any form or by any means electronic or mechanical, including photocopying, without permission in writing from the publisher. All inquiries should be addressed to Reference & Information Publishing, Random House, Inc., 201 East 50th Street, New York, NY 10022-7703. Published in the United States by Ballantine Books, a division of Random House, Inc., New York and simultaneously in Canada by Random House of Canada, Limited. This is a revised and completely retypeset edition of *The New International Bartender's Guide* originally published in 1984 by Random House, Inc.

Library of Congress Catalog Card Number: 96-96995

ISBN 0-345-40544-7

http://www.randomhouse.com

This edition published by arrangement with Reference & Information Publishing, Random House, Inc.

First Ballantine Books Edition: November 1996

OPM   17   16   15   14   13   12   11   10   9   8

CONTENTS

Page

EQUIPMENT
AND MIXING

BASIC EQUIPMENT

There are numerous items on the market that fall into the category of bar equipment. Some are functional, and some are simply attractive gadgets. Listed below is the *basic* equipment that should be a part of the home bar. Following the basic list are other *desirable* items that would make attractive and often useful additions but are not essential. A manual or electric ice crusher is certainly a handy gadget, but ice can usually be crushed satisfactorily by wrapping cubes or chunks in a sturdy bowl and hitting them with a mallet or hammer.

- bottle and can opener (including beer-can opener)
- corkscrew
- double-ended measure with half and quarter ounces clearly marked; a jigger (1½–2 oz) on one end, a pony (1 oz) on the other
- measuring cup and set of spoons
- Long-handled bar spoon (10 inches); some have a muddler on the end of the handle (see *muddling*, p. 12)
- juice squeezer
- cutting board and sharp paring knife
- ice bucket and tongs
- 2-piece mixing glass and shaker set; glass and metal
- strainer, preferably coil-rimmed
- bottle sealers and a champagne stopper
- cocktail napkins and coasters
- swizzle sticks, straws (including short straws for sipping frappés), and cocktail picks

1

- towels
- glassware (see p. 4)

DESIRABLE EQUIPMENT

- ice crusher (manual or electric)
- electric blender (a must for any *frozen* drink)
- wooden muddler
- ice chipper or pick
- twist cutter or vegetable peeler for fruit peels
- funnel
- ice scoop
- nutmeg grater
- bowls of sugar and salt (for coating rim of glasses)

STOCKING THE BAR

Below is a list of liquors, mixes, etc., the average host will need to make the drinks that are most often requested (Martini, Manhattan, Bloody Mary, etc.). Tastes are variable, and you must know your crowd. Some parties could get by with nothing more than gin, whisky, vermouth, and soda; a younger group might never need a whisky or other dark liquor but would require various fruit juices and flavored liqueurs for exotic concoctions such as the Sex on the Beach. Bear in mind that no bartender can anticipate every request, and that even the most professional bar may be unable to meet every demand (a specific brand of whiskey or gin, an exotic liqueur, etc.). So be content with the basic provisions, perhaps adding to them from time to time, and meanwhile learning to combine these basics with as much skill, precision, and ingenuity as befits an experienced host.

BASIC LIQUORS
WINES, ETC.

The number of bottles to be stocked will of course depend on the number of guests expected, their anticipated requirements, and the amount of time to be devoted to drinking (a drink or two before dinner, a three-hour cocktail party, etc.). A section follows on *Bottle Sizes and Contents* to help you estimate your requirements. In general, the well-stocked bar should have at least the following:

- gin (London dry)
- vodka
- rye or Canadian whiskey
- bourbon
- Scotch whiskey
- rum (light)
- vermouth, dry and sweet
- tequila
- white wine (dry)
- red wine (dry)
- beer
- cognac or other brandy
- liqueurs (see *Drink Categories,* p. 15)

BASIC MIXERS, FLAVORINGS,
GARNISHES, ETC.

- club soda
- tonic water
- ginger ale
- 7-Up
- cola

- tomato juice
- orange juice
- pineapple juice
- cranberry juice
- grapefruit juice

- bitters (Angostura)
- grenadine
- Maraschino liqueur
- Worcestershire sauce
- Tabasco sauce

- toothpicks
- short straws
- swizzle sticks

- milk
- heavy cream

- maraschino cherries
- green olives (small)
- cocktail onions
- lemons, limes, and oranges

- sugar
- salt and pepper

- coffee

GLASSWARE

No host could be expected to have the precisely correct glass for serving every drink. To do so would require that one own several hundred items of glassware. There has been a trend in recent years toward the use of stemmed glassware for many drinks. Thus the wine glass or the larger, all-purpose balloon glass have become increasingly useful. There has been a greater flexibility in the use of glassware, too. It is not unusual to see Bloody Marys served on the rocks in a beer goblet, sherry served on the rocks in an Old-Fashioned glass, or a Martini brought around in a wine glass or even a brandy snifter.

Regardless of the shape of glass used, *never fill a glass to the brim.* A fairly full champagne glass is fine, but when serving wine, never fill the glass more than half full.

The most common types of glasses are the following:

- Old-Fashioned (4–5 or 6–10 oz)
- all-purpose wine (8–10 oz)
- cocktail or Martini (3–4 oz)
- collins (8–13 oz) or highball (up to 13 oz)

Beer Mug

Flute Champagne

Hollow Stem Champagne

Pilsner Beer Glass

Beer Goblet

Saucer Champagne

Tulip Champagne

10-oz Collins

13-oz Collins

Small Brandy Snifter

Balloon Snifter

1½-oz Shot Glass (Jigger)

Irish Coffee

Punch Cup

Cocktail Glass

Champagne Bottle

Wine Rack

Mateus Wine

Bungundy Wine

Bordeaux Wine

Ice Bucket

Punch Bowl and Cups

Boston Cocktail Shaker

- balloon wine, red wine, white wine, German wine
- champagne: flute or tulip; the saucer and hollow-stem glasses should be avoided
- brandy snifter (6 oz)
- cordial (1 oz)
- sherry (2½ oz)
- shot, or jigger (1½–2 oz)

THE BASICS

These glasses are the absolute musts for the average home bar:

- Old-Fashioned (4–5 oz)
- highball (or collins)
- wine glasses (especially for red wine)

With a half dozen or so of each of these, a host can easily serve almost any kind of drink. If one is likely to serve punches, buy a punch bowl with at least a 4-qt capacity and 10 to 12 handled cups. The other glasses described above are often desirable, however, and should be added when feasible. An adequate supply of the proper glassware is as much a complement to the bartender's art as a well-stocked bar.

MEASUREMENTS AND MEASURING

When making a drink for the first time it is best to be precise when measuring out the ingredients called for in a recipe. Freehand pouring can quickly ruin a drink by making it too weak, too strong, or unbalanced with the dominating flavor of a particular ingredient. Be creative on your own if you wish, but try to refrain from experimenting on your guests. These are the standard measurements used in the recipes:

- drop
- dash—2 or 3 drops
- teaspoon—⅙ oz
- tablespoon—½ oz (3 teaspoons)
- ounce—2 tablespoons
- pony—1 oz (2 tablespoons)
- jigger—1½–2 oz (3–4 tablespoons)
- cup—8 oz
- pound—16 oz (2 cups)
- pint—16 oz (2 cups)
- quart—32 oz (4 cups)
- gallon—128 oz (4 quarts)

BOTTLE SIZES AND CONTENTS

	U.S. Measures	Metric Measure	Yield*
split (champagne)	6.3 oz	187 milliliters	2 glasses
fifth	25.6 oz	750 milliliters	17–17 drinks
wine bottle	25.3 oz	750 milliliters	6 glasses
champagne bottle	25.3 oz	750 milliliters	6–12 glasses
quart	32 oz	.9464 liter	16–21 drinks
liter	33.8 oz	1000 milliliters	17–22 drinks
magnum (wine)	50.7 oz	1.5 liters	12 glasses
half gallon	64 oz	1.75 liters	32–42 drinks
gallon (liquor or wine)	128 oz	3.5 liters	64–85 drinks or 32 glasses

*Based on a jigger of 1½–2 oz and a wine glass filled approximately half full (4 oz)

CHILLING AND FROSTING GLASSWARE

Using a chilled glass is extremely important in producing a good cocktail, since it ensures the drink will be as cold as possible. Glasses can be chilled by storing them in the refrigerator for an hour or in a freezer for 5–10 minutes. If there is not adequate space in the refrigerator or freezer, glasses should be chilled by filling them with ice *and water* and letting them sit while you are mixing the drinks.

Some drink recipes call for a *frosted* glass instead of a chilled one, particularly for a Mint Julep or Planter's Punch. Glasses are frosted by dipping them in water and placing them in the freezer for half an hour. Mugs with handles are convenient to hold and are attractive for serving such tall cold drinks as Pimm's Cup and Moscow Mule. Silver or other metal mugs will frost better than glass ones.

ICE

Never skimp in ice when preparing a cocktail. The ice, in whatever form called for, should be hard, clear, and free of odors (never store ice where it can absorb odors from food). When removing ice cubes from a tray, avoid running water over the cubes as this may cause them to stick together.

When a recipe calls for stirring or shaking ingredients with ice, use ice cubes to avoid diluting the drink. Always put the ice cubes into the mixing container before the liquor (see *Mixing*).

Cracked and crushed ice can be made with an electric or manual ice crusher or simply by wrapping the ice in a towel and breaking it up with a hammer or a cooking pot. Crushed ice is in smaller, finer pieces than cracked ice and is usually used for frappés and other drinks sipped through a straw.

COATING THE RIM
OF A GLASS

To sugar-rim a glass, simply rub the rim of a chilled glass with a piece of citrus fruit (or dip the rim into citrus juice), then dip the glass into a bowl of superfine sugar. Gently shake off any excess. Some recipes call for dipping the rim of the glass into a liqueur before dipping it into sugar. Some glasses, as for a Margarita cocktail, are dipped (lightly) into salt instead of sugar.

STIRRING vs
SHAKING

A cocktail that is stirred rather than shaken will retain its clarity, and recipes using clear liquors (Martinis, Manhattans, etc.) are usually mixed in this manner, regardless of what James Bond would have you believe. A stirred drink will also remain free of ice chips. A cocktail must be stirred enough to mix the ingredients but not so much that the ice begins to dilute the liquor; 12 to 15 stirs are usually sufficient for proper mixing. If a carbonated beverage is used in a recipe, stir *gently* and *briefly* to retain the sparkle.

Recipes using fruit juices, eggs, cream, or other hard-to-mix ingredients should be shaken *vigorously* to ensure that they are thoroughly mixed. For extra frothiness, use a blender.

MIXING

When filling a cocktail shaker, always put the ice in first and the liquor last. There are no hard and fast rules about the order of ingredients added between the ice and the liquor (fruit juices, bitters, etc.). By putting the ice in the shaker or mixing container first, all the ingredients to follow will be chilled as they pass over the ice. The liquor is added last so that there will be less chance of dilution.

FLOATING

When a recipe calls for *floating* a liqueur on top of a drink, it is most easily done by allowing the liqueur to trickle slowly over the back of a demitasse spoon held over or placed in the glass. The purpose of floating is to keep each ingredient—liqueur, cream, brandy, etc.—in its own separate layer, so that it does not mix with the other ingredients. The Pousse Café is a good example of a drink in which several ingredients are floating.

MUDDLING

Muddling is the mixing (or crushing) of ingredients, such as the sugar cube, bitters, and water in an Old-Fashioned, or the mint leaves, sugar, and water in a Mint Julep. The muddling can be done with a special *muddler* or with the back of a long-handled bar spoon.

POURING

When pouring a drink never fill the glass more than three-quarters full. A wineglass should never be filled more than half full to allow the bouquet to collect in the top of the glass. When making an "on the rocks" drink, always pour the liquor into the glass *over* the ice. When pouring beer, pour it first down the side of the glass (to avoid an excess of foam) and then into the middle to aerate the beer and release the flavor.

FRUIT JUICES

Fresh citrus juice may of course be used whenever "fruit juice" is called for in a recipe. However, some connoisseurs insist that liquor tends to overpower fresh orange juice, for example, and prefer the frozen concentrated variety. Your own taste reactions will have to decide the issue. When using fresh fruit, soak the fruit in hot water or roll it on a cutting board before squeezing to allow the juice to flow more freely. Rose's Lime Juice is sweetened; you can't use fresh lime juice to replace it unless you add sugar.

FRUIT PEELS

When a recipe calls for a twist of peel from a fruit, use only the colored peel of the fruit, not the white pith, which is bitter. There are special *twist cutters* on the market, but a sharp paring knife or a vegetable peeler will also do the job. Cut a section of peel about 1 inch by ½ inch, twist the peel over the drink to release a drop or so of the oil, then drop the peel into the drink. If desired, rub the rim of the glass with the peel before twisting.

GARNISHES

These are used to enhance both the flavor and appearance of a drink. Among the most popular are cocktail onions, olives, maraschino cherries, and fresh fruits. When garnishing with a slice of fresh fruit (lemon, lime, orange) cut a ¼- to ½-inch wedge or slice. In order to fix the slice to the rim of the glass, make a slit toward the center so that it can straddle the rim. Garnishes of onions or cherries can be dropped into the drink or skewered on a cocktail pick that also serves as a swizzle stick.

CREAM

Heavy cream should be used in all recipes calling for "cream" unless otherwise specified. In recipes calling for lemon juice and cream, mix the drink as close to serving time as possible. Cream tends to thicken when mixed with lemon juice, especially if it is allowed to stand for more than a few minutes. Always be certain that the cream to be used is absolutely fresh.

EGGS

Always break an egg into a separate dish and not directly into a drink, in order to be certain of its freshness and to keep out any bits of eggshell. If the yolk remains whole and the white is thick, the egg is fresh. In general, use medium or smaller eggs so that the egg flavor of a drink is not overpowering. (Such "eggy" drinks as eggnogs, of course, do not need precautions.)

SUGAR SYRUP

Sugar syrup, also called gomme syrup, can be substituted for loose sugar in a drink recipe. In fact, some
recipes call specifically for sugar syrup because it does
not take excessive stirring or shaking to dissolve. To
make the syrup, add 1 cup sugar to 1 cup boiling
water and let it simmer for two or three minutes until all the sugar is dissolved and the mixture is clear.
Bottle the mixture after it has cooled and store it in
a cool place.

PROOF

Proof is the measure of absolute alcohol in a distilled
beverage. The American system is based upon the
percentage of absolute alcohol in the liquor at 60 degrees F; the proof measurement is double the percentage of alcohol (100 proof = 50% alcohol).

DRINK CATEGORIES

BEFORE-DINNER DRINKS

Generally speaking, an apéritif can be any drink tak-
en before a meal to stimulate the appetite. In the United States the most common form of before-dinner
drink is the cocktail, for which the reader will find
hundreds of recipes in the pages that follow. Sometimes, however, a guest may prefer simply beer (see
page 23), a glass of wine (see page 20), or a drink
containing no alcohol (see page 347) before a meal.
As another alternative, there are a number of ready-

to-serve apéritif wines that have become increasingly popular. These are of relatively low alcoholic content (usually below 20%) and may be served "straight up" (the dry sherries in particular) or "on the rocks," often with a twist of peel or slice of orange, lemon, etc., as a garnish.

Among the most popular apéritifs are the sherries. A white wine fortified with brandy, sherry comes from Spain and is categorized roughly, according to sweetness, as dry, medium, or rich. The dry and very dry sherries (manzanilla, fino, amontillado, etc.) are best served well chilled without ice. The medium drys (some olorosos, such as the popular Dry Sack) may be chilled slightly or served at room temperature. Increasingly, however, these medium-dry sherries are served on the rocks with a twist of lemon peel. The rich sherries (other olorosos, amoroso, Harvey's Bristol Cream, etc.) are full-bodied and are generally not chilled. For this reason most people prefer them as an after-dinner drink (see page 17) as a substitute for port or a liqueur.

France produces a number of very popular apéritif wines and liqueurs. Among those readily available are:

- Byrrh—reddish color with an aromatic flavor

- Dubonnet—red with quinine flavor, also available in white

- Lillet—orange-flavored white vermouth from Bordeaux, also available in red

- Pernod or Ricard—anise-flavored liqueurs, similar to absinthe, a drink that is now banned because of the toxic wormwood used in its manufacture

- St. Raphael—red, quinine-flavored, often served on the rocks.

Other suggested apéritifs are *Campari,* a bitter red wine from Italy, often served with soda; *Cynar,* also Italian, made from artichokes; *Ouzo,* a strong anise-flavored liqueur from Greece, usually served on the rocks in the United States; *Raki* (or *Arrack*), from the Middle East, similar to Ouzo; *Sake,* a Japanese rice wine, usually served warm; *Aquavit,* a potent, sometimes caraway-flavored drink of Scandinavia; and *Vermouth,* either sweet or dry, served on the rocks with a slice of lemon or bit of orange peel.

AFTER-DINNER DRINKS

Chief among after-dinner drinks are brandies, ports, and liqueurs, the latter available in almost any conceivable flavor. Another favorite is one of the full-bodied sherries, such as an oloroso or Harvey's Bristol Cream. All of these are usually served at room temperature. After a particularly rich or heavy meal, the after-dinner drink may even take the place of dessert. Some experienced diners would be quite content with a snifter of fine brandy, a glass of vintage port, or a well-chilled glass of dessert wine, such as Sauternes. And don't forget the exotic coffees, made with brandy, rum, or liqueurs (Café Brûlot, Café Royale, etc.).

The best-known types of brandy are Cognac and Armagnac, both named after the districts in western France where they are produced. Cognac is generally more subtle than Armagnac and is more popular. Both need time to mature and are seldom drinkable under five years of age. Calvados, made in Normandy, is said to be the world's best apple brandy. In any case, it is a considerably more refined drink than its American cousin, applejack. There are many other types of fruit-flavored brandy, with peach, apricot, and blackberry being among the most popular.

Port is a sweet fortified wine produced in Portugal. A fine vintage port will bear the year of its making and will require 10 to 15 years or more to reach maturity. Tawny ports are aged in the bottle and need no special preparation. Other ports include late-bottled vintage and ruby. Ruby port is generally the most popular because of its rich color and fruity sweetness. White port is generic and should usually be avoided. Enjoy port, which should be served at room temperature, with walnuts or Stilton cheese.

There is a vast variety of liqueurs, and their flavorings are almost endless. Among the favorites are the following:

- Advocaat—Dutch liqueur similar to brandy eggnog

- Amaretto—almond-flavored liqueur of Italy

- Anisette—anise-flavored liqueur of France

- Benedictine—herb-flavored liqueur of France, often mixed with brandy and known as "B & B"

- Chambord—black-raspberry-flavored liqueur of France

- Chartreuse—herbed liqueur, in green or yellow, created by the Carthusian monks of France

- Cointreau—orange-flavored liqueur of France, a brand of curaçao

- Crème de Cacao—brandy-based liqueur flavored with cacao beans.

- Crème de Cassis—French liqueur flavored with black currants

- Crème de Menthe—mint-flavored liqueur in green or white

- Crème de Violette—lavender-colored liqueur flavored with violets

- Crème Yvette—American liqueur with strong taste of violets

- Curaçao—originally a Dutch liqueur made of West Indian oranges

- Galliano—Italian liqueur flavored with herbs and spices

- Godiva—chocolate-flavored liqueur

- Goldwasser—liqueur of France and Germany flavored with herbs and spices (esp. caraway in the German version) and flecked with bits of gold leaf

- Grand Marnier—liqueur of champagne and curaçao

- Irish Mint—liqueur combining Irish whiskey with cream

- Kahlúa—coffee-flavored liqueur from Mexico

- Kümmel—caraway-flavored liqueur of Germany

- Mandarine Napoléon—tangerine-flavored liqueur with a brandy base, made in Belgium

- Midori—melon-flavored liqueur from Japan

- Ouzo—anise-flavored liqueur of Greece, usually served on the rocks

- Peter Heering—cherry-flavored liqueur of Denmark

- Prunelle—plum-flavored liqueur of France

- Sabra—Israeli liqueur flavored with orange and chocolate

- Sambuca—Italian liqueur with taste of wild elderberries

- ■ Southern Comfort—American bourbon-based liqueur with peach flavor

- ■ Strega—Italian liqueur flavored with orange peel and spices

- ■ Tia Maria—coffee-flavored liqueur of Jamaica

- ■ Triple Sec—orange-flavored liqueur, a type of curaçao.

WINE AND CHAMPAGNE

Wine, in general, falls into the categories of *fortified wines* (sherry, port, madeira, etc., with an alcohol content of 17–21%) and *table wines* (wines with 14% or less alcohol content). Table wines are further divided into the categories of red, white, and rosé, and are either dry, sweet, or semisweet. A home bar should stock at least several bottles of dry white, one full-bodied red, one semisweet rosé (such as white zinfandel), and one fortified wine.

When serving wine as an accompaniment to meals, it is traditional that red wine is served with red meat and white wine is served with white meat (veal or pork), poultry, and fish. This tradition has relaxed somewhat in recent years, and many people now believe that the choice of red or white wine should be dictated by personal preference. A good rule to follow is that the richer the food, the richer and more full-bodied the wine should be. The preparation, then, becomes the important factor: chicken sautéd with white wine and cream should be served with a white wine, but if it is roasted and served with a mushroom sauce, a red wine is called for. Even the stronger fish can be served with a red: grilled salmon or tuna go especially well with red wine. Use your judgment, and the possibilities are endless.

Wine bottles should be stored on their sides so that the corks are kept moist, thereby maintaining a watertight seal on the bottle. An ideal storage area is one that is well ventilated and has a fairly constant temperature of 50–60 degrees F. White and rosé wines should be served chilled—either 2 hours of storage in the refrigerator or 20 minutes in a bucket of ice water. Red wines should be served a bit cooler than room temperature; twenty minutes in the refrigerator should do the trick. Stronger red wines can benefit from *breathing* for an hour or so before being poured in order to develop the bouquet and soften any tannic astringency. A wine will breathe by simply being uncorked, or it can be decanted into a decanter, carafe, pitcher, etc.

Removing the cork from a wine bottle can be accomplished easily with a bit of practice. With a knife (some openers are equipped with a small blade) remove the paper or foil covering the cork and the top of the bottle. Then insert the corkscrew so that it penetrates straight down into the cork. When the corkscrew is firmly inserted, pull upward and the cork should slide out of the bottle with a pleasant popping sound. Then let the wine breathe, decant it, or serve it immediately, as appropriate.

The leading wine producers for the American market are France, Italy, Germany, Spain, and the state of California. The most popular French wines are named after the regions in which they are produced: Bordeaux (the dry reds of St. Emilion, Médoc, etc.), Burgundy (the reds Côte de Beaune and Beaujolais, for instance, and the whites of Chablis and Montrachet), Rhône (the robust reds of Châteauneuf-du-Pape), and Loire (Sancerre, Muscadert, Vouvray). From Italy there are the red wines of Chianti, Barolo, Barbaresco, Valpolicella, Bardolino, and Lambrusco, and the dry white wines of Soave and Frascati. German wines are underrated, but go very well with food; the elegant white wines from the Moselle or Rhine Valley range from crisp and dry to sweet. Among the better-known California wines are the highly regarded reds Cabernet Sauvignon and Pinot Noir and the whites Chardonnay and Sauvignon Blanc.

The term "vintage" simply refers to the year in which the grapes for the wine were harvested. Good recent vintage years in Bordeaux, for example, include 1982, 1983, 1985, 1986, 1988, 1989, and 1990; for Burgundy, 1982, 1985, 1986 (white), 1988, 1989, 1990, and 1992 (white). Since good vintages are clearly the exception rather than the rule, wines of these years are much sought-after and are relatively higher in price.

There are many good, pleasing wines, however, selling for moderate prices. You can easily find the wines that best suit your taste and budget by trial and error or through the recommendations of a knowledgeable friend or wine dealer. Most wines are meant to be drunk soon after they are made, so vintages are less important for less expensive wines.

Unused wine that is left over should be recorked as soon as possible, because air will turn wine sour after a while. After being recorked, wines should be refrigerated, with reds allowed to warm up before serving. It is best not to buy wine in half-gallon or larger bottles unless it is to be consumed on one occasion.

Champagne. Most champagne sold in the United States is labeled either *brut* (extremely dry) or *extra dry* (meaning that it has no more than 2% added sugar), though sweeter varieties are available. The only French wines allowed to be labeled "Champagne" are those produced in the Champagne district of Northeast France under strict government controls. However, champagne-type wines are produced in other countries, including Spain, Italy, Germany, and the United States, where California and New York State produce popular brands.

Champagne should always be served well chilled. This is most easily done by refrigerating it for an hour or two prior to serving. Once removed from the refrigerator, the bottle can be nestled down into an ice bucket filled with cracked ice and water. To open, first remove the foil covering the head of the bottle, cover the cork with a dishtowel to prevent accidents, and then untwist the wires of the cage that secures the cork. When this is removed, hold the cork firmly with one hand on top of the dishtowel while rotating the bottle clockwise until the cork jumps out of the bottle with a gentle popping sound. Point the bottle away from you and your guests when opening it as the cork, and even some of the champagne, may erupt rather forcefully and dangerously. Pour and serve the champagne as soon as it is opened, then keep the opened bottle in the ice bucket.

Champagne is best served in either a well-chilled flute or tulip goblet. The traditional saucer-shaped goblet, sometimes hollow-stemmed, is attractive but spills easily, and its wide-open mouth tends to dissipate the wine's effervescence in a very short time.

BEER AND ALE

Most of the beer consumed in the United States—the world's largest beer producer—is *lager,* a light, dry, pale, heavily carbonated beer with an alcohol content of between 3 and 4.5%. *Pilsner beer,* a type of lager originally developed in Czechoslovakia, is a term now loosely applied to many dry, gold-colored beers with alcohol content of 4 to 5%. *Dry beer* is a type of lager brewed to be less bitter, and the newer *ice beer* has a high alcohol content. *Light beer* is lower in calories, alcohol content (2.3 to 4%), and taste than lager. These beers are typically served well chilled.

Ale is an English style of beer with a heavier flavor and a copper color. Ales are made with a different type of yeast and fermented at different temperatures than lager. There are many different varieties of ale. *Bitter ale,* favored in England, has a heavy hop flavor. *Pale ale,* also known as *India pale ale,* is slightly acidic and has a strong hop flavor. *Porter* is heavy, dark brown ale. *Brown ale,* becoming popular in America, is medium dark and richly (but not excessively) flavored. Ales should be served cool, not cold (but never at "room temperature," which would be too warm).

Bock beer, a German product now made also in the United States, is dark brown in color and has an alcohol content of around 6%. Formerly, it was available only during the Lenten season and was prized as the heavy, rich, sediment-filled beer that was first drawn off when the vats were tapped in early spring.

Stout, especially the Irish version called *bitter stout,* is the darkest and strongest of the beers, with an alcohol content between 4 and 7%. (It is no higher in calories than other beers, however.) Traditionally the national drink of Ireland, it is generally served at a cool temperature.

SINGLE-MALT SCOTCH

There are two major varieties of Scotch: single malts, which are made solely from malted barley in a single distillery, and blends, which consist of many single malts mixed with neutral grain alcohol. While all the major brands of Scotch are blends, single malts are becoming increasingly popular due to their individuality.

The character of a Scotch varies greatly with its region. The Lowland malts are typically mild and soft with a light body; two examples are Auchentoshan and Glenkinchie. The Highlands is the largest and best-known region and its whiskies are elegant and well-balanced. The Speyside area in the Highlands includes the light-bodied Glenfiddich, Glenlivet, and Knockando; heavier Scotches are Macallan and Glenfarclas. The other important region is the Islands, which generally produce very smoky, powerful whiskies. Some examples are Laphroaig and Lagarulin from the island of Islay, and the seaweedy Talisker from the island of Skye.

Single-malt Scotch should be drunk neat and at room temperature; ice, lemon, or soda obscure the taste and should only be used for cheaper blends. A small amount of water can help bring out the flavor in the stronger Scotches.

ABBREVIATIONS

tsp	teaspoon
Tbsp	tablespoon
oz	ounce
pt	pint
qt	quart
lb	pound
gal	gallon

METRIC EQUIVALENTS

1 tsp	(⅙ oz)	.4929 centiliter
1 tbsp	(½ oz)	1.4786 centiliters
1 oz		2.9573 centiliters
1 jigger	(1½ oz)	4.4360 centiliters
1 cup	(8 oz)	23.6584 centiliters
1 pt	(16 oz)	.4732 liter
1 qt	(32 oz)	.9464 liter
1 gal	(128 oz)	3.7854 liters

RECIPES

Unless otherwise specified, all recipes given are for one drink.

A

Abbey Cocktail

1½ oz (3 Tbsp) gin
1 oz (2 Tbsp) orange juice
1 dash orange bitters
maraschino cherry

Shake liquid ingredients with ice and strain into a chilled cocktail glass. Garnish with the cherry.

Absinthe Cocktail

1¾ oz (3½ Tbsp) Pernod or other
absinthe substitute
1 oz (2 Tbsp) water
1 tsp anisette
1–2 dashes orange bitters

Shake ingredients with ice and strain into a chilled cocktail glass.

Absinthe Suissesse

A more elegant absinthe cocktail, named in honor of a "Swiss girl."

1½ oz (3 Tbsp) Pernod or other
absinthe substitute

1 dash anisette
½ oz (1 Tbsp) white crème de menthe
1 egg white

Shake ingredients vigorously with ice and strain into a chilled cocktail glass.

─────── **Acapulco** ───────

(serves 2)

2 oz (4 Tbsp) light rum
1 oz (2 Tbsp) Cointreau or triple sec
1 oz (2 Tbsp) lime juice
2 tsp sugar
1 egg white
fresh mint leaves

Shake first 5 ingredients with ice and strain into chilled cocktail glasses over ice cubes. Garnish with mint.

Variations: can be served in highball glasses and topped off with chilled club soda. Pineapple or grape-fruit juice can be substituted for the lime. Garnish with fresh pineapple.

Tequila Acapulco: substitute tequila for Cointreau.

─────── **Adonis Cocktail** ───────

2 oz (4 Tbsp) dry sherry
1 oz (2 Tbsp) sweet vermouth
2 dashes Angostura bitters

Stir ingredients with ice and strain into a chilled cocktail glass.

Variation: substitute orange bitters for Angostura and garnish with an orange peel.

Affinity Cocktail

1 oz (2 Tbsp) Scotch
1 oz (2 Tbsp) dry vermouth
1 oz (2 Tbsp) sweet vermouth
2 dashes Angostura bitters
twist of lemon peel
maraschino cherry (optional)

Stir liquid ingredients with ice and strain into a chilled cocktail glass. Garnish with the lemon peel and cherry.

Variation: substitute orange bitters for Angostura.

Afterglow

1½ oz (3 Tbsp) blended whiskey
1 oz (2 Tbsp) Southern Comfort
½ oz (1 Tbsp) banana liqueur
1 tsp grenadine
1 tsp lemon juice
1–2 dashes orange bitters
pineapple stick (optional)

Place first 6 ingredients in shaker with 5 or 6 ice cubes, cover, and shake vigorously several times. Strain into large Old-Fashioned glass half-filled with cracked ice. Garnish with pineapple stick, if desired.

Alabama Fizz

1½ oz (3 Tbsp) gin
juice of ½ lemon
1 tsp sugar
chilled club soda
sprig of fresh mint

(continued)

Shake first 3 ingredients with ice and strain into a chilled collins glass over ice cubes. Top with soda and garnish with mint.

——— **Alabama Slammer** ———

1½ oz (3 Tbsp) Amaretto
1 oz (2 Tbsp) Southern Comfort
1 oz (2 Tbsp) sloe gin
½ oz (1 Tbsp) lemon juice

Place all ingredients in shaker with ice and shake vigorously to combine. Strain into an ice-filled Old-Fashioned glass or into several shot glasses and serve.

——— **Alaska Cocktail** ———

2 oz (4 Tbsp) gin
½ oz (1 Tbsp) yellow Chartreuse
2 dashes orange bitters

Stir ingredients with ice and strain into a chilled cocktail glass.

Variation: add ½ oz (1 Tbsp) dry sherry. Substitute a twist of lemon peel for the bitters.

——— **Alexander Cocktail** ———

1 oz (2 Tbsp) gin
1 oz (2 Tbsp) white crème de cacao
1 oz (2 Tbsp) cream
nutmeg

Shake liquid ingredients vigorously with ice and strain into a chilled cocktail glass. Sprinkle with nutmeg.

Variations: substitute vodka for gin. Substitute coffee liqueur or prunelle for crème de cacao. If using prunelle, sprinkle with cinnamon instead of nutmeg.

Alexander's Sister Cocktail: substitute crème de menthe for crème de cacao.

Brandy Alexander: substitute 2 oz (4 Tbsp) brandy for the gin.

——— **Alexander's Sister Cocktail** ———

See under *Alexander Cocktail.*

——— **Alfonso Cocktail** ———

1 oz (2 Tbsp) Dubonnet
1 lump sugar
2 dashes Angostura bitters
chilled champagne
twist of lemon peel

Put sugar lump into a chilled highball or wine glass and shake bitters over it. Add ice and Dubonnet. Stir and top off with champagne. Garnish with lemon twist.

——— **Alfonso Special** ———

1½ oz (3 Tbsp) Grand Marnier
¾ oz gin
¾ oz dry vermouth
4 dashes sweet vermouth
1 dash Angostura bitters

Stir or shake ingredients with ice and strain into a chilled cocktail glass.

(continued)

Variation: use equal parts (1 oz (2 Tbsp) each) of Grand Marnier, gin, and dry vermouth.

─────── **Algonquin** ───────

This drink originated at the famous Algonquin Hotel in New York City.

> 2 oz (4 Tbsp) rye whiskey
> 1 oz (2 Tbsp) dry vermouth
> 1 oz (2 Tbsp) pineapple juice

Shake ingredients with ice and strain into a chilled cocktail glass or into an Old-Fashioned glass over ice cubes.

─────── **All-American Fizz** ───────

> 1¼ oz (2½ Tbsp) gin
> 1 oz (2 Tbsp) brandy
> juice of ½ lemon
> 2 dashes grenadine
> chilled club soda

Shake gin, brandy, lemon, and grenadine with ice and strain into a chilled collins or highball glass over ice cubes. Fill with soda and stir.

─────── **Allegheny** ───────

> 1 oz (2 Tbsp) bourbon
> 1 oz (2 Tbsp) dry vermouth
> ¼ oz (½ Tbsp) blackberry brandy
> ¼ oz (½ Tbsp) lemon juice
> 1 dash Angostura bitters
> twist of lemon peel

Shake liquid ingredients with ice and strain into a chilled cocktail glass. Garnish with lemon twist.

Allen Cocktail

1½ oz (3 Tbsp) gin
½ oz (1 Tbsp) Maraschino liqueur
1½ tsp lemon juice

Stir or shake ingredients with ice and strain into a chilled cocktail glass.

Variation: for a sweeter drink, increase maraschino to ¾ oz (1½ Tbsp).

Allies Cocktail

1 oz (2 Tbsp) gin
1 oz (2 Tbsp) dry vermouth
2 dashes kümmel

Stir ingredients with ice and strain into a chilled cocktail glass.

All-White Frappé

¾ oz (1½ Tbsp) white crème de menthe
¾ oz (1½ Tbsp) anisette
¾ oz (1½ Tbsp) peppermint schnapps
¾ oz (1½ Tbsp) lemon juice

Shake ingredients with ice. Strain into a large chilled cocktail glass over crushed ice.

Variation: substitute white crème de cacao for the peppermint schnapps.

——— **Amaretto Café** ———

1 cup hot black coffee
1 oz (2 Tbsp) amaretto
whipped cream (optional)

Add amaretto to coffee and top with whipped cream.

Variation: decrease amaretto to ½ oz (1 Tbsp) and
add ½ oz (1 Tbsp) Kahlúa or Tia Maria.

——— **Amaretto Cream** ———

1½ oz (3 Tbsp) amaretto
1½ oz (3 Tbsp) cream

Shake ingredients with ice and strain into a chilled
cocktail glass.

——— **Ambrosia Cocktail** ———

Said to have originated in New Orleans, quite possi-
bly at Arnaud's restaurant, about the time Prohibition
ended.

juice of 1 lemon
1 oz (2 Tbsp) applejack
1 oz (2 Tbsp) brandy
½ oz (1 Tbsp) Cointreau
cold champagne

Shake together the lemon juice, applejack, brandy,
and Cointreau. Pour into a chilled hollow-stemmed
champagne glass and top with champagne.

——— **Americana** ———

1 oz (2 Tbsp) bourbon
½ tsp sugar

1 dash Angostura bitters
chilled champagne
slice of fresh peach

Stir bourbon, sugar, and bitters in a chilled champagne glass. Fill with champagne and garnish with peach.

--------- **American Beauty Cocktail** ---------

1 oz (2 Tbsp) brandy
1 oz (2 Tbsp) dry vermouth
1 oz (2 Tbsp) orange juice
1 dash grenadine
1 dash white créme de menthe
½ oz (1 Tbsp) port

Shake all ingredients, except the port, with ice. Strain into a large chilled cocktail glass or Old-Fashioned glass. Float the port on top.

--------- **Americano** ---------

2 oz (4 Tbsp) sweet vermouth
2 oz (4 Tbsp) Campari
chilled club soda
twist of lemon or orange peel

Pour vermouth and Campari over ice cubes in a highball or large wine glass. Fill with soda and garnish with fruit peel.

--------- **Amer Picon Cocktail** ---------

1 oz (2 Tbsp) Amer Picon
1 oz (2 Tbsp) sweet vermouth

(continued)

Shake ingredients with ice and strain into a chilled cocktail glass.

Variation: increase Amer Picon to 1½ oz (3 Tbsp) and substitute juice of 1 lime and 1 tsp grenadine for the vermouth.

——— **Andalusia** ———

1½ oz (3 Tbsp) dry sherry
½ oz (1 Tbsp) brandy or cognac
½ oz (1 Tbsp) light rum
1 dash Angostura bitters (optional)

Stir ingredients with ice and strain into a chilled cocktail glass.

——— **Angel Face** ———

1 oz (2 Tbsp) gin
1 oz (2 Tbsp) apricot brandy
1 oz (2 Tbsp) apple brandy or Calvados

Shake ingredients with ice and strain into a chilled cocktail glass.

——— **Angel's Delight** ———

½ oz (1 Tbsp) grenadine
½ oz (1 Tbsp) triple sec
½ oz (1 Tbsp) sloe gin
½ oz (1 Tbsp) cream

Pour ingredients, in order given, into a Pousse-Café glass, being careful that the ingredients remain in layers and do not mix.

——— **Angel's Dream** ———

1½ oz (3 Tbsp) dark crème de cacao
½ tsp cream

Pour crème de cacao into a 2-oz liqueur glass. Float cream on top.

——— **Angel's Kiss** ———

½ oz (1 Tbsp) white or dark crème de cacao
½ oz (1 Tbsp) sloe gin
½ oz (1 Tbsp) brandy
½ oz (1 Tbsp) cream

Pour ingredients, in order given, into a Pousse-Café glass, being careful that the ingredients remain in layers and do not mix.

——— **Angel's Tip** ———

1 oz (2 Tbsp) white crème de cacao
½ oz (2 Tbsp) cream
maraschino cherry (optional)

Pour crème de cacao into a cordial glass. Slowly float cream on top so the two will be in layers and not mix. Insert a toothpick into the cherry and place on top.

——— **Angel's Wing** ———

⅓ oz (2 Tbsp) white crème de cacao
⅓ oz (2 Tbsp) brandy
⅓ oz (2 Tbsp) cream

(continued)

Pour ingredients, in order given, into a Pousse-Café glass, being careful that the ingredients remain in layers and do not mix.

———— Apple Blow Fizz ————

2 oz (4 Tbsp) apple brandy
1 tsp lemon juice
1 tsp sugar
1 egg white
chilled club soda

Shake ingredients with ice and strain into a chilled highball glass over several ice cubes. Top with soda.

———— Apple Brandy Cocktail ————

1½ oz (3 Tbsp) apple brandy
1 tsp lemon juice
1 tsp grenadine

Shake ingredients with ice and strain into a chilled cocktail glass.

Variation: omit lemon juice and grenadine and add ¾ oz (1½ Tbsp) brandy, ¾ oz (1½ Tbsp) gin, and 1½ oz (3 Tbsp) sweet cider. Stir with ice and strain into a large chilled cocktail or wine glass.

———— Applecar ————

1 oz (2 Tbsp) apple brandy
1 oz (2 Tbsp) Cointreau or triple sec
1 oz (2 Tbsp) lemon juice

Shake ingredients with ice and strain into a chilled cocktail glass.

Variation: substitute lime juice for lemon juice.

———— Applejack Collins ————

See under *Tom Collins*.

———— Applejack Cooler ————

1½ oz (3 Tbsp) applejack
juice of ½ lemon
1 tsp sugar
chilled club soda

Shake ingredients, except soda, with ice and strain into a chilled collins or highball glass over ice cubes. Top with soda and stir gently.

Variation: add ½ tsp brandy.

———— Applejack Punch ————

(serves 10–12)

2 qts apple brandy
6 oz grenadine
1 pt lemon juice
1 pt orange juice
2 qts chilled ginger ale
1 apple, sliced

Stir all ingredients, except ginger ale, in a punch bowl with a large block of ice. Add ginger ale just before serving.

———— **Applejack Rabbit** ————

1½ oz (3 Tbsp) apple brandy
½ oz (1 Tbsp) lemon juice
½ oz (1 Tbsp) orange (or lime) juice
½ tsp maple syrup

Shake ingredients vigorously with ice. Strain into a chilled cocktail glass or into an Old-Fashioned glass over ice cubes.

Variation: sugar-rim the glass by dipping into maple syrup and then into sugar.

———— **Applejack Sour** ————

See under *Whiskey Sour*.

———— **Apple Pie Cocktail** ————

1 oz (2 Tbsp) light rum
1 oz (2 Tbsp) sweet vermouth
1 tsp apple brandy
½ tsp grenadine
1 tsp lemon juice

Shake ingredients with ice and strain into a chilled cocktail glass.

———— **Apricot Anise Collins** ————

1½ oz (3 Tbsp) gin
½ oz (1 Tbsp) apricot brandy
½ oz (1 Tbsp) anisette
½ oz (1 Tbsp) lemon juice
chilled club soda
slice of apricot or lemon

Shake gin, brandy, anisette, and lemon juice with ice. Strain into a chilled collins glass over ice cubes. Top with soda and garnish with apricot or lemon.

——— **Apricot Cocktail** ———

1½ oz (3 Tbsp) apricot brandy
1 tsp gin
⅔ oz (1¼ Tbsp) orange juice
⅔ oz (1¼ Tbsp) lemon juice

Shake ingredients with ice and strain into a chilled cocktail glass.

——— **Apricot Cooler** ———

2 oz (4 Tbsp) apricot brandy
½ tsp sugar
juice of ½ lemon
juice of ½ lime
1 dash grenadine (optional)
chilled club soda
twist of lemon peel

Shake liquid ingredients, except soda, with ice. Strain into a chilled highball glass over ice cubes. Top with soda and garnish with lemon peel.

——— **Apricot Fizz** ———

2 oz (4 Tbsp) apricot brandy
juice of ¾ lime
½ tsp sugar
chilled club soda

Shake brandy, lime, and sugar with ice and strain into a chilled collins or highball glass. Fill with soda and stir gently.

———— **Apricot Lady** ————

(serves 2)

2 oz (4 Tbsp) light rum
2 oz (4 Tbsp) apricot brandy
½ oz (1 Tbsp) Cointreau or triple sec
1 egg white
1 oz (2 Tbsp) lime juice
2 slices of orange

Shake liquid ingredients vigorously with ice. Strain
into chilled Old-Fashioned glasses over ice cubes and
garnish with orange slices.

———— **Apricot Sour** ————

1 oz (2 Tbsp) lemon juice
1 tsp sugar syrup
2 oz (4 Tbsp) apricot brandy
orange slice and maraschino cherry

Pour juice and syrup into shaker and stir to combine
thoroughly. Add brandy and 5 or 6 ice cubes. Cover
and shake vigorously several times. Strain into chilled
sour or cocktail glass and garnish.

———— **Aqueduct** ————

1½ oz (3 Tbsp) vodka
¼ oz curaçao
¼ oz apricot brandy
½ oz (1 Tbsp) lime juice
twist of orange peel

Shake liquid ingredients with ice and strain into a
chilled cocktail glass. Garnish with orange peel.

—————— **Archbishop** ——————

2 oz (4 Tbsp) gin
1 oz (2 Tbsp) ginger wine
½ oz (1 Tbsp) B & B
thin slice lime

Fill an Old-Fashioned glass halfway with cracked ice.
Add liquors and stir gently to combine. Float lime
slice on top.

—————— **Artillery Punch** ——————

(serves 12–16)

1 qt bourbon
8 oz Jamaican rum
6 oz apricot brandy
1 qt strong black tea
1 qt orange juice
8 oz lemon juice
¼ cup sugar

Blend ingredients and refrigerate for an hour. Pour
into a punch bowl over a block of ice.

Variation: add 1 qt red wine.

—————— **Ashley Wilkes** ——————

2 oz (4 Tbsp) bourbon
1 oz (2 Tbsp) peach brandy
2 tsp powdered sugar
1 tsp lime juice
3 or 4 fresh mint sprigs

Place mint sprigs, lime juice, and sugar in bottom of
metal julep glass. With bar spoon bruise mint leaves
and mix. Fill glass with crushed ice and pour in

(continued)

brandy followed by bourbon. Stir gently and garnish
with mint sprig.

—————— **Aunt Jemima** ——————

1 oz (2 Tbsp) brandy
1 oz (2 Tbsp) white crème de cacao
1 oz (2 Tbsp) Benedictine

In the order given above, pour slowly into a Pousse-
Café glass so that the layers do not mix.

B

—————— **Babbie's Special Cocktail** ——————

2 oz (4 Tbsp) apricot brandy
1 oz (2 Tbsp) cream
½ tsp gin

Shake ingredients with ice and strain into a chilled
cocktail glass.

—————— **Bacardi Cocktail** ——————

See under *Daiquiri.*

—————— **Bacio Punch** ——————

(serves 8–10)

"Bacio" (pronounced bah' cho) is the Italian word
for "kiss." Many think the drink is aptly named.

8 oz gin
3 oz (6 Tbsp) anisette
8 oz grapefruit juice

slices of oranges and lemons
1 qt chilled club soda
1 split chilled champagne

Pour gin, anisette, and grapefruit juice over a block
of ice in a punch bowl and add fruit slices. Before
serving add soda and champagne. Serve in chilled
punch cups.

───────── **Back Bay** ─────────

2 oz (4 Tbsp) Jamaican rum
1 oz (2 Tbsp) brandy
½ oz (1 Tbsp) peach brandy
1 tsp lime juice

Shake all ingredients with ice and strain into Old-
Fashioned glass half-filled with cracked ice.

───────── **Ballerina I** ─────────

2 oz (4 Tbsp) white rum
½ oz (1 Tbsp) chocolate-orange liqueur
½ oz (1 Tbsp) curaçao
2 tsp champagne cognac

Place ingredients in shaker with ½ cup cracked ice.
Cover and shake vigorously several times. Strain into
chilled wineglass.

───────── **Ballerina II** ─────────

4 oz (8 Tbsp) dry white wine chilled
½ oz (1 Tbsp) amaretto
orange zest

(continued)

Pour wine into chilled wineglass. Add amaretto and stir gently. Twist zest over glass to release oils and drop it in.

——————   **Baltimore Bracer Cocktail**   ——————

1 oz (2 Tbsp) anisette
1 oz (2 Tbsp) brandy
1 egg white

Shake ingredients vigorously with ice and strain into a chilled cocktail glass.

——————   **Baltimore Eggnog**   ——————

See under *Eggnog I*.

——————   **Bamboo Cocktail**   ——————

1 oz (2 Tbsp) dry sherry
1 oz (2 Tbsp) dry vermouth
1 dash orange bitters
twist of lemon peel (optional)

Shake liquid ingredients with ice and strain into a chilled cocktail glass. Garnish with lemon peel.

Variation: substitute Angostura bitters for orange bitters.

——————   **Banana Bliss**   ——————

1 oz (2 Tbsp) light rum
1 oz (2 Tbsp) banana liqueur
½ oz (1 Tbsp) orange juice
1 dash Angostura bitters
1 oz (2 Tbsp) cream

dash of grenadine
banana slices

Shake all ingredients, except grenadine and banana
slices, vigorously with ice. Strain into a chilled Old-
Fashioned glass. Garnish with a few drops of grenadine and the banana.

Variation: a simplified version is to mix 1 oz (2
Tbsp) rum (or brandy) with 1 oz (2 Tbsp) banana
liqueur and serve in a cordial glass.

Banana Colada

2 oz (4 Tbsp) golden rum
4 oz (8 Tbsp) pineapple juice
1 oz (2 Tbsp) coconut cream
1 ripe banana sliced in 4 or 5 sections
maraschino cherry (optional)
pineapple slice (optional)

In blender place first 4 ingredients with ½ cup cracked
ice. Blend at high speed 15–20 seconds. Pour into
chilled highball glass and garnish, if desired, with
cherry and/or pineapple slice.

Banana Daiquiri

See under *Daiquiri.*

B & B

This liqueur is commercially available as a ready-
mix. For those who prefer to mix their own, the proportions are equal.

1 oz (2 Tbsp) Benedictine
1 oz (2 Tbsp) brandy or cognac

(continued)

Mix and serve in a cordial glass with or without crushed ice.

Variation: pour slowly into the glass so that the drink will be in layers.

--------- **Banana Rum Cream** ---------

2 oz (4 Tbsp) golden rum
½ oz (1 Tbsp) banana liqueur
1 oz (2 Tbsp) light cream

Place ingredients in shaker with 4 or 5 ice cubes. Add other ingredients, cover, and shake briskly several times. Strain into chilled wineglass.

--------- **Banana Rum Frappé** ---------

1 oz (2 Tbsp) white rum
½ oz (1 Tbsp) banana liqueur
1 oz (2 Tbsp) orange juice

Combine all ingredients in blender with 4 or 5 ice cubes. Cover and blend at high speed till ice cubes are just frappéed. Pour into chilled wineglass.

--------- **Barbados Rum Swizzle** ---------

2 oz (4 Tbsp) Barbados rum
juice and rind of ½ lime
1–2 dashes Angostura bitters
½ tsp sugar

Squeeze lime into a chilled collins or highball glass and drop in the rind. Fill the glass nearly full with shaved ice and add bitters, rum, and sugar. Stir and serve with a swizzle stick.

—————— **Barbara** ——————

1½ oz (3 Tbsp) vodka
¾ oz crème de cacao
¾ oz cream

Shake ingredients vigorously with ice and strain into
a chilled cocktail glass.

—————— **Barbary Coast Cocktail** ——————

¾ oz (1½ Tbsp) gin
¾ oz (1½ Tbsp) Scotch
¾ oz (1½ Tbsp) crème de cacao
¾ oz (1½ Tbsp) cream

Shake ingredients vigorously with ice and strain into
a chilled cocktail glass.

Variation: add ¾ oz (1½ Tbsp) light rum.

—————— **Barton Special** ——————

1 oz (2 Tbsp) apple brandy
½ oz (1 Tbsp) Scotch
½ oz (1 Tbsp) gin
twist of lemon peel

Shake liquid ingredients with ice and strain into a
chilled cocktail glass or into an Old-Fashioned glass
over ice cubes. Garnish with lemon peel.

—————— **Beachcomber** ——————

1½ oz (3 Tbsp) light rum
½ oz (1 Tbsp) Cointreau or triple sec
½ oz (1 Tbsp) lime juice
1 dash of Maraschino liqueur

(continued)

Sugar-rim a chilled cocktail glass by rubbing with lime and dipping into sugar. Shake ingredients with ice and strain into the glass.

Beef-A-Mato Cocktail

4 oz (8 Tbsp) tomato juice
2 oz (4 Tbsp) full-strength beef bouillon
1–2 dashes Worcestershire sauce
1½ oz (3 Tbsp) vodka
lemon zest

Place 3 or 4 ice cubes in highball glass and add liquid ingredients. Stir gently to combine. Twist zest over glass and add to drink.

Beekman Place

1 oz (2 Tbsp) gin
2 oz (4 Tbsp) sloe gin
1 tsp lemon juice
1 oz (2 Tbsp) grenadine

In chilled wineglass pour grenadine to cover bottom. Add crushed ice to fill halfway. Shake together gins and juice with ice and strain into glass. Do not stir. Serve with small straw.

Beer Buster

1½ oz (3 Tbsp) chilled vodka
chilled beer or ale
2 dashes Tabasco sauce

Put vodka and Tabasco into a chilled highball glass or beer mug, fill with beer, and stir lightly.

——— **Bee's Knees** ———

2 oz (4 Tbsp) white rum
½ oz (1 Tbsp) Cointreau or triple sec
2 tsp fresh lemon juice
1 tsp sugar
orange slice (optional)

Shake first 4 ingredients with ice cubes and strain into Old-Fashioned glass filled with cracked ice. Garnish, if desired, with half orange slice on rim.

——— **Bel Air Cocktail** ———

2 oz (4 Tbsp) gin
1 oz (2 Tbsp) apricot brandy
1 tsp grenadine
1 egg white

Shake together vigorously with ice cubes and strain into chilled wineglass.

——— **Bellini** ———

2 oz (4 Tbsp) peach juice
4 oz (8 Tbsp) chilled champagne
1 dash grenadine (optional)
slice of fresh peach

Pour peach juice over crushed ice in a large wineglass. Top with champagne, add grenadine, and garnish with peach slice.

———— **Bellini Punch** ————

(serves 16–18)

2 ripe peaches, seeded and peeled
½ oz (1 Tbsp) fresh lemon juice
⅓ cup sugar
3 (or more) bottles of champagne
block of ice

In blender purée peaches, lemon juice, and sugar. Cover and refrigerate overnight if possible (do not freeze). When ready to serve, put block of ice in large punch bowl and spread purée on bottom of bowl around block. Pour 3 or 4 bottles of champagne over ice and ladle into punch cups.

———— **Belmont Cocktail** ————

2 oz (4 Tbsp) gin
1 tsp grenadine
¾ oz (1½ Tbsp) cream

Shake ingredients vigorously with ice and strain into a chilled cocktail glass.

Variation: substitute raspberry syrup for grenadine.

———— **Belvedere** ————

A belvedere is a summerhouse, a quiet retreat. And here's the perfect refreshment.

1½ oz (3 Tbsp) gin
½ oz (1 Tbsp) Galliano
½ oz (1 Tbsp) banana liqueur
½ oz (1 Tbsp) grapefruit juice

Place all ingredients in shaker with cracked ice. Cover and shake vigorously several times. Strain into chilled cocktail glass.

───────── **Bennett Cocktail** ─────────

1½ oz (3 Tbsp) gin
½ oz (1 Tbsp) lime juice
½ tsp sugar
2 dashes Angostura bitters

Shake ingredients with ice and strain into a chilled cocktail glass.

Variation: substitute orange bitters for Angostura. Increase sugar to 1 tsp.

───────── **Bentley** ─────────

1½ oz (3 Tbsp) apple brandy or Calvados
1½ oz (3 Tbsp) Dubonnet
twist of lemon peel

Stir liquid ingredients with ice and strain into a chilled cocktail glass. Garnish with lemon peel.

───────── **Bermuda Highball** ─────────

¾ oz (1½ Tbsp) gin
¾ oz (1½ Tbsp) dry vermouth
¾ oz (1½ Tbsp) brandy
chilled ginger ale or club soda
twist of lemon peel

Pour gin, vermouth, and brandy into a chilled highball glass over ice cubes. Top with ginger ale or soda and garnish with lemon peel.

——————— **Bermuda Rose Cocktail** ———————

1¼ oz (2½ Tbsp) gin
1½ tsp apricot brandy
1½ tsp lime juice
1 dash grenadine

Shake ingredients with ice and strain into a chilled cocktail glass.

Variation: substitute lemon juice for lime.

——————— **Betsy Ross Cocktail** ———————

1½ oz (3 Tbsp) brandy
1½ oz (3 Tbsp) port
1 dash Cointreau or triple sec
1 dash Angostura bitters (optional)

Stir ingredients with ice and strain into a chilled cocktail glass.

——————— **Between-the-Sheets Cocktail** ———————

1 oz (2 Tbsp) brandy
1 oz (2 Tbsp) light rum
1 oz (2 Tbsp) Cointreau or triple sec
1 oz (2 Tbsp) lemon juice
twist of lemon peel

Shake liquid ingredients with ice and strain into a large chilled cocktail glass. Garnish with lemon peel.

Variation: substitute lime juice for lemon and garnish with a twist of lime peel.

——— **Biffy Cocktail** ———

1½ oz (3 Tbsp) gin
¾ oz (1½ Tbsp) Swedish punch
¾ oz (1½ Tbsp) lemon juice

Shake ingredients with ice and strain into a chilled cocktail glass.

——— **Bijou Cocktail** ———

1 oz (2 Tbsp) gin
1 oz (2 Tbsp) green Chartreuse
1 oz (2 Tbsp) sweet vermouth
1 dash orange bitters
maraschino cherry (optional)
twist of lemon peel (optional)

Stir liquid ingredients with ice and strain into a chilled cocktail glass. Garnish with cherry or lemon.

——— **Bird of Paradise I** ———

1½ oz (3 Tbsp) tequila
½ oz (1 Tbsp) white crème de cacao
½ oz (1 Tbsp) Galliano
1 oz (2 Tbsp) orange juice
½ oz (1 Tbsp) heavy cream

Put ingredients in blender with ½ cup cracked ice and blend about 10 seconds, or just till ice is puréed. Pour into chilled hollow-stemmed champagne glass.

——— **Bird of Paradise II** ———

1 oz (2 Tbsp) chocolate liqueur
½ oz (1 Tbsp) peppermint schnapps

(continued)

2 oz (4 Tbsp) heavy cream
sprig of mint (optional)

Place first three ingredients into blender with ½ cup cracked ice and blend at high speed 10–15 seconds or until ice is just puréed. Pour into chilled wineglass and garnish, if desired, with mint sprig.

————— Bishop —————

Burgundy wine
juice of ¼ lemon
juice of ¼ orange
1 tsp sugar
3 dashes light rum or brandy (optional)
slices of orange and lemon

Mix sugar, lemon, and orange juice in a highball glass. Add ice cubes and fill with Burgundy. Add rum or brandy if desired and garnish with fruit.

Variations: to serve hot, mix ingredients and heat in a pan to just below boiling. Serve in a heated mug.

The Cardinal: substitute Bordeaux wine for Burgundy.

The Pope: substitute champagne for Burgundy.

————— Bittersweet —————

1½ oz (3 Tbsp) sweet vermouth
1½ oz (3 Tbsp) dry vermouth
1 dash orange bitters
1 dash Angostura bitters
twist of orange peel

Shake liquid ingredients with ice and strain into a chilled cocktail glass. Garnish with orange peel.

Variation: substitute 2 oz (4 Tbsp) whiskey and 1 oz (2 Tbsp) orange juice for the sweet and dry vermouths.

────── **Black Devil** ──────

2 oz (4 Tbsp) light rum
½ oz (1 Tbsp) dry vermouth
black olive

Shake liquid ingredients with ice and strain into a chilled cocktail glass. Garnish with the olive.

────── **Black Hawk Cocktail** ──────

1½ oz (3 Tbsp) bourbon
1½ oz (3 Tbsp) sloe gin
maraschino cherry

Stir liquid ingredients with ice and strain into a chilled cocktail glass. Garnish with the cherry.

Variation: add ½ oz (1 Tbsp) lemon juice and shake instead of stirring.

────── **Blackjack** ──────

1 oz (2 Tbsp) brandy
½ oz (1 Tbsp) kirsch
1 oz (2 Tbsp) cold black coffee
twist of lemon peel

Stir liquid ingredients with ice and strain into a chilled cocktail glass or into an Old-Fashioned glass over ice cubes. Garnish with lemon peel.

Variation: substitute gin for brandy.

Black Maria

2 oz (4 Tbsp) coffee brandy
2 oz (4 Tbsp) light rum
2 tsp sugar
4 oz (8 Tbsp) cold strong coffee

Stir ingredients in a large brandy snifter and add cracked ice.

Blackout

2 oz (4 Tbsp) dark Jamaican rum
1 oz (2 Tbsp) Kahlúa or other coffee liqueur
1 tsp fresh lemon juice

Place ingredients in shaker with 4 or 5 ice cubes, cover, and shake vigorously several times. Strain into Old-Fashioned glass filled with cracked ice.

Black Rose

1½ oz (3 Tbsp) rum
1 tsp sugar
cold black coffee

Mix rum and sugar in a chilled collins glass. Add ice cubes, fill with coffee, and stir.

Black Russian

2 oz (4 Tbsp) vodka
1 oz (2 Tbsp) Kahlúa, Tia Maria,
or coffee brandy

Pour ingredients into a chilled Old-Fashioned glass over ice cubes.

Variation: stir ingredients with ice and strain into a chilled cocktail glass. Add a few drops of lemon juice.

--------- **Blackthorn** ---------

1½ oz (3 Tbsp) sloe gin
1 oz (2 Tbsp) sweet vermouth
2 dashes orange bitters (optional)
twist of lemon peel

Stir liquid ingredients with ice and strain into a chilled cocktail glass. Garnish with lemon peel.

See also *Irish Blackthorn.*

--------- **Black Velvet** ---------

6 oz chilled stout
6 oz chilled dry champagne

Pour ingredients simultaneously into a chilled high-ball glass.

Variation: pour carefully, in the order given above, into a chilled glass. Do not stir.

--------- **Blanche** ---------

1 oz (2 Tbsp) white curaçao
1 oz (2 Tbsp) anisette
1 oz (2 Tbsp) Cointreau or triple sec

Shake ingredients with ice and strain into a chilled cocktail glass.

———————— **Blarney Stone** ————————

2 oz (4 Tbsp) Irish whiskey
2 tsp Pernod
2 tsp white curaçao
1 tsp clear Maraschino liqueur
dash bitters
1 strip orange peel

Shake first 5 ingredients with ice cubes and strain into chilled cocktail glass. Twist peel to release oils and drop into drink.

———————— **Blended Comfort** ————————

2 oz (4 Tbsp) bourbon
1 oz (2 Tbsp) Southern Comfort
½ oz (1 Tbsp) dry vermouth
1 oz (2 Tbsp) lemon juice
¼ cup skinned peach slices
1 tsp sugar
1 oz (2 Tbsp) orange juice (optional)
½ cup crushed ice
slice of peach and orange for garnish

Put ingredients, except for fruit slices, in a blender and blend at low speed until smooth. Pour into a chilled collins or highball glass and add ice cubes. Garnish with peach and orange slices.

———————— **Blonde Bombshell** ————————

1½ oz (3 Tbsp) gin
½ oz (1 Tbsp) white curaçao
1 tsp white crème de menthe
2 tsp heavy cream

Place all ingredients in shaker with 5 or 6 ice cubes. Cover and shake vigorously several times. Strain into chilled cocktail glass.

Blood & Sand Cocktail

1 oz (2 Tbsp) Scotch
1 oz (2 Tbsp) cherry brandy
1 oz (2 Tbsp) sweet vermouth
½ oz (1 Tbsp) orange juice

Shake ingredients with ice and strain into a chilled cocktail glass.

Bloodhound Cocktail

1 oz (2 Tbsp) gin
½ oz (1 Tbsp) dry vermouth
½ oz (1 Tbsp) sweet vermouth
½ oz (1 Tbsp) strawberry liqueur
2 fresh strawberries

Shake liquid ingredients with ice and strain into a chilled cocktail glass. Garnish with strawberries.

Bloody Caesar

See under *Bloody Mary.*

Bloody Maria

See under *Bloody Mary.*

———— **Bloody Mary** ————

Perhaps named for Queen Mary I of England, whose relentless pursuit of the Protestants earned her the nickname "Bloody Mary," the drink is thought to have made its debut in the United States in the mid-1930s. The Bloody Mary is a popular brunch drink (or a morning-after hangover cure). Some individuals prefer a mild version, others are heavy-handed with the Tabasco and Worcestershire sauce.

2 oz (4 Tbsp) vodka
4 oz (8 Tbsp) tomato juice
2 dashes lemon juice
2 dashes Worcestershire sauce
2–3 drops Tabasco sauce
½ tsp sugar (optional)
1 dash celery salt
salt and pepper to taste
celery stalk for garnish (optional)

Shake ingredients with ice and strain into a large chilled wineglass. Sprinkle with salt, celery salt, and pepper. Garnish with celery stalk.

Variations: serve "on the rocks" by straining into a chilled highball glass or beer goblet over ice cubes.

Bloody Caesar: substitute Clamato juice for tomato juice.

Bloody Maria: substitute 1½ oz (3 Tbsp) tequila for the vodka, use only 3 oz (6 Tbsp) tomato juice, 1 dash lemon juice, 1 dash Tabasco sauce, and 1 dash Worcestershire sauce. Omit sugar, salt, and pepper. Garnish with slice of lemon.

——— **Blue Angel** ———

½ oz (1 Tbsp) blue curaçao
½ oz (1 Tbsp) brandy
½ oz (1 Tbsp) parfait d'amour
½ oz (1 Tbsp) cream
1 dash lemon juice

Shake ingredients with ice and strain into a chilled cocktail glass.

——— **Blue Blazer** ———

3 oz (6 Tbsp) warmed whiskey
3 oz (6 Tbsp) boiling water
1½ tsp sugar or honey
twist of lemon peel

Using 2 metal mugs, pour whiskey into one mug and dissolve sugar or honey in boiling water in the second mug. Ignite whiskey and while it blazes mix ingredients by pouring back and forth several times from one mug to the other. Serve in a heated wineglass or mug. Garnish with lemon peel.

Variation: substitute Irish whiskey or Scotch for the whiskey.

——— **Blue Devil** ———

1½ oz (3 Tbsp) gin
¾ tsp blue curaçao
¾ oz lemon or lime juice
½ oz (1 Tbsp) Maraschino liqueur

Shake ingredients with ice and strain into a chilled cocktail glass.

───────── **Bluegrass Cocktail** ─────────

2 oz (4 Tbsp) bourbon
½ oz (1 Tbsp) apricot brandy
1 tsp lemon juice
1 tsp sugar syrup
chilled club soda
stemmed maraschino cherry

Place first 4 ingredients in highball glass filled with ice cubes. Top with chilled soda and stir gently. Garnish with cherry.

───────── **Blue Hawaiian** ─────────

2 oz (4 Tbsp) light rum
½ oz (1 Tbsp) blue curaçao
½ oz (1 Tbsp) Cointreau or triple sec
¾ oz (1½ Tbsp) cream
1 tsp coconut cream

Shake ingredients with ice and strain into a chilled cocktail glass.

Variation: substitute ½ oz (1 Tbsp) pineapple juice for the Cointreau.

───────── **Blue Lady** ─────────

(serves 2)

3 oz (6 Tbsp) blue curaçao
1½ oz (3 Tbsp) light rum
1½ oz (3 Tbsp) lemon juice
1 egg white

Shake ingredients vigorously with ice and strain into chilled cocktail glasses.

Variation: substitute gin for the rum.

Blue Lagoon

1½ oz (3 Tbsp) vodka
½ oz (1 Tbsp) blue curaçao
4 oz (8 Tbsp) white grape juice
orange slice

Place 3 or 4 ice cubes in highball glass. Add liquid ingredients in order given and stir to combine. Garnish with half slice of orange on rim.

Blue Monday

Nothing sad about this one, and it's refreshing anytime.

2 oz (4 Tbsp) vodka
½ oz (1 Tbsp) Cointreau
½ oz (1 Tbsp) blue curaçao
zest of lemon

Add liquors to shaker with half a cup of cracked ice. Cover and shake vigorously several times and strain into chilled cocktail glass. Twist lemon zest over glass to release oils and add to drink.

Blue Moon Cocktail

1½ oz (3 Tbsp) gin
¾ oz blue curaçao
twist of lemon

Shake liquid ingredients with ice and strain into a chilled cocktail glass. Garnish with lemon peel.

Variation: substitute 1 egg white and ½ oz (1 Tbsp) maraschino for the curaçao and eliminate the lemon twist.

——— **Blush Wine Cooler** ———

4 oz (8 Tbsp) white zinfandel
1 tsp lime juice
1 tsp grenadine
chilled club soda
thin slice lime

In mixing glass stir to combine first 3 ingredients.
Pour into highball glass half filled with cracked ice.
Top with a little soda and stir. Garnish with lime slice.

——— **Bobby Burns Cocktail** ———

1½ oz (3 Tbsp) Scotch
1½ oz (3 Tbsp) sweet vermouth
2 dashes Benedictine
twist of lemon peel

Stir liquid ingredients with ice and strain into a chilled
cocktail glass. Garnish with lemon peel.

Variation: reduce sweet vermouth to 1 oz (2 Tbsp)
and add 1 oz (2 Tbsp) dry vermouth.

——— **Body & Soul** ———

1½ oz (3 Tbsp) gin
½ oz (1 Tbsp) Maraschino liqueur
2 tsp lemon juice
1 egg white

Place ingredients in shaker with 5 or 6 ice cubes.
Cover and shake vigorously several times. Strain into
chilled cocktail glass.

—— **Boilermaker** ——

Serve 2 oz (4 Tbsp) whiskey in a shot glass or cordial glass with a glass of beer on the side as a chaser.

—— **Bolero Cocktail** ——

1½ oz (3 Tbsp) light rum
¾ oz (1½ Tbsp) apple brandy
2 dashes sweet vermouth

Stir ingredients with ice and strain into a chilled cocktail glass.

Variation: substitute cognac for apple brandy.

—— **Bolo** ——

3 oz (6 Tbsp) light rum
1 tsp sugar
juice of ½ orange
juice of ½ lemon or lime

Shake ingredients with ice and strain into a chilled cocktail glass.

See also *English Bolo.*

—— **Bolshoi** ——

2 oz (4 Tbsp) vodka
1 oz (2 Tbsp) Campari
lemon zest

Pour vodka and Campari into Old-Fashioned glass with 3 or 4 ice cubes. Stir to blend. Twist peel over glass to release oil and add to drink.

────── Bombardier ──────

4 oz (8 Tbsp) beef bouillon
1½ oz (3 Tbsp) bourbon
fresh lemon juice

Add first 2 ingredients to highball glass half-filled with cracked ice. Top with a few drops lemon juice and stir gently.

────── Bombay Cocktail ──────

1½ oz (3 Tbsp) brandy
¾ oz (1½ Tbsp) sweet vermouth
¾ oz (1½ Tbsp) dry vermouth
1 dash Pernod
2 dashes orange curaçao

Stir ingredients with ice and strain into chilled cocktail glass.

Variation: substitute Cointreau or triple sec for the curaçao.

────── Bombay Punch ──────

(serves 16–20)

1 qt dry sherry
1 qt brandy
½ cup maraschino
½ cup Cointreau or triple sec
2 qts chilled club soda
4 bottles chilled champagne
juice of 12 lemons
1 oz (2 Tbsp) sugar

Mix sugar and lemon juice. Pour the mixture over a block of ice in a large punch bowl. Add sherry, brandy, maraschino, and Cointreau and stir well. Just before serving add soda and champagne.

Variation: add 2 packages frozen peaches, half-thawed, or other fruit in season.

———— **Bonanza Cocktail** ————

1½ oz (3 Tbsp) rye
1 tsp fresh lime juice
½ oz (1 Tbsp) triple sec
dash of bitters
maraschino cherry

Place first 4 ingredients in shaker with 4 or 5 ice cubes. Cover and shake vigorously. Strain into chilled cocktail glass and add cherry.

———— **Boomerang** ————

1½ oz (3 Tbsp) dry vermouth
1 dash Angostura bitters
twist of lemon peel

Stir liquid ingredients with ice and strain into a chilled cocktail glass.

Variation: substitute rye whiskey for gin.

———— **Borinquen** ————

1½ oz (3 Tbsp) light rum
½ oz (1 Tbsp) passionfruit syrup
¾ oz (1½ Tbsp) lime juice
¾ oz (1½ Tbsp) orange juice
1 tsp 151-proof rum
½ cup crushed ice

(continued)

Put ingredients in a blender and blend at low speed for 10–15 seconds. Pour into a chilled Old-Fashioned glass.

——————— **Bosom Caresser** ———————

2 oz (4 Tbsp) brandy
1 oz (2 Tbsp) madeira
1 oz (2 Tbsp) curaçao
1 tsp grenadine
1 egg yolk

Shake ingredients with ice and strain into a chilled wineglass.

Variations: eliminate grenadine and egg yolk; stir brandy, madeira, and curaçao with ice and strain into a chilled cocktail glass. Cointreau or triple sec can be substituted for curaçao.

——————— **Bossa Nova** ———————

1 oz (2 Tbsp) dark rum
1 oz (2 Tbsp) Galliano
½ oz (1 Tbsp) apricot brandy
3 oz (6 Tbsp) passionfruit juice

Put ingredients in a blender with 4 ice cubes. Blend for 15 seconds and pour into a chilled highball or wine glass.

Variation: substitute pineapple juice for passionfruit juice.

——————— **Boston Bullet** ———————
See under *Martini.*

———— **Boston Cocktail** ————

1½ oz (3 Tbsp) gin
1½ oz (3 Tbsp) apricot brandy
2 dashes grenadine
1 tsp lemon juice
twist of lemon peel

Shake liquid ingredients with ice and strain into a
chilled cocktail glass. Garnish with lemon peel.

———— **Boston Cooler** ————

2 oz (4 Tbsp) light rum
juice of ⅓ lemon
½–1 tsp sugar
chilled club soda or ginger ale
twist of lemon peel

Shake rum, lemon, and sugar with ice and strain into
a chilled collins or highball glass over ice cubes. Top
with soda, stir gently, and garnish with lemon peel.

Variation: substitute cognac for rum and add a
dash of rum over the top of the drink.

———— **Boston Sidecar** ————

See under *Sidecar.*

———— **Boston Sour** ————

2 oz (4 Tbsp) bourbon
juice of ½ lemon
1 tsp sugar
1 egg white
slice of lemon
maraschino cherry

(continued)

Shake ingredients, except lemon slice and cherry, vigorously with ice and strain into a chilled cocktail or sour glass. Garnish with lemon slice and cherry.

Variation: strain into a chilled collins glass over ice cubes and top with chilled club soda.

————— **Bourbon Cobbler** —————

½ oz (1 Tbsp) lemon juice
2 tsp sugar syrup
2 oz (4 Tbsp) bourbon
club soda
lemon slice or mint sprig (optional)

In highball glass thoroughly blend lemon juice and sugar syrup. Add 4 or 5 ice cubes, then pour in bourbon. Top with club soda and stir gently. Garnish, if desired, with lemon slice or mint.

————— **Bourbon Cocktail** —————

2 oz (4 Tbsp) bourbon
⅓ oz curaçao
⅓ oz Benedictine
⅓ oz lemon juice
1 dash Angostura bitters
twist of lemon peel

Shake liquid ingredients with ice and strain into a chilled cocktail glass or into an Old-Fashioned glass over ice cubes. Garnish with lemon peel.

Bourbon Daisy

There are other versions, but we like this one.

1½ oz (3 Tbsp) bourbon
½ oz (1 Tbsp) lemon juice
½ oz (1 Tbsp) grenadine
½ oz (1 Tbsp) Southern Comfort
orange slice and maraschino cherry (optional)

Place liquors and juices into shaker with 5 or 6 ice cubes. Cover and shake vigorously several times. Strain into Old-Fashioned glass filled two-thirds with cracked ice. Garnish, if desired, with orange slice and cherry.

Bourbon Eggnog

(serves 8)

A Christmastime favorite. Makes one quart, but can easily be doubled or tripled.

6 eggs, separated
½ cup sugar
½ cup bourbon (or rye) whiskey
½ cup brandy
3 cups heavy cream
grated nutmeg

Beat egg yolks with sugar until light yellow. Add bourbon and brandy and blend well. Refrigerate several hours or overnight. Whip cream till slightly thickened and fold into yolk mixture. Beat egg whites till peaks form and fold into mixture. Chill till ready to serve. Serve in punch cups with a few gratings of nutmeg. Makes eight 4-oz servings.

———— Bourbon Mist ————

See under *Scotch Mist.*

———— Boxcar ————

1½ oz (3 Tbsp) gin
1 oz (2 Tbsp) Cointreau
1 tsp lime or lemon juice
½ tsp grenadine
1 egg white
1 tsp sugar syrup

In a shaker with 5 or 6 ice cubes combine all liquid ingredients and egg white. Cover and shake vigorously several times. Strain into chilled sour glass.

———— Brandied Cranberry Punch ————

(serves 20–24)

A great favorite at Christmastime.

1 qt cranberry juice
1 bottle dry white wine
1 cup brandy
1 lemon thinly sliced
¼–½ cup sugar, to taste
1 or 2 bottles club soda, to taste
block of ice

In large crock combine cranberry juice, wine, brandy, lemon slices, and ¼ cup of the sugar. Stir to combine well and taste tartness. Add more sugar if needed. Cover and refrigerate overnight. When ready to serve, place block of ice in large punch bowl and pour in cranberry mix. Pour one bottle soda over ice. Stir and taste. If a lighter punch is desired, add second bottle. Ladle into punch cups.

──── Brandied Ginger ────

1½ oz (3 Tbsp) brandy
½ oz (1 Tbsp) ginger brandy
1 tsp lime juice
1 tsp orange juice
1 piece preserved ginger

Shake liquid ingredients with ice and strain into a chilled cocktail glass. Garnish with piece of ginger.

Variation: sprinkle with grated chocolate.

──── Brandied Madeira ────

1 oz (2 Tbsp) madeira
1 oz (2 Tbsp) brandy
½ oz (1 Tbsp) dry vermouth
twist of lemon peel

Stir liquid ingredients with ice and strain into a chilled cocktail glass or into an Old-Fashioned glass over ice cubes. Garnish with lemon peel.

──── Brandied Port ────

1 oz (2 Tbsp) brandy
1 oz (2 Tbsp) tawny port
½ oz (1 Tbsp) lemon juice
1 tsp Maraschino liqueur
slice of orange

Shake liquid ingredients with ice and strain into an Old-Fashioned glass over ice cubes. Garnish with orange slice.

——— **Brandy Alexander** ———

See under *Alexander Cocktail.*

——— **Brandy Blazer** ———

3 oz (6 Tbsp) warmed brandy
1 lump sugar
1 strip lemon peel
1 strip orange peel

Muddle sugar, lemon and orange peels, and brandy in an Old-Fashioned glass. Ignite brandy and serve.

——— **Brandy Cassis** ———

1¾ oz (3½ Tbsp) brandy
1 oz (2 Tbsp) lemon juice
2–3 dashes crème de cassis
twist of lemon peel

Shake ingredients with ice and strain into a chilled cocktail glass. Garnish with lemon peel.

——— **Brandy Cobbler** ———

2 oz (4 Tbsp) brandy
1 tsp sugar
2 oz (4 Tbsp) chilled club soda
fruits in season

In a highball glass dissolve sugar in soda. Fill ¾ full of cracked ice and add brandy. Stir and garnish with fruits in season.

Variation: add 1 tsp curaçao.

──────── **Brandy Cocktail** ────────

3 oz (6 Tbsp) brandy
½ tsp sugar
2 dashes orange bitters
twist of lemon peel

Stir liquid ingredients to dissolve sugar. Shake with ice and strain into a chilled cocktail glass. Garnish with lemon peel.

Variation: substitute Angostura bitters for orange bitters and add ¾ oz sweet vermouth or ¾ oz curaçao. Garnish with a maraschino cherry.

──────── **Brandy Collins** ────────

See under *Tom Collins.*

──────── **Brandy Crusta Cocktail** ────────

2 oz (4 Tbsp) brandy
½ oz (1 Tbsp) triple sec
1 tsp lemon juice
1 tsp Maraschino liqueur
1 dash Angostura bitters
peel of ½ lemon (cut in a continuous spiral)

Sugar-rim a chilled cocktail glass by rubbing with lemon and dipping into sugar. Put lemon peel in the glass. Shake liquid ingredients with ice and strain into the glass.

──────── **Brandy Daisy** ────────

2 oz (4 Tbsp) brandy
juice of ½ lemon
1 tsp grenadine or raspberry syrup

(continued)

> chilled club soda
> fresh fruit for garnish

Shake brandy, lemon, and grenadine. Strain into a highball or large wine glass that has been filled with ice cubes. Top with soda and garnish with fruit.

Variation: eliminate club soda.

─────── **Brandy Eggnog** ───────

See under *Eggnog I.*

─────── **Brandy Fix** ───────

> 2½ oz (5 Tbsp) brandy
> 1 tsp sugar
> 1 tsp water
> juice of ½ lemon
> slice of lemon

Mix sugar, water, and lemon juice in a highball glass. Fill glass with shaved ice, add brandy, and mix. Garnish with lemon slice.

Variation: reduce brandy to 1½ oz (3 Tbsp) and add 1 oz (2 Tbsp) cherry brandy.

─────── **Brandy Fizz** ───────

> 2 oz (4 Tbsp) brandy
> 1 tsp sugar
> juice of ½ lemon
> chilled club soda

Shake brandy, sugar, and lemon with ice. Strain into a chilled highball glass over ice cubes and top with soda.

———— Brandy Flip ————

2 oz (4 Tbsp) brandy
1 whole egg
1 tsp sugar
2 tsp cream (optional)
nutmeg

Shake first 4 ingredients vigorously with ice. Strain into a chilled cocktail glass and sprinkle with nutmeg.

———— Brandy Float ————

Widely favored as a mild after-dinner drink.

1½ oz (3 Tbsp) white crème de menthe
½ oz (1 Tbsp) brandy

Fill a small brandy snifter or Old-Fashioned glass halfway with crushed ice. Pour crème de menthe over the ice, followed by the brandy poured very slowly so that the liquors stay in two separate layers. Serve with a short straw.

———— Brandy Gump Cocktail ————

2 oz (4 Tbsp) brandy
juice of ½ lemon
2 dashes grenadine

Shake ingredients with ice and strain into a chilled cocktail glass.

———— Brandy Milk Punch ————

3 oz (6 Tbsp) brandy
6 oz chilled milk

(continued)

1 tsp sugar
nutmeg

Shake first 3 ingredients vigorously with ice. Strain into a chilled highball glass and sprinkle with nutmeg.

-------- **Brandy Puff** --------

2 oz (4 Tbsp) brandy
2 oz (4 Tbsp) milk
2 ice cubes
club soda or tonic water

Place ice cubes in a small tumbler and add brandy and milk. Fill with soda or tonic water, stir lightly, and serve.

Variations: substitute rum, whiskey, or gin for the brandy.

-------- **Brandy Punch** --------

(serves 12–16)

juice of 4 oranges
juice of 12 lemons
3 tsp sugar
1 qt chilled club soda
1 cup grenadine
2 qts brandy
1 cup Cointreau or triple sec
fresh fruit in season

Mix first 5 ingredients and pour into a punch bowl over a block of ice. Add brandy and Cointreau and stir well. Garnish with fruit.

Variation: add 2 cups strong black tea when adding the brandy and Cointreau.

Brandy Sangaree

See under *Sangaree.*

Brandy Shrub

(serves 12–16)

2 qts brandy
juice of 6 lemons
peel of 3 lemons
1 lb sugar
8 oz sherry (optional)

Mix the lemon juice, lemon peel, and brandy and store in a covered container for 3 days. Add the sugar and sherry, strain the mixture, and bottle it. Store in a cool place for at least a week. (Longer storage will improve the flavor.) Serve as a punch, over a block of ice, or as an individual drink, either straight or diluted with water, in a brandy snifter.

Brandy Sling

2 oz (4 Tbsp) brandy
1 tsp sugar
1 tsp water
juice of ½ lemon
twist of lemon peel

Dissolve sugar in water and lemon juice in a chilled Old-Fashioned glass. Add ice cubes and brandy and garnish with lemon peel.

(continued)

Variation: add 1 dash Angostura bitters, serve in a chilled highball glass, and top with plain chilled water.

——— **Brandy Smash** ———

Actually, a smash is a small-size julep, usually served in an Old-Fashioned glass.

2 oz (4 Tbsp) brandy
1 lump sugar
1 oz (2 Tbsp) chilled club soda
4 sprigs fresh mint
mint for garnish

Muddle sugar, soda, and mint sprigs in a chilled Old-Fashioned glass. Add ice cubes and brandy. Garnish with additional mint.

Variation: gin, whiskey, or other liquor may be substituted for the brandy, and the smash is then named for the liquor used (Gin Smash, etc.).

——— **Brandy Sour** ———

See under *Whiskey Sour.*

——— **Brandy Vermouth Cocktail** ———

3 oz (6 Tbsp) brandy
¾ oz (1½ Tbsp) sweet vermouth
1 dash Angostura bitters

Stir ingredients with ice and strain into a chilled cocktail glass.

Brave Bull

1½ oz (3 Tbsp) tequila
1½ oz (3 Tbsp) Kahlúa or Tia Maria
twist of lemon peel

Stir liquid ingredients with ice and strain into a chilled Old-Fashioned glass over ice cubes. Garnish with lemon peel.

Brazil Cocktail

1½ oz (3 Tbsp) dry sherry
1½ oz (3 Tbsp) dry vermouth
1 dash Pernod
1 dash Angostura bitters
twist of lemon peel

Stir liquid ingredients with ice and strain into a chilled cocktail glass. Garnish with lemon peel.

Breakfast Eggnog

See under *Eggnog I*.

Brewster Special

2 oz (4 Tbsp) vodka
sweet cider
strip of orange peel
orange slice (optional)

Place 2 or 3 ice cubes in a collins glass, add orange peel, and pour vodka over it. Top with cider and garnish with orange slice if desired.

Variation: Float ½ oz (1 Tbsp) Galliano on top.

──────── **Brighton Punch** ────────

1 oz (2 Tbsp) bourbon
1 oz (2 Tbsp) brandy
1 oz (2 Tbsp) Benedictine
juice of ½ orange
juice of ½ lemon
chilled club soda
slices of orange and lemon

Shake first 5 ingredients with ice. Strain into a chilled highball glass over ice cubes and top with soda. Stir gently and garnish with orange and lemon.

Variation: eliminate Benedictine, reduce bourbon to ½ oz (1 Tbsp), and substitute ¾ oz (1½ Tbsp) peach brandy and ¾ oz (1½ Tbsp) apricot brandy for the 1 oz (2 Tbsp) brandy.

──────── **Broken Spur Cocktail** ────────

1½ oz (3 Tbsp) white port
¾ oz (1½ Tbsp) sweet vermouth
¼ oz Cointreau or triple sec

Stir ingredients with ice and strain into a chilled cocktail glass.

Variation: substitute ¾ oz (1½ Tbsp) gin for the Cointreau and add 1 egg yolk. Shake with ice and strain.

──────── **Bronx Cocktail** ────────

A classic cocktail, the Bronx is named after the New York borough and was invented around 1919 when gin was substituted for whiskey in a Manhattan.

1½ oz (3 Tbsp) gin
½ oz (1 Tbsp) dry vermouth
½ oz (1 Tbsp) sweet vermouth
juice of ¼ orange
slice of orange

Shake liquid ingredients with ice and strain into a chilled cocktail glass or into an Old-Fashioned glass over ice cubes. Garnish with orange slices.

Bronx Golden Cocktail: add 1 egg yolk, shake vigorously, and strain.

Dry Bronx Cocktail: eliminate the sweet vermouth.

See also *Bronx Silver Cocktail.*

——— **Bronx River** ———

2 oz (4 Tbsp) gin
¾ oz (1½ Tbsp) sweet vermouth
½ tsp sugar
juice of lemon

Stir ingredients with ice and strain into a chilled cocktail glass.

——— **Bronx Silver Cocktail** ———

1 oz (2 Tbsp) gin
½ oz (1 Tbsp) dry vermouth
1 egg white
juice of ½ orange

Shake ingredients vigorously with ice and strain into a chilled cocktail glass.

Bronx Terrace Cocktail

1½ oz (3 Tbsp) gin
½ oz (1 Tbsp) dry vermouth
juice of ½ lime
maraschino cherry

Shake liquid ingredients with ice and strain into a chilled cocktail glass. Garnish with cherry.

Brooklyn

2 oz (4 Tbsp) rye whiskey
1 oz (2 Tbsp) dry vermouth
1 dash Angostura bitters
1 dash Maraschino liqueur

Stir ingredients with ice and strain into a chilled cocktail glass.

Variations: substitute sweet vermouth for the dry. Add 1 dash Amer Picon. Eliminate bitters.

Buck's Fizz

2 oz (4 Tbsp) chilled orange juice
chilled champagne

Put 2–3 ice cubes in a chilled collins or large wine glass. Add orange juice and top with champagne.

Variation: add a dash of grenadine and stir very gently.

Bulldog Cocktail I

2 oz (4 Tbsp) gin
juice of 1 orange
chilled ginger ale

Pour gin and orange juice into a chilled highball glass over ice cubes. Top with ginger ale and stir gently.

Bulldog Cocktail II

1½ oz (3 Tbsp) cherry brandy
½ oz (1 Tbsp) light rum
juice of ½ lime

Shake ingredients with ice and strain into a chilled cocktail glass.

Variation: substitute gin for rum.

Bullfrog

2 oz (4 Tbsp) vodka
2 tsp Cointreau
4 oz (8 Tbsp) lemonade
lemon slice

Place 3 or 4 ice cubes in highball glass. Add liquid ingredients in order given and stir to combine well. Float lemon slice.

Bullshot

Often regarded as a good "hair-of-the-dog" morning-after hangover cure, the Bullshot is a fairly recent drink. It is an offshoot of the Bloody Mary, but the exact origin is unknown.

2½ oz (5 Tbsp) vodka
5 oz strong chilled beef bouillon
1 dash Worcestershire sauce
salt and pepper to taste

(continued)

Shake ingredients with ice and strain into a large chilled wineglass. Sprinkle with salt and pepper.

Variation: add a dash of Tabasco sauce, 2 dashes lemon juice, and a dash of celery salt. Can also be served over ice cubes.

––––––– **Burgundy Bishop** –––––––

See under *Bishop.*

––––––– **Bushranger** –––––––

1 oz (2 Tbsp) light rum
1 oz (2 Tbsp) Dubonnet
1 dash Angostura bitters
twist of lemon peel

Shake ingredients with ice and strain into a chilled cocktail glass. Garnish with lemon peel.

––––––– **Button Hook Cocktail** –––––––

¾ oz (1½ Tbsp) brandy
¾ oz (1½ Tbsp) apricot brandy
¾ oz (1½ Tbsp) white crème de menthe
¾ oz (1½ Tbsp) Pernod

Shake ingredients with ice and strain into a chilled cocktail glass.

––––––– **B.V.D.** –––––––

Originally equal parts of brandy, vermouth, and Dubonnet, hence the initials.

¾ oz (1½ Tbsp) light rum
¾ oz (1½ Tbsp) dry vermouth
¾ oz (1½ Tbsp) gin

Stir ingredients with ice and strain into a chilled cocktail glass.

Variation: substitute ¾ oz (1½ Tbsp) Dubonnet for the gin.

——— **Byrrh Cassis** ———

1½ oz (3 Tbsp) Byrrh
1 oz (2 Tbsp) crème de cassis
chilled club soda

Mix Byrrh and crème de cassis in a large chilled wineglass. Add ice cubes and top with soda.

——— **Byrrh Cocktail** ———

1 oz (2 Tbsp) Byrrh
1 oz (2 Tbsp) rye whiskey
1 oz (2 Tbsp) dry vermouth

Stir ingredients with ice and strain into a chilled cocktail glass.

Variation: substitute gin and bourbon for the rye.

C

——— **Cabaret Cocktail** ———

1½ oz (3 Tbsp) gin
½ oz (1 Tbsp) dry vermouth
2 dashes Benedictine

(continued)

1 dash Angostura bitters
maraschino cherry

Stir liquid ingredients with ice and strain into a chilled
cocktail glass. Garnish with the cherry

Variation: substitute Dubonnet for dry vermouth.

─────── **Cablegram Highball** ───────

2 oz (4 Tbsp) rye whiskey
1 tsp sugar
juice of ½ lemon
chilled ginger ale

Mix whiskey, sugar, and lemon juice in a chilled highball glass. Add ice cubes and top with ginger ale.

─────── **Cactus Rose** ───────

2 oz (4 Tbsp) tequila
1 oz (2 Tbsp) Drambuie
1 tsp lemon juice

Place ingredients in shaker with 4 or 5 ice cubes,
cover, and shake vigorously several times. Strain into
chilled cocktail glass.

─────── **Cadiz** ───────

¾ oz (1½ Tbsp) dry sherry
¾ oz (1½ Tbsp) blackberry brandy
½ oz (1 Tbsp) triple sec
½ oz (1 Tbsp) cream

Shake ingredients with ice and strain into a chilled
Old-Fashioned glass over ice cubes.

─────── Café Amaretto ───────

See under *Amaretto Café*.

─────── Café Brûlot ───────

(serves 8)

1–2 sticks cinnamon
12 whole cloves
peel of 2 oranges and 2 lemons cut into thin
strips
4 lumps sugar
8 oz brandy or cognac
2 oz (4 Tbsp) curaçao (optional)
1 qt hot strong black coffee

In a chafing dish or a large bowl, mash together the cinnamon, cloves, fruit peels, and sugar. Stir in the brandy and curaçao. Ignite carefully and gradually add black coffee, stirring until the flames go out. Serve in heated cups or goblets.

─────── Café de Paris Cocktail ───────

2 oz (4 Tbsp) gin
1 tsp Pernod
1 tsp cream
1 egg white

Shake ingredients with ice and strain into a chilled cocktail glass.

─────── Café Kirsch ───────

1½ oz (3 Tbsp) kirsch
1 tsp sugar

(continued)

1 egg white
1½ oz (3 Tbsp) cold black coffee

Shake ingredients with ice and strain into a chilled cocktail glass.

——— Café Royale ———

2 oz (4 Tbsp) cognac
1 lump sugar
1 cup hot black coffee
cream (optional)

Pour steaming hot coffee into a cup or mug. Rest a teaspoon on top of the cup and place the sugar lump in it. Soak the lump with cognac and after the spoon heats up ignite the lump and slide it into the coffee. Float cream on top.

Variation: pour cognac directly into the coffee without flaming.

——— Cajun Mimosa ———

(serves 8)

A variation on the Mimosa cocktail, and one your guests are not likely to forget. The perfect prelude to a cajun meal.

1 qt orange juice
6 bottled jalapeño peppers, drained
2 bottles chilled Champagne
or other sparkling wine
crushed ice

Place orange juice in quart bottle with tight-fitting lid. Drain peppers thoroughly and pat dry. Slice into rounds and add to juice. Cap, shake well, and refrigerate 3 days. When ready to serve, strain juice and discard peppers. Fill highball glasses half full of crushed ice, then fill half full with orange juice and top off with cold champagne. Makes eight 8-oz drinks, with a little extra champagne to freshen the glasses.

——— **Cajun Party Punch** ———

(serves 40)

1 qt strong tea
1½ cups sugar
10 mint sprigs
4 cinnamon sticks (about 3″ each)
1 tsp whole cloves
1 qt dark rum
2 cups unsweetened pineapple juice
1 cup fresh lime juice
2 qt bottles club soda, chilled
block of ice
1 lemon, thinly sliced
1 lime, thinly sliced
1 orange, thinly sliced

In 3-qt saucepan place tea and bring heat to medium. Add sugar, mint, cinnamon, and cloves. Cook, stirring, till sugar dissolves. Cool slightly, then chill in refrigerator. When ready to serve, place block of ice in large punch bowl. Strain tea into bowl and discard spices. Add rum, juices, and soda and stir till blended. Add fruit slices. Ladle into punch cups.

——— **California Lemonade** ———

2 oz (4 Tbsp) rye whiskey
1 dash grenadine

(continued)

½ oz (1 Tbsp) sugar
juice of 1 lime
juice of 1 lemon
chilled club soda
slices of fruit
maraschino cherry

Shake rye, grenadine, sugar, and fruit juices with ice.
Strain into a collins glass over shaved ice and top
with soda. Garnish with slices of fruit and cherry.

──────── **Calisay Cocktail** ────────

1½ oz (3 Tbsp) Calisay
1½ oz (3 Tbsp) sweet vermouth
3 dashes lime juice
3 dashes sugar syrup

Shake ingredients with ice and strain into a chilled
cocktail glass.

──────── **Calm Voyage** ────────

(serves 2)

1 oz (2 Tbsp) Galliano or Strega
1 oz (2 Tbsp) light rum
1 oz (2 Tbsp) passionfruit syrup
4 tsp lemon juice
1 egg white
1 cup crushed ice

Put ingredients in a blender and blend at low speed
15 seconds. Pour into chilled champagne glasses.

——— Calvados Cocktail ———

1½ oz (3 Tbsp) Calvados
1½ oz (3 Tbsp) orange juice
4 oz (1½ Tbsp) Cointreau or triple sec
½ oz (1 Tbsp) orange bitters

Shake ingredients with ice and strain into a chilled cocktail glass.

——— Canadian Cherry ———

1½ oz (3 Tbsp) Canadian whiskey
½ oz (1 Tbsp) cherry brandy
2 tsp lemon juice
2 tsp orange juice

Sugar-rim a chilled cocktail glass by dipping it into cherry brandy and then into sugar. Shake ingredients with ice and strain into the glass.

——— Canadian Cocktail ———

1½ oz (3 Tbsp) Canadian whiskey
1½ tsp Cointreau or triple sec
1 dash Angostura bitters
1 tsp sugar

Shake ingredients with ice and strain into a chilled cocktail glass.

Variation: substitute 2 dashes curaçao for the Cointreau or triple sec.

——— Canadian Pineapple ———

1½ oz (3 Tbsp) Canadian whiskey
2 tsp pineapple juice

(continued)

2 tsp lemon juice
2 tsp Maraschino liqueur
stick of fresh pineapple

Shake liquid ingredients with ice and strain into a
chilled cocktail glass. Garnish with the pineapple stick.

––––––– **Cape Codder** –––––––

2 oz (4 Tbsp) vodka
4 oz (8 Tbsp) cranberry juice
juice of ½ lime
chilled club soda (optional)

Shake first 3 ingredients with ice and strain into a
chilled collins glass over ice cubes. Top with soda if
desired.

Variation: substitute light rum for vodka.

––––––– **Cara Sposa** –––––––

1 oz (2 Tbsp) Tia Maria or coffee brandy
1 oz (2 Tbsp) triple sec
1 oz (2 Tbsp) cream

Shake ingredients with ice and strain into a chilled
Old-Fashioned glass over ice cubes.

Variations: put ingredients into a blender with ½
cup crushed ice, blend for 10 seconds, and pour into
a sugar-rimmed cocktail glass. Orange curaçao can be
substituted for triple sec.

––––––– **Cardinal, The** –––––––
See under *Bishop.*

——————— **Cardinal Punch** ———————

(serves 16–20)

1 qt chilled club soda
1 lb sugar
juice of 12 lemons
2 qts claret
1 pt brandy
1 pt rum
8 oz sweet vermouth
1 split chilled champagne or sparkling wine
fresh fruit for garnish

Mix soda, sugar, and lemon juice and pour into a punch bowl over a block of ice. Add rest of ingredients, except champagne and fruit, and stir well. Add champagne just before serving and garnish with fruit.

Variation: eliminate lemon juice and increase club soda to 2 qts. Add 1 pt strong black tea.

——————— **Caribbean Champagne** ———————

½ tsp light rum
½ tsp banana liqueur
1 dash Angostura or orange bitters (optional)
4 oz (8 Tbsp) chilled champagne
slice of banana

Pour rum, banana liqueur, and bitters into a chilled champagne glass. Fill with champagne and stir gently. Garnish with banana slice.

——————— **Caribe Cocktail** ———————

juice of 1 orange
½ oz (1 Tbsp) lemon juice
2 oz (4 Tbsp) dark rum

(continued)

½ oz (1 Tbsp) raw sugar
orange zest (optional)

Combine juices, rum, and sugar in cocktail shaker with cracked ice. Shake well and strain into chilled cocktail glass. Garnish, if desired, with orange zest.

──────── **Carrol Cocktail** ────────

2 oz (4 Tbsp) brandy
1 oz (2 Tbsp) sweet vermouth
maraschino cherry or cocktail onion

Stir liquid ingredients with ice and strain into a chilled cocktail glass. Garnish with cherry or onion.

──────── **Caruso** ────────

1½ oz (3 Tbsp) gin
1 oz (2 Tbsp) dry vermouth
½ oz (1 Tbsp) green crème de menthe

Stir ingredients with ice and strain into a chilled cocktail glass.

Variation: use equal parts of all 3 ingredients (1 oz (2 Tbsp) of each).

──────── **Casa Blanca** ────────

2 oz (4 Tbsp) light rum
1½ tsp Cointreau or triple sec
1½ tsp lime juice
1½ tsp maraschino
slice of orange (optional)

Shake liquid ingredients with ice and strain into a chilled cocktail glass. Garnish with the orange slice.

Variation: substitute vodka for rum and Galliano for Cointreau.

Casino Cocktail

3 oz (6 Tbsp) gin
¼ tsp lemon juice
¼ tsp Maraschino liqueur
2 dashes orange bitters
maraschino cherry

Shake liquid ingredients with ice and strain into a chilled cocktail glass. Garnish with the cherry.

Champagne Cobbler

½ tsp lemon juice
½ tsp curaçao
thin slice of orange
chilled champagne

Fill a large goblet or wineglass half full of cracked ice. Add lemon juice, curaçao, and orange slice. Stir and fill glass with champagne. Stir again gently.

Champagne Cocktail

4–5 oz chilled champagne
1 lump sugar
1 dash Angostura bitters

Put lump of sugar into a chilled champagne glass. Add bitters and fill with champagne.

Variation: add twist of lemon or orange peel. Float 1 oz (2 Tbsp) brandy on top of champagne.

–––––––– **Champagne Cooler** ––––––––

1 oz (2 Tbsp) brandy
1 oz (2 Tbsp) Cointreau or triple sec
chilled champagne
sprig of fresh mint

Fill a large chilled wineglass or highball glass half full of ice cubes. Add brandy and Cointreau. Fill with champagne and stir gently. Garnish with mint.

–––––––– **Champagne Cup** ––––––––

(serves 4–6)

1 fifth chilled champagne
4 oz (8 Tbsp) brandy
2 oz (4 Tbsp) Benedictine
3 oz (6 Tbsp) Maraschino liqueur
1 qt chilled club soda
3 dashes grenadine (optional)
1 cup mixed fruit, sliced and chilled

Place fruit in a chilled pitcher or bowl and add brandy, Benedictine, Maraschino liqueur, and grenadine. Add ice cubes or a block of ice and stir. Just before serving add soda and champagne and stir gently. Serve in chilled wineglasses or punch cups.

–––––––– **Champagne Julep** ––––––––

chilled champagne
1 sugar cube
2 sprigs of fresh mint
slices of fresh fruit (optional)

Put sugar cube and mint in a chilled highball glass or stemmed goblet. Add 2 cubes of ice and slowly pour in champagne while stirring constantly. Garnish with fresh fruit if desired.

Variation: add 1 oz (2 Tbsp) brandy.

Champagne Normande

1 tsp Calvados
½ tsp sugar
1 dash Angostura bitters
chilled champagne
slice of orange or lime

Stir Calvados, sugar, and bitters in a chilled champagne glass until sugar dissolves. Fill with champagne and stir gently. Garnish with orange or lime.

Champagne Pick-Me-Up

2 oz (4 Tbsp) brandy
1 oz (2 Tbsp) orange juice
½ oz (1 Tbsp) lemon juice
1 tsp grenadine
4 oz (8 Tbsp) chilled champagne
twist of lemon peel

Shake brandy, fruit juices, and grenadine with ice. Strain into a large chilled wineglass. Fill with champagne and garnish with lemon peel.

Champagne Punch

(serves 10–14)

juice of 12 lemons
sugar to sweeten
½ cup Maraschino liqueur
1 cup triple sec

(continued)

2 cups brandy
2 cups chilled club soda
2 fifths chilled champagne
fresh fruit for garnish

Mix first 5 ingredients in a punch bowl and add a block of ice. Just before serving pour in soda and champagne. Garnish with fruit.

Claret Punch: substitute chilled claret for champagne.

———— **Champagne Sherbet Punch** ————

(serves 10–12)

1 qt frozen lemon sherbet
2 fifths chilled champagne
¾ tsp Angostura bitters
slices of lemon

Pour champagne over sherbet in a chilled punch bowl. Add bitters and stir. Garnish with lemon slices.

Variation: substitute pineapple sherbet for the lemon and garnish with slices of pineapple.

———— **Champagne Velvet** ————

See *Black Velvet.*

———— **Champs Elysées Cocktail** ————

1½ oz (3 Tbsp) brandy
½ oz (1 Tbsp) yellow Chartreuse
juice of ¼ lemon
1 dash Angostura bitters
½ tsp sugar (optional)

Shake ingredients with ice and strain into a chilled cocktail glass.

Chapala

1½ oz (3 Tbsp) tequila
½ oz (1 Tbsp) orange juice
½ oz (1 Tbsp) lemon juice
2 tsp grenadine
1 dash orange-flower water
slice of orange

Shake liquid ingredients with ice and strain into a chilled Old-Fashioned glass over ice cubes. Garnish with orange slice.

Chapel Hill

1½ oz (3 Tbsp) bourbon
½ oz (1 Tbsp) triple sec
½ oz (1 Tbsp) lemon juice
twist of lemon peel

Shake liquid ingredients with ice and strain into a chilled cocktail glass or into an Old-Fashioned glass over ice cubes. Garnish with orange peel.

Cherry Blossom Cocktail

2 oz (4 Tbsp) brandy
1 oz (2 Tbsp) cherry brandy
1 dash grenadine
1 dash lemon juice
1 dash orange curaçao

Sugar-rim a chilled cocktail glass by dipping first into cherry brandy and then into sugar. Shake ingredients with ice and strain into the glass.

——————— **Cherry Brandy Cooler** ———————

2 oz (4 Tbsp) cherry brandy
chilled cola
slice of lemon

Pour brandy and cola into a chilled collins or highball glass over ice and stir gently. Garnish with the lemon slice.

Variation: substitute cherry-flavored vodka for the brandy.

——————— **Cherry Cobbler** ———————

1½ oz (3 Tbsp) gin
¾ oz cherry brandy
½ oz (1 Tbsp) lemon juice
1 tsp sugar
slice of lemon
maraschino cherry

Fill a chilled highball or collins glass ⅔ full of crushed ice. Add liquid ingredients and sugar and stir until sugar dissolves. Top with more ice if necessary and garnish with lemon and cherry.

——————— **Cherry Fizz** ———————

2 oz (4 Tbsp) cherry brandy
juice of ½ lemon
½ tsp sugar (optional)
chilled club soda
maraschino cherry

Shake brandy, lemon juice, and sugar with ice and strain into a chilled collins or highball glass over ice cubes. Top with soda, stir gently, and garnish with the cherry.

——— **Cherry Rum** ———

1½ oz (3 Tbsp) light rum
¾ oz cherry brandy
½ oz (1 Tbsp) cream

Shake ingredients with ice and strain into a chilled cocktail glass.

Variation: put ingredients in a blender with ⅓ cup crushed ice. Blend at low speed for 15 seconds and pour into a chilled cocktail glass.

——— **Chicago Cocktail** ———

2 oz (4 Tbsp) cognac
1 dash triple sec
1 dash Angostura bitters

Sugar-rim a chilled cocktail glass by rubbing with lemon and dipping into sugar. Stir ingredients with ice and strain into the glass.

Variation: substitute curaçao for triple sec. Stir ingredients with ice, strain into a chilled wineglass, and top with champagne.

——— **Chinese Cocktail** ———

1½ oz (3 Tbsp) Jamaican rum
½ oz (1 Tbsp) grenadine
3 dashes triple sec or curaçao
3 dashes Maraschino liqueur
1 dash Angostura bitters

Shake ingredients with ice and strain into a chilled cocktail glass.

─────── **Chiquita** ───────

1½ oz (3 Tbsp) golden rum
½ oz (1 Tbsp) banana liqueur
1 tsp grenadine
1 oz (2 Tbsp) light cream

Place all ingredients in blender with ½ cup cracked ice. Cover and blend at high speed about 10 seconds or just until ice is thoroughly blended. Pour into chilled wineglass.

─────── **Chocolate Cocktail** ───────

1½ oz (3 Tbsp) port
½ oz (1 Tbsp) yellow Chartreuse
1 egg yolk
1 tsp cocoa powder or grated dark chocolate

Shake ingredients vigorously with ice and strain into a chilled cocktail glass.

─────── **Chocolate Rum** ───────

1 oz (2 Tbsp) light rum
½ oz (1 Tbsp) crème de cacao
½ oz (1 Tbsp) white crème de menthe
½ oz (1 Tbsp) cream
1 tsp 151-proof rum

Shake ingredients with ice and strain into a chilled cocktail glass or into an Old-Fashioned glass over ice cubes.

Variation: float 151-proof rum on top instead of shaking it with the other ingredients.

Cider Cup

(serves 2–3)

1 pt chilled apple cider
2 oz (4 Tbsp) brandy
2 oz (4 Tbsp) Cointreau or triple sec
6 oz chilled club soda
4 tsp sugar
sliced fresh fruit
mint sprigs

Mix first 5 ingredients in a pitcher with ice cubes or a chunk of ice. Garnish with fruit and mint. Serve in chilled punch cups or wineglasses.

Claret Cup: substitute claret for cider.

Cinderella

1½ oz (3 Tbsp) white rum
½ oz (1 Tbsp) port wine
1 egg white
2 tsp fresh lemon juice
1 tsp sugar syrup

Place all ingredients in shaker with several ice cubes. Cover and shake vigorously. Strain into chilled wineglass or hollow-stemmed champagne glass.

Claret Cobbler

"Claret" is an old term for red Bordeaux wine; you can use any Cabernet Sauvignon or similar red wine for this recipe.

1 tsp sugar
1 tsp lemon juice (optional)
2 oz (4 Tbsp) chilled club soda

(continued)

4 oz (8 Tbsp) chilled red wine
sliced fresh fruit in season

Dissolve sugar in soda and lemon juice in a large chilled wineglass. Add red wine and cracked ice. Garnish with fruit.

––––––––– **Claret Cup** –––––––––

See under *Cider Cup*.

––––––––– **Claret Lemonade I** –––––––––

½ oz (1 Tbsp) lemon juice (½ lemon)
1 tsp sugar
1 cup red wine
1 thin slice of lemon

Put lemon juice and sugar in a highball glass. Stir to dissolve sugar. Fill glass halfway with cracked ice and add red wine. Stir briefly and garnish with lemon slice. Serve with a straw.

––––––––– **Claret Lemonade II** –––––––––

1 oz (2 Tbsp) fresh lemon juice
2 tsp sugar syrup
2 oz (4 Tbsp) red wine
club soda
thin slice lemon

Put juice and syrup into a collins glass and stir to combine. Fill glass with crushed ice and pour in soda to three-quarters full. Float wine and lemon slice atop that. Serve with long straw.

─────── **Claret Punch** ───────

See under *Champagne Punch.*

─────── **Claridge Cocktail** ───────

1 oz (2 Tbsp) gin
1 oz (2 Tbsp) dry vermouth
½ oz (1 Tbsp) Cointreau or triple sec
½ oz (1 Tbsp) apricot brandy

Shake or stir ingredients with ice and strain into a
chilled cocktail glass.

─────── **Classic Cocktail** ───────

2 oz (4 Tbsp) brandy
½ oz (1 Tbsp) orange curaçao
½ oz (1 Tbsp) Maraschino liqueur
½ oz (1 Tbsp) lemon juice
twist of lemon peel

Shake liquid ingredients with ice and strain into a
chilled cocktail glass. Garnish with lemon peel.

Variation: sugar-rim the glass by rubbing with
lemon and dipping into sugar.

─────── **Close-Up** ───────

4 oz (8 Tbsp) dry white wine
1 oz (2 Tbsp) peach brandy
½ oz (1 Tbsp) apple brandy
dash orange bitters

Stir ingredients together in mixing glass and pour
into chilled wineglass.

——— **Clover Club Cocktail** ———

1½ oz (3 Tbsp) gin
juice of ½ lime or lemon
1 egg white
2 tsp grenadine
sprig of fresh mint

Shake liquid ingredients with ice and strain into a chilled cocktail glass or wineglass. Garnish with mint.

——— **Clover Leaf** ———

2 oz (4 Tbsp) gin
juice of 1 lime
1 or 2 tsp grenadine
1 egg white
mint sprig (optional)

Shake first 4 ingredients vigorously with cracked ice and strain into chilled cocktail glass. Garnish, if desired, with mint sprig.

——— **Cobbler** ———

See *Sherry Cobbler.*

——— **Coconut Tequila** ———

1½ oz (3 Tbsp) tequila
2 tsp cream of coconut
2 tsp lemon juice
1 tsp Maraschino liqueur
½ cup crushed ice

Put ingredients in a blender and blend at low speed for 15 or 20 seconds. Pour into a chilled champagne glass.

——— **Coffee Cocktail** ———

2½ oz medium-dry sherry
1½ oz (3 Tbsp) brandy
1 whole egg
1 tsp sugar
nutmeg

Shake first 4 ingredients vigorously with ice and strain into a chilled wineglass. Sprinkle with nutmeg.

Variation: substitute 1½ oz (3 Tbsp) port for the sherry.

——— **Coffee Flip** ———

1½ oz (3 Tbsp) brandy
1½ oz (3 Tbsp) port
1 whole egg
1 tsp sugar
2 tsp cream
½ tsp instant coffee
nutmeg

Shake ingredients, except nutmeg, vigorously with ice and strain into a chilled wineglass. Sprinkle with nutmeg.

Variation: substitute 1½ oz (3 Tbsp) coffee-flavored brandy for the brandy and instant coffee.

——— **Coffee Grasshopper** ———

See under *Grasshopper Cocktail.*

——— Cognac Coupling ———

2 oz (4 Tbsp) cognac
1 oz (2 Tbsp) tawny port
½ oz (1 Tbsp) Pernod
1 tsp lemon juice
2 dashes Peychaud's bitters (optional)

Shake ingredients with ice and strain into a chilled Old-Fashioned glass over ice cubes.

——— Cold Duck ———

(serves 15–18)

2 bottles German white wine
1 bottle champagne
1½ oz (3 Tbsp) lemon juice
¼–⅓ cup sugar
1 lemon thinly sliced

Mix sugar with lemon juice and pour over block of ice in large punch bowl. Add wine and champagne and stir gently. Float lemon slices.

——— Colleen ———

1½ oz (3 Tbsp) Irish whiskey
1 oz (2 Tbsp) Irish Mist
½ oz (1 Tbsp) Cointreau
1 tsp fresh lemon juice

Place all ingredients in shaker with 4 or 5 ice cubes. Cover and shake briskly. Strain into chilled cocktail glass.

Collins

See *Tom Collins*.

Colonial Cocktail

1½ oz (3 Tbsp) gin
¾ oz (1½ Tbsp) grapefruit juice
2–3 dashes Maraschino liqueur
green olive

Shake liquid ingredients with ice and strain into a chilled cocktail glass. Garnish with the olive.

Columbia Cocktail

1½ oz (3 Tbsp) light rum
¾ oz (1½ Tbsp) raspberry syrup
½ oz (1 Tbsp) lemon juice

Sugar-rim a chilled cocktail glass by rubbing with lemon and dipping into sugar. Shake ingredients with ice and strain into the glass.

Variation: add 1 tsp kirschwasser.

Combo

2½ oz (5 Tbsp) dry vermouth
1 tsp brandy
½ tsp curaçao
½ tsp sugar
1 dash Angostura bitters

Shake ingredients with ice and strain into a chilled Old-Fashioned glass over ice cubes.

—— Commodore Cocktail ——

2 oz (4 Tbsp) rye whiskey
2 dashes orange bitters
1 tsp sugar
juice of ½ lime

Shake ingredients with ice and strain into a chilled cocktail glass.

Variation: substitute juice of ¼ lemon for the lime juice.

—— Commuter Cocktail ——

1½ oz (3 Tbsp) bourbon
½ oz (1 Tbsp) sweet vermouth
½ oz (1 Tbsp) grenadine

Shake all ingredients with cracked ice and strain into chilled cocktail glass.

—— Cooch Behar ——

Thought to have been invented by a maharajah of Cooch Behar, India. To make pepper vodka, put a hot (Mexican) pepper into a bottle of vodka and let it steep for a week or two.

2 oz (4 Tbsp) pepper vodka
4 oz (8 Tbsp) tomato juice

Pour vodka and tomato juice into a chilled Old-Fashioned glass over ice cubes. Stir gently.

—— Cooler ——

See *Strawberry Cream Cooler.*

——————— **Cooperstown Cocktail** ———————

1½ oz (3 Tbsp) gin
¾ oz (1½ Tbsp) dry vermouth
¾ oz (1½ Tbsp) sweet vermouth
sprig of fresh mint

Shake liquid ingredients with ice and strain into a chilled cocktail glass. Garnish with mint.

——————— **Copenhagen** ———————

1½ oz (3 Tbsp) gin
1 oz (2 Tbsp) Aquavit
1 tsp dry vermouth
green olive (optional)

Place 4 or 5 ice cubes in shaker and add liquors. Cover and shake vigorously several times. Strain into chilled cocktail glass and add green olive, if desired.

——————— **Corkscrew** ———————

1½ oz (3 Tbsp) light rum
½ oz (1 Tbsp) dry vermouth
½ oz (1 Tbsp) peach brandy
slice of lime

Shake liquid ingredients with ice and strain into a chilled cocktail glass. Garnish with lime.

——————— **Cornell Cocktail** ———————

1½ oz (3 Tbsp) gin
1 egg white
1 tsp Maraschino liqueur

(continued)

Shake ingredients with ice and strain into a chilled cocktail glass.

Variation: add ½ tsp lemon juice.

Coronation Cocktail

1½ oz (3 Tbsp) dry sherry
1½ oz (3 Tbsp) dry vermouth
2 dashes orange bitters
1 dash Maraschino liqueur

Stir ingredients with ice and strain into a chilled cocktail glass.

Variation: add 4 oz (8 Tbsp) chilled white wine to above ingredients. Stir with ice and strain into a chilled highball glass. Top with chilled club soda.

Corpse Reviver I

1 oz (2 Tbsp) gin
1 oz (2 Tbsp) Cointreau or triple sec
1 oz (2 Tbsp) Swedish punch
1 oz (2 Tbsp) lemon juice
1 dash Pernod

Shake ingredients with ice and strain into a large chilled cocktail glass.

Corpse Reviver II

1 oz (2 Tbsp) brandy or cognac
1 oz (2 Tbsp) white crème de menthe
1 oz (2 Tbsp) Fernet-Branca

Shake ingredients with ice and strain into a chilled cocktail glass.

Variation: substitute peppermint schnapps for the crème de menthe.

Cosmopolitan

1 oz (2 Tbsp) vodka
½ oz (1 Tbsp) triple sec
1 oz (2 Tbsp) cranberry sauce
½ oz (1 Tbsp) lime juice

Place all ingredients in shaker with cracked ice. Cover and shake vigorously and strain into a chilled Martini glass. Twist lemon zest to release oils and add to drink.

Cossack

1 oz (2 Tbsp) cognac
1 oz (2 Tbsp) vodka
1 oz (2 Tbsp) lime juice
½ tsp sugar

Shake ingredients with ice and strain into a chilled cocktail glass.

Country Club Cooler

2 oz (4 Tbsp) dry vermouth
½ tsp grenadine
chilled club soda
twists of lemon and orange peel

Mix grenadine with a little soda in a chilled highball glass. Add ice cubes and vermouth. Top with soda and garnish with fruit peels.

Variation: substitute chilled ginger ale for club soda.

Cowboy Cocktail

3 oz (6 Tbsp) rye whiskey
1 oz (2 Tbsp) cream

Shake ingredients with ice and strain into a chilled cocktail glass.

Cranberry Frost

4 oz (8 Tbsp) cranberry juice
½ oz (1 Tbsp) calvados or other apple brandy
1 tsp lime juice
1 tsp sugar syrup

Place ingredients in shaker glass with 5 or 6 ice cubes and stir. Strain into highball glass half filled with cracked ice.

Cranberry Punch

(serves 12–16)

1 pkg (16 oz) whole cranberries
1 cup sugar
2 cups apple juice
1 cup cranberry juice
½ cup lemon juice (2 large lemons)
1 cup pineapple chunks and juice
1 fifth of vodka
1 qt club soda

Combine cranberries with the sugar and 2 cups of water in a large saucepan and bring to a boil. Reduce heat and simmer until berries are soft, stirring constantly. Put through strainer, mashing skins with a wooden spoon to extract the juice, and discard the skins. Combine with other ingredients (except the soda) and refrigerate for several hours or overnight.

When ready to serve, pour mixture over a block of ice in a punch bowl, add soda, and stir gently.

–––––––––– **Cranberry Wine Punch** ––––––––––

(serves 15)

3 cups vodka
1 cup Burgundy (or other dry red wine)
4 cups cranberry juice
orange slices
sliced strawberries

Pour all ingredients, except fruit, into a punch bowl over a large block of ice. Garnish with fruit slices and serve in chilled punch cups.

Variation: See Brandied Cranberry Punch.

–––––––––– **Creamy Orange** ––––––––––

1 oz (2 Tbsp) cream sherry
1 oz (2 Tbsp) orange juice
½ oz (1 Tbsp) brandy
½ oz (1 Tbsp) cream

Shake ingredients with ice and strain into a chilled cocktail glass.

–––––––––– **Creamy Screwdriver** ––––––––––

2 oz (4 Tbsp) vodka
1 egg yolk
1 tsp sugar
6 oz chilled orange juice
½ cup crushed ice

(continued)

Put ingredients in a blender and blend at low speed 15–20 seconds. Pour into a chilled collins glass over ice cubes.

────────── **Crème de Menthe Frappé** ──────────

2 oz (4 Tbsp) green crème de menthe
shaved ice

Fill a cocktail, Old-Fashioned, or small wine glass with the ice. Add crème de menthe and serve with short straws.

Variation: substitute white crème de menthe for the green.

────────── **Creole** ──────────

1½ oz (3 Tbsp) light rum
1 tsp lemon juice
1 dash Tabasco sauce
chilled beef bouillon
salt and pepper to taste

Shake rum, lemon, and Tabasco with ice. Strain into a chilled Old-Fashioned glass over ice cubes. Fill with bouillon and stir. Sprinkle with salt and pepper.

────────── **Creole Champagne Punch** ──────────

(serves 25–30)

1 ripe pineapple, peeled and cored
1 pt lemon juice (approx. 15 lemons)
1 cup sugar
½ cup Cointreau
½ cup brandy

2 bottles chilled champagne
or other sparkling wine
1 bottle dry white wine
1 liter chilled club soda
1 cup thinly sliced strawberries
block of ice

Halve pineapple. Finely chop one half, slice the other and reserve. In large crock combine chopped pineapple, lemon juice, sugar, Cointreau, and brandy. Cover and refrigerate overnight. When ready to serve, place block of ice in large punch bowl and pour in chilled mix. Add champagne and wine and stir gently. Float pineapple slices and strawberries. Just before serving pour club soda over ice. Ladle into punch cups.

———— **Creole Mint Julep** ————

A milder drink than the traditional bourbon julep, but decidedly refreshing.

1 6 oz water
3–6 tsp sugar, to taste
½ oz (1 Tbsp) brandy or whiskey
½ oz (1 Tbsp) lemon juice
zest of lemon and/or orange
6 (or more) sprigs of mint
3 or 4 ripe strawberries

Fill highball glass half full of water, add mint sprigs and 3 sugar lumps. With bar spoon bruise mint leaves and stir till sugar dissolved. Add liquor and stir well. Add peel and fill glass with crushed ice. Decorate with another sprig or two of mint and the strawberries. Sprinkle with crushed sugar before serving.

——— **Crusta** ———

2 oz (4 Tbsp) brandy
½ oz (1 Tbsp) lemon juice
1 tsp Maraschino liqueur
1 tsp curaçao
2 dashes Angostura bitters
peel of 1 whole lemon cut in
a continuous spiral

Sugar-rim a chilled wine glass by rubbing with lemon and dipping into sugar. Place the lemon peel around the rim. Shake liquid ingredients with ice and strain into the glass.

Variation: substitute gin for the brandy.

——— **Cuba Libre** ———

3 oz (6 Tbsp) light rum
juice of ½ lime
6 oz chilled cola
slice of lime

Pour rum, lime juice, and cola into a chilled collins glass over ice cubes. Stir and garnish with lime slice.

——— **Cuban Cocktail** ———

2 oz (4 Tbsp) brandy
1 oz (2 Tbsp) apricot brandy
1 oz (2 Tbsp) lime juice

Shake ingredients with ice and strain into a chilled cocktail glass.

Variation: add 1 tsp light rum.

─────── **Culross** ───────

1½ oz (3 Tbsp) light rum
½ oz (1 Tbsp) apricot brandy
½ oz (1 Tbsp) Lillet
1 tsp lemon juice

Shake ingredients with ice and strain into a chilled cocktail glass or into an Old-Fashioned glass over ice cubes.

─────── **Cup** ───────

See *Champagne Cup*.

─────── **Czarina** ───────

2 oz (4 Tbsp) vodka
½ oz (1 Tbsp) dry vermouth
½ oz (1 Tbsp) apricot brandy
dash bitters

Add all ingredients to shaker with half cup of cracked ice. Cover and shake vigorously several times. Strain into chilled cocktail glass.

D

─────── **Daiquiri** ───────

The Daiquiri was invented around 1900 in Daiquiri, Cuba, and has become one of the most popular rum drinks in the United States. The following is the original version, but with the invention of the blender the Frozen Daiquiri (usually made with fresh fruit) has gained almost as much popularity.

(continued)

2 oz (4 Tbsp) light rum
juice of ½ lime
1 tsp sugar

Shake ingredients vigorously with ice and strain into
a chilled cocktail glass.

Variations: add 1 tsp of egg white before shaking
for a foamier drink. Add 1 tsp Cointreau or triple sec.
Add a dash of apricot brandy. Substitute lemon juice
for the lime. Add 1 tsp grapefruit juice. Add 2 dashes grenadine. Garnish with a maraschino cherry or
twist of lemon peel.

Bacardi Cocktail: use 2 oz (4 Tbsp) Bacardi rum.
Substitute ¾ oz (1½ Tbsp) lime juice for juice of ½
lime and 1 tsp grenadine for the sugar.

Banana Daiquiri: use only 1½ oz (3 Tbsp) rum,
substitute 1½ oz (3 Tbsp) lime juice for juice of ½
lime, add ½ oz (1 Tbsp) Cointreau or triple sec, 1 cup
crushed ice, and 1 medium-size ripe banana. Blend
at medium speed for 15 seconds and serve in a large
chilled wineglass with a straw.

Derby Daiquiri: use only 1½ oz (3 Tbsp) rum,
substitute 1 oz (2 Tbsp) orange juice and ½ oz (1
Tbsp) lime juice for the juice of ½ lime, add ½ cup
crushed ice, put ingredients in blender and blend at
low speed for 20 seconds. Pour into a chilled wineglass.

Frozen Daiquiri: substitute 2 oz (4 Tbsp) lime juice
for the juice of ½ lime, add 1 tsp Cointreau or triple
sec and ¾ cup crushed ice, put in blender, blend at
medium speed for 20 seconds, and pour into a chilled
champagne, sour, or wine glass.

Frozen Kiwi Daiquiri: see *Gino's Kiwi Daiquiri.*

Frozen Mint Daiquiri: substitute ½ oz (1 Tbsp) lime juice for juice of ½ lime, add 6 mint leaves (crushed) and ½ cup crushed ice, put in blender, blend at low speed for 15–20 seconds, and pour into a chilled Old-Fashioned or champagne glass.

Frozen Peach Daiquiri: use only 1½ oz (3 Tbsp) rum. Add ½ fresh peeled peach or ½ canned peach. Increase sugar to 1½ tsp if using fresh peach. Put ingredients into blender with ½ cup crushed ice and blend at medium speed for 10–15 seconds. Pour into a chilled goblet.

Frozen Pineapple Daiquiri: substitute 1½ oz (3 Tbsp) rum for 2 oz (4 Tbsp) rum, 1 tsp lime juice for juice of ½ lime, add 4 chunks canned pineapple and ½ cup crushed ice, put in blender, blend at low speed for 15 seconds, and pour into a chilled Old-Fashioned or champagne glass.

Frozen Strawberry Daiquiri: combine 1 oz (2 Tbsp) light rum, ½ oz (1 Tbsp) strawberry liqueur, ¼ cup strawberries, 1 oz (2 Tbsp) lime juice, and 1 tsp sugar with ⅓ cup crushed ice, blend at medium speed until smooth, and serve in a chilled goblet or champagne glass.

Frozen Watermelon Daiquiri: substitute 1½ oz (3 Tbsp) rum for 2 oz (4 Tbsp) rum and ½ oz (1 Tbsp) lime juice for juice of ½ lime, add ½ cup seeded watermelon pieces, 1 tsp Cointreau or triple sec, and ⅓ cup crushed ice, put in blender, blend at medium speed for 10 seconds, and pour into a chilled champagne glass.

Daisy

See *Gin Daisy*.

——— Danish Gin Fizz ———

1½ oz (3 Tbsp) gin
½ oz (1 Tbsp) Peter Heering
1 tsp kirschwasser
½ oz (1 Tbsp) lime juice
1 tsp sugar
chilled club soda
slice of lime
maraschino cherry

Shake first 5 ingredients vigorously with ice. Strain into a chilled highball glass over ice cubes. Top with soda and garnish with cherry and lime.

——— Dark & Stormy ———

2 oz (4 Tbsp) rum
4 oz (8 Tbsp) ginger beer

Put 2 or 3 ice cubes in a chilled highball glass or copper mug. Add rum, fill with ginger beer, and stir.

——— Deauville Cocktail ———

¾ oz (1½ Tbsp) brandy
½ oz (1 Tbsp) apple brandy
½ oz (1 Tbsp) triple sec
½ oz (1 Tbsp) lemon juice

Shake ingredients with ice and strain into a chilled cocktail glass.

——— Delmonico ———

1½ oz (3 Tbsp) gin
½ oz (1 Tbsp) dry vermouth
½ oz (1 Tbsp) sweet vermouth

½ oz (1 Tbsp) brandy
dash bitters
zest of lemon

In shaker with 5 or 6 ice cubes place liquors and bitters. Cover and shake vigorously several times. Strain into chilled cocktail glass. Twist lemon zest over the drink to release oils and drop into drink.

Delta

1½ oz (3 Tbsp) blended whiskey
½ oz (1 Tbsp) Southern Comfort
1 tsp lime juice
1 tsp sugar syrup
orange slice and peach slice

In shaker add liquid ingredients with several ice cubes. Cover and shake vigorously, then strain into Old-Fashioned glass half filled with crushed ice. Garnish with peach slice and orange slice.

Dempsey Cocktail

1 oz (2 Tbsp) gin
1 oz (2 Tbsp) Calvados or apple brandy
½ tsp Pernod
2 dashes grenadine

Stir ingredients with ice and strain into a chilled cocktail glass.

Depth Bomb I

1½ oz (3 Tbsp) brandy
1½ oz (3 Tbsp) apple brandy
2 dashes lemon juice
1 dash grenadine

(continued)

Shake ingredients with ice and strain into a chilled Old-Fashioned glass over ice cubes. Also called a Depth Charge.

——— **Depth Bomb II** ———

This drink was a special favorite of servicemen during World War II.

1 shot glass of whiskey
1 glass of beer

Serve ingredients separately. Carefully drop the glass of whiskey into the glass of beer, and the drink is ready.

——— **Derby Cocktail** ———

1½ oz (3 Tbsp) bourbon
½ oz (1 Tbsp) B & B
½ oz (1 Tbsp) pineapple juice

Place ingredients in shaker with ½ cup cracked ice. Cover and shake briefly. Strain into chilled cocktail glass.

——— **Derby Daiquiri** ———

See under *Daiquiri*.

——— **Derby Fizz** ———

1½ oz (3 Tbsp) rye whiskey
juice of ½ lemon
1 whole egg
1 tsp sugar

3 dashes curaçao
chilled club soda

Shake ingredients, except soda, with ice. Strain into a chilled highball glass over ice cubes and top with soda.

Variation: substitute Scotch for rye and Cointreau or triple sec for curaçao.

——— **Derby Special** ———

2 oz (4 Tbsp) white or golden rum
½ oz (1 Tbsp) Cointreau
2 tsp lime juice
1 oz (2 Tbsp) orange juice

Place ingredients in blender with ½ cup cracked ice and blend at high speed 10–15 seconds. Pour into chilled wineglass.

——— **Desert Rose** ———

See under *Tequila Solo.*

——— **Devil's Cocktail** ———

1½ oz (3 Tbsp) port
1½ oz (3 Tbsp) dry vermouth
½ tsp lemon juice

Stir ingredients with ice and strain into a chilled cocktail glass.

——— **Devil's Tail** ———

1½ oz (3 Tbsp) light rum
1 oz (2 Tbsp) vodka

(continued)

¼ oz apricot brandy
½ oz (1 Tbsp) lime juice
2–3 dashes grenadine
½ cup crushed ice
twist of lemon peel

Put first 6 ingredients in a blender and blend at low speed for 15 seconds. Pour into a chilled wine or champagne glass and garnish with lemon peel.

——— Diablo ———

1½ oz (3 Tbsp) dry white port
1 oz (2 Tbsp) dry vermouth
¼ tsp lemon juice
twist of lemon peel (optional)

Shake liquid ingredients with ice and strain into a chilled cocktail glass. Garnish with lemon peel.

Variation: substitute sweet vermouth for dry.

——— Diana Cocktail ———

2 oz (4 Tbsp) white crème de menthe
3 tsp brandy

Fill a cocktail glass or small wineglass with crushed ice and pour in crème de menthe. Float brandy on top.

Variation: substitute peppermint schnapps for the crème de menthe.

——— Diplomat Cocktail ———

2 oz (4 Tbsp) dry vermouth
1 oz (2 Tbsp) sweet vermouth

2 dashes Maraschino liqueur
1 dash Angostura bitters (optional)
twist of lemon peel
maraschino cherry

Stir liquid ingredients with ice and strain into a chilled cocktail glass. Garnish with lemon peel and cherry.

——— **Dixie Cocktail** ———

1 oz (2 Tbsp) gin
½ oz (1 Tbsp) dry vermouth
½ oz (1 Tbsp) Pernod
juice of ¼ orange
2 dashes grenadine (optional)

Shake ingredients with ice and strain into a chilled cocktail glass.

——— **Dolly Hoskins** ———

1½ oz (3 Tbsp) gin
1 oz (2 Tbsp) peach brandy
1 tsp grenadine
½ oz (1 Tbsp) heavy cream

Place ingredients in shaker with 5 or 6 ice cubes, cover, and shake vigorously several times. Pour into chilled wineglass.

——— **Dolores Cocktail** ———

Said to have been created in tribute to the beautiful Mexican actress Dolores Del Rio.

¾ oz (1½ Tbsp) Spanish brandy
¾ oz (1½ Tbsp) cherry brandy

(continued)

¾ oz (1½ Tbsp) white or dark crème de cacao
maraschino cherry (optional)

Shake ingredients with ice and strain into a chilled
cocktail glass. Garnish with the cherry if desired.

Variation: add 1 egg white and shake vigorously.

──────── **Dream Cocktail** ────────

1½ oz (3 Tbsp) brandy
¾ oz Cointreau or triple sec
1 dash Pernod

Shake ingredients with ice and strain into a chilled
cocktail glass.

Variation: substitute curaçao for the Cointreau.

──────── **Dry Manhattan** ────────

See under *Manhattan*.

──────── **Dry Martini** ────────

See under *Martini*.

──────── **Dubarry Cocktail** ────────

1½ oz (3 Tbsp) gin
¾ oz (1½ Tbsp) dry vermouth
½ tsp Pernod
1 dash Angostura bitters
thin slice of orange

Stir liquid ingredients with ice and strain into a chilled
cocktail glass. Garnish with orange slice.

——— **Dubonnet Cocktail** ———

2 oz (4 Tbsp) red Dubonnet
1 oz (2 Tbsp) gin
twist of lemon peel

Stir liquid ingredients with ice and strain into a chilled cocktail glass. Garnish with lemon peel.

Variation: add a fresh dash of orange bitters, omit the lemon twist, and rub the rim of the glass with an orange peel (do not add the orange peel to the drink).

——— **Dubonnet Fizz** ———

2 oz (4 Tbsp) red Dubonnet
1 oz (2 Tbsp) cherry brandy
1 oz (2 Tbsp) orange juice
½ oz (1 Tbsp) lemon juice
1 tsp kirschwasser (optional)
chilled club soda
slice of lemon

Shake Dubonnet, brandy, juices, and kirschwasser with ice. Strain into a chilled highball glass and top with soda. Garnish with lemon slice.

——— **Duchess** ———

1 oz (2 Tbsp) Pernod
1 oz (2 Tbsp) dry vermouth
1 oz (2 Tbsp) sweet vermouth

Shake ingredients with ice and strain into a chilled cocktail glass.

─────── **Duke Cocktail** ───────

½ oz (1 Tbsp) Cointreau
2 tsp lemon juice
1 tsp orange juice
½ tsp white Maraschino liqueur
1 egg white
cold champagne

Shake first 5 ingredients vigorously with several ice cubes. Strain into chilled burgundy wine glass and top with champagne.

E

─────── **Earthquake** ───────

1 oz (2 Tbsp) rye or bourbon
1 oz (2 Tbsp) gin
1 oz (2 Tbsp) Pernod

Shake ingredients with ice and strain into a chilled cocktail glass.

─────── **East India Cocktail** ───────

1 oz (2 Tbsp) brandy
½ oz (1 Tbsp) curaçao
½ oz (1 Tbsp) pineapple juice
1 dash Angostura or orange bitters
twist of lemon peel (optional)
maraschino cherry (optional)

Shake liquid ingredients with ice and strain into a chilled cocktail glass. Garnish with lemon peel and cherry.

Variation: strain into a chilled highball glass over ice cubes and top with chilled club soda. Add 1 tsp Jamaican rum. Add a dash of Maraschino liqueur or raspberry syrup.

———— **East Indian** ————

1½ oz (3 Tbsp) dry sherry
1½ oz (3 Tbsp) dry vermouth
1 dash orange bitters

Shake ingredients with ice and strain into a chilled cocktail glass.

———— **Edwardian** ————

1½ oz (3 Tbsp) vodka
1½ oz (3 Tbsp) Dubonnet
1 tsp fresh lime juice
1 tsp grenadine

Place ingredients in shaker with ice cubes, cover, and shake briskly. Strain into chilled cocktail glass.

———— **Eggnog I** ————

(serves 1)

2 oz (4 Tbsp) rye whiskey
1 whole egg
1 tsp sugar
4 oz (8 Tbsp) chilled milk
nutmeg

Shake first 4 ingredients with ice and strain into a chilled collins glass or large wine glass. Sprinkle with nutmeg.

(continued)

Variation: add 1½ oz (3 Tbsp) Jamaican rum.

Baltimore Eggnog: substitute 1 oz (2 Tbsp) brandy or cognac and 1 oz (2 Tbsp) Jamaican rum for the whiskey and add 1 oz (2 Tbsp) madeira wine and 2 oz (4 Tbsp) heavy cream.

Brandy Eggnog: substitute brandy for whiskey.

Breakfast Eggnog: substitute 2 oz (4 Tbsp) brandy or apricot brandy for the whiskey and ½ oz (1 Tbsp) Cointreau or triple sec for the sugar.

Hot Eggnog: substitute 1 oz (2 Tbsp) rum and 1 oz (2 Tbsp) brandy for the whiskey and 6–8 oz hot milk for the chilled milk. Mix egg and sugar in a heated mug, add rum, brandy, and milk, stirring constantly. Sprinkle with nutmeg.

———— Eggnog II ————

(serves 12)

10 whole eggs (separated)
⅓ cup sugar
1 qt chilled heavy cream
1 pt chilled milk
1 fifth rye or bourbon whiskey
12 oz (4 Tbsp) Jamaican rum (optional)
nutmeg

Beat egg whites with all but 1 oz (2 Tbsp) of the sugar until thick and foamy. In a separate bowl beat egg yolks. Add egg white mixture to this and beat together until thoroughly combined. Put heavy cream [with 1 oz (2 Tbsp) sugar] in a punch bowl and beat until cream doubles in volume. While continuing to beat, slowly add egg mixture. When thoroughly combined continue beating while adding whiskey, rum, and milk. Sprinkle with nutmeg and chill for 2–3 hours (overnight is fine). Eggnog will thicken as it chills.

------- **Egg Toddy** -------

A hot drink, similar to eggnog.

2 egg yolks
½ oz (1 Tbsp) brown sugar
½ cup hot milk
½ oz (1 Tbsp) golden or dark rum
nutmeg (optional)

Whisk egg yolks with sugar till creamy. Gradually whisk in hot milk, then the rum. Pour into a warmed mug and, if desired, sprinkle top with a few gratings of nutmeg.

------- **El Diablo** -------

1½ oz (3 Tbsp) tequila
½ oz (1 Tbsp) crème de cassis
juice and rind of ½ lime
chilled ginger ale

Put lime juice and rind into a chilled collins glass over ice cubes. Add tequila and crème de cassis. Fill with ginger ale and stir gently.

See also *Diablo*.

------- **El Presidente** -------

3 oz (6 Tbsp) light rum
½ oz (1 Tbsp) dry vermouth
1 dash Angostura bitters

(continued)

Stir ingredients with ice and strain into a chilled cocktail glass.

Variation: substitute sweet vermouth or the juice of 1 lime for the dry vermouth. Add ½ oz (1 Tbsp) curaçao. Add a dash of grenadine.

Elk (Elk's Own) Cocktail

1½ oz (3 Tbsp) rye whiskey
¾ oz (1½ Tbsp) port
1 tsp sugar
1 egg white
juice of ¼ lemon
small wedge of fresh pineapple

Shake first 5 ingredients vigorously with ice and strain into a chilled cocktail glass. Garnish with pineapple.

Embassy Royal

1 oz (2 Tbsp) bourbon
1 oz (2 Tbsp) Drambuie
½ oz (1 Tbsp) sweet vermouth
2 dashes orange juice
twist of orange peel

Shake liquid ingredients with ice and strain into a chilled cocktail glass. Garnish with orange peel.

Emerald Isle Cocktail

2½ oz (5 Tbsp) gin
1 tsp green crème de menthe
3 dashes Angostura bitters
green cherry (optional)

Stir liquid ingredients with ice and strain into a chilled cocktail glass. Garnish with the cherry.

English Bolo

4 oz (8 Tbsp) dry sherry
1 tsp sugar
1½ oz (3 Tbsp) lemon juice
1 stick cinnamon

Muddle the cinnamon, sugar, and lemon juice in an Old-Fashioned glass. Add sherry and stir.

See also *Bolo.*

English Rose

1½ oz (3 Tbsp) gin
½ oz (1 Tbsp) dry vermouth
½ oz (1 Tbsp) apricot brandy
1 tsp lemon juice
1 tsp grenadine
maraschino cherry (optional)

Combine all ingredients in shaker with ½ cup cracked ice. Cover and shake vigorously several times. Strain into chilled cocktail glass and garnish, if desired.

Espresso Royal

(serves 6)

Coffee, dessert, and after-dinner drink all in one.

1 cup sugar
2 cups water
1 cup brewed espresso (extra strength)

(continued)

Kahlúa, Tia Maria, or other
coffee-flavored liqueur
whipped cream

In saucepan dissolve sugar in water over low heat.
Add espresso and stir to combine thoroughly. Remove
from heat and cool. Freeze 3 to 4 hours till slushy.
Spoon into chilled wineglasses and top with a tablespoon or two of liqueur and a dollop of whipped
cream.

Everybody's Irish Cocktail

2 oz (4 Tbsp) Irish whiskey
1 tsp green Chartreuse
3 dashes green crème de menthe
green olive

Stir liquid ingredients with ice and strain into a chilled
cocktail glass. Garnish with the olive.

Executive Suite

2 oz (4 Tbsp) brandy
1 oz (2 Tbsp) Grand Marnier
1–2 dashes orange bitters
cold champagne

To chilled hollow-stemmed champagne glass add ingredients in order given. Stir gently.

Eye-Opener Cocktail

1½ oz (3 Tbsp) light rum
1 tsp white crème de cacao
1 tsp orange curaçao
1 tsp Pernod

1 egg yolk
½ tsp sugar

Shake ingredients vigorously with ice and strain into
a chilled cocktail glass.

F

--------   **Fair-And-Warmer Cocktail**   --------

2 oz (4 Tbsp) light rum
1 oz (2 Tbsp) sweet vermouth
3 dashes curaçao
twist of lemon peel (optional)

Stir liquid ingredients with ice and strain into a chilled
cocktail glass. Garnish with lemon peel if desired.

--------   **Fallen Angel Cocktail**   --------

1½ oz (3 Tbsp) gin
¼ oz (1 Tbsp) white crème de menthe
½ oz (1 Tbsp) lemon juice
1 dash Angostura bitters
maraschino cherry (optional)

Shake liquid ingredients with ice and strain into a
chilled cocktail glass. Garnish with the cherry if desired.

Variation: substitute lime juice for lemon.

--------   **Fandango**   --------

2 oz (4 Tbsp) fino (dry sherry)
1 oz (2 Tbsp) golden rum
1–2 dashes orange bitters

(continued)

Place ingredients in shaker with 5 or 6 ice cubes, cover, and shake vigorously several times. Strain into chilled cocktail glass.

Fantasia

1½ oz (3 Tbsp) brandy
1 oz (2 Tbsp) dry vermouth
1 tsp white crème de menthe
1 tsp Maraschino liqueur
maraschino cherry (optional)

Shake first 4 ingredients together with cracked ice and strain into chilled cocktail glass. Garnish, if desired, with cherry.

Fare Thee Well

1½ oz (3 Tbsp) gin
½ oz (1 Tbsp) dry vermouth
2 dashes sweet vermouth
2 dashes curaçao

Shake ingredients with ice and strain into a chilled cocktail glass.

Favorite Cocktail

1 oz (2 Tbsp) gin
1 oz (2 Tbsp) apricot brandy
½ oz (1 Tbsp) dry vermouth
½ tsp fresh lemon juice

Shake all ingredients with cracked ice and strain into chilled cocktail glass.

─────── **Fernet Cocktail** ───────

1½ oz (3 Tbsp) Fernet-Branca
1½ oz (3 Tbsp) brandy
1 tsp sugar
1 dash Angostura bitters (optional)
twist of lemon or orange peel

Stir liquid ingredients with ice and strain into a chilled
cocktail glass. Garnish with lemon or orange peel.

─────── **Fifth Avenue** ───────

1 oz (2 Tbsp) dark crème de cacao
1 oz (2 Tbsp) apricot brandy
½ oz (1 Tbsp) cream

Pour ingredients carefully and slowly, in the order
given, into a cordial or Pousse-Café glass. Ingredients should be in layers.

─────── **Fifty-Fifty Cocktail** ───────

1½ oz (3 Tbsp) gin
1½ oz (3 Tbsp) dry vermouth
green olive

Stir liquid ingredients with ice and strain into a chilled
cocktail glass. Garnish with the olive.

─────── **Fine-And-Dandy Cocktail** ───────

1½ oz (3 Tbsp) gin
¾ oz (1½ Tbsp) Cointreau or triple sec
½ oz (1 Tbsp) lemon juice
1 dash Angostura bitters
maraschino cherry

(continued)

Stir liquid ingredients with ice and strain into a chilled cocktail glass. Garnish with the cherry.

───────── **Fino Martini** ─────────

See under *Martini*.

───────── **Firemen's Sour** ─────────

2 oz (4 Tbsp) rum
juice of 1 lime
½ tsp sugar
½ oz (1 Tbsp) grenadine
slice of lemon
maraschino cherry

Shake liquid ingredients with ice and strain into a chilled cocktail glass. Garnish with lemon and cherry.

───────── **Fish House Punch** ─────────

(serves 18–24)

1½ cups sugar
3 cups lemon juice (12 large lemons)
2 qts Jamaican rum
6 cups chilled water
6 oz peach brandy
1 qt brandy
1 cup sliced peaches (optional)

Dissolve sugar in lemon juice in a large punch bowl. Add rum, water, and brandies and stir. Allow to stand at room temperature for several hours, stirring occasionally. Before serving, add block of ice and peaches.

Variation: substitute light rum for Jamaican rum for a less "heavy" punch.

Fix

See *Brandy Fix.*

Fizz

See *Gin Fizz.*

Flamingo Cocktail

1½ oz (3 Tbsp) gin
½ oz (1 Tbsp) apricot brandy
½ oz (1 Tbsp) lime juice
1 tsp grenadine

Shake ingredients with ice and strain into a chilled cocktail glass.

Flip

See *Sherry Flip.*

Florida

½ oz (1 Tbsp) gin
1½ tsp kirschwasser
1½ tsp Cointreau or triple sec
1½ oz (3 Tbsp) orange juice
1 tsp lemon juice

Shake ingredients with ice and strain into a chilled cocktail glass or into an Old-Fashioned glass over ice cubes.

——— **Florida Special** ———

1½ oz (3 Tbsp) light rum
1 tsp dry vermouth
1 tsp sweet vermouth
1 oz (2 Tbsp) grapefruit juice

Stir ingredients with ice and strain into a chilled cocktail glass.

——— **Flying Dutchman** ———

3 oz (6 Tbsp) gin
1 dash triple sec or curaçao
1 dash orange bitters (optional)

Stir ingredients with ice and strain into a chilled cocktail glass.

——— **Flying Grasshopper Cocktail** ———

1 oz (2 Tbsp) vodka
¾ oz (1½ Tbsp) green crème de menthe
¾ oz (1½ Tbsp) white crème de menthe

Stir ingredients with ice and strain into a chilled cocktail glass.

——— **Flying Scotchman Cocktail** ———

1½ oz (3 Tbsp) Scotch
1½ oz (3 Tbsp) sweet vermouth
¼ tsp sugar syrup
1 dash Angostura bitters

Stir ingredients with ice and strain into a chilled cocktail glass.

Fog Cutter

1½ oz (3 Tbsp) light rum
⅔ oz brandy
½ oz (1 Tbsp) gin
⅔ oz orange juice
1 oz (2 Tbsp) lemon juice
1 tsp orgeat syrup
1 tsp sweet sherry

Shake all ingredients, except sherry, with ice and
strain into a chilled collins glass over ice cubes. Float
sherry on top.

Fog Horn

2 oz (4 Tbsp) gin
juice of 1 lime
chilled ginger ale

In chilled highball glass with 4 or 5 ice cubes squeeze
lime juice and add the squeezed halves. Pour in gin
and top with chilled ginger ale. Stir before serving.

Fort Lauderdale

1½ oz (3 Tbsp) light rum
¾ oz (1½ Tbsp) sweet vermouth
juice of ¼ lime
juice of ¼ orange
slice of orange
maraschino cherry (optional)

Shake liquid ingredients with ice and strain into a
chilled Old-Fashioned glass over ice cubes. Garnish
with orange and cherry.

———— **Foxhound** ————

1½ oz (3 Tbsp) brandy
¾ oz cranberry juice
1 tsp kümmel
1 dash lemon juice
slice of lemon

Shake liquid ingredients with ice and strain into a chilled Old-Fashioned glass over ice cubes. Garnish with lemon slice.

———— **Fox River Cocktail** ————

2 oz (4 Tbsp) rye whiskey
½ oz (1 Tbsp) crème de cacao
3–4 dashes Angostura bitters
twist of lemon peel

Stir liquid ingredients with ice and strain into a chilled cocktail glass. Garnish with lemon peel.

Variation: substitute peach bitters for Angostura.

———— **Fraise Fizz** ————

1½ oz (3 Tbsp) gin
1 oz (2 Tbsp) strawberry liqueur
½ oz (1 Tbsp) lemon juice
1 tsp sugar
chilled club soda
twist of lemon peel
1 fresh strawberry

Shake gin, liqueur, lemon juice, and sugar with ice. Strain into a chilled highball glass (with or without ice cubes) and top with soda. Stir and garnish with lemon peel and strawberry.

———— Frankenjack Cocktail ————

1 oz (2 Tbsp) gin
1 oz (2 Tbsp) dry vermouth
½ oz (1 Tbsp) apricot brandy
1 tsp Cointreau or triple sec
maraschino cherry

Stir liquid ingredients with ice and strain into a chilled cocktail glass. Garnish with the cherry.

———— Frappé ————

See *Crème de Menthe Frappé.*

———— Freedom Fighter ————

1½ oz (3 Tbsp) sloe gin
½ oz (1 Tbsp) crème yvette
2 tsp lemon juice
1 egg white

Place all ingredients in shaker with 4 or 5 ice cubes. Cover and shake vigorously. Strain into chilled cocktail or wine glass.

———— French Connection ————

2 oz (4 Tbsp) brandy
1 oz (2 Tbsp) amaretto

Pour ingredients into Old-Fashioned or sour glass half-filled with cracked ice. Serve with small straw.

———— French Manhattan ————

See under *Manhattan.*

────── French Rose ──────

3 oz (6 Tbsp) rosé wine
½ oz (1 Tbsp) cherry brandy
½ oz (1 Tbsp) cherry liqueur

Put ingredients in shaker with cracked ice. Cover and shake quickly 2 or 3 times. Strain into chilled champagne glass.

────── French "75" ──────

1 oz (2 Tbsp) lemon juice
1 tsp sugar
1 oz (2 Tbsp) gin or cognac
3 oz (6 Tbsp) chilled champagne

Stir lemon and sugar together in a tall chilled glass, add 3–4 cubes of ice; gin or cognac, and champagne.

Variation: mix lemon, sugar, gin, and champagne with 1 egg white, ½ oz (1 Tbsp) heavy cream, and ice. Shake vigorously and strain into a large chilled champagne or wine glass. Add twist of lemon peel and/or a cherry as garnish.

────── Frisco Sour ──────

2½ oz (5 Tbsp) rye whiskey
¾ oz (1½ Tbsp) Benedictine
¼ oz (½ Tbsp) lemon juice
¼ oz (½ Tbsp) lime juice
slice of lime and lemon

Shake liquid ingredients with ice and strain into a chilled cocktail or sour glass. Garnish with lemon and lime.

Frobisher

1½ oz (3 Tbsp) gin
2 or 3 dashes bitters
cold champagne
zest of lemon (optional)

In highball glass with 6 or 8 ice cubes add gin and bitters. Top very slowly with champagne. Garnish with lemon zest, if desired.

Froth Blower Cocktail

2 oz (4 Tbsp) gin
1 egg white
1 tsp grenadine

Shake ingredients with ice and strain into a chilled cocktail glass.

Froupe Cocktail

1½ oz (3 Tbsp) brandy
1½ oz (3 Tbsp) sweet vermouth
1 tsp Benedictine

Stir ingredients with ice and strain into a chilled cocktail glass.

Frozen Apple

(serves 2)

3 oz (6 Tbsp) applejack
1 oz (2 Tbsp) lime juice
2 tsp sugar
1 egg white
1 cup crushed ice

(continued)

Put ingredients into a blender and blend at low speed for 15 seconds. Pour into chilled Old-Fashioned or champagne glasses.

─────── **Frozen Berkeley** ───────

1½ oz (3 Tbsp) light rum
½ oz (1 Tbsp) brandy
1 tsp lemon juice
1 tsp passionfruit juice
½ cup crushed ice

Put ingredients into a blender and blend at low speed for 10–15 seconds. Pour into a chilled champagne or sour glass.

─────── **Frozen Brandy & Rum** ───────

1½ oz (3 Tbsp) brandy
1 oz (2 Tbsp) light rum
½ oz (1 Tbsp) lemon juice
1 egg yolk
1 tsp sugar
½ cup crushed ice

Put ingredients into a blender and blend at low speed for 15 seconds. Pour into a chilled Old-Fashioned or champagne glass.

─────── **Frozen Daiquiri** ───────

See under *Daiquiri*.

─────── **Fuzzy Navel** ───────

1½ oz (3 Tbsp) peach schnapps
orange juice, to taste

Pour schnapps into an ice-filled collins glass. Fill with orange juice and stir to combine.

G

Gauguin

2 oz (4 Tbsp) light rum
½ oz (1 Tbsp) passionfruit syrup
½ oz (1 Tbsp) lemon juice
½ oz (1 Tbsp) lime juice
½ cup crushed ice
maraschino cherry

Put first 5 ingredients in a blender and blend at low speed for 15 seconds. Pour into chilled Old-Fashioned or champagne glass. Garnish with the cherry.

Gazebo

A delicious drink named for the summertime retreat.

1½ oz (3 Tbsp) gin
½ oz (1 Tbsp) Cointreau
½ oz·(1 Tbsp) blue Curaçao
dash or two of bitters
zest of lemon and maraschino cherry
(optional)

In shaker combine liquors and bitters with 4 or 5 ice cubes. Cover and shake vigorously several times. Strain into cocktail glass filled with crushed ice. Add zest and cherry.

––––––– **General Harrison's Eggnog** –––––––

1 egg
1 tsp sugar syrup
8 oz hard cider

Place ingredients in blender with 1 cup of cracked ice and blend at high speed 10–15 seconds. Pour into chilled highball glass and serve with straw.

Variation: substitute dry red wine for hard cider.

––––––– **Genoa** –––––––

¾ oz (1½ Tbsp) gin
¾ oz (1½ Tbsp) grappa
2 tsp sambuca
2 tsp dry vermouth
green olive

Stir liquid ingredients with ice and strain into a chilled cocktail glass or into an Old-Fashioned glass over ice cubes. Garnish with the olive.

Variation: eliminate the gin and increase the grappa to 1½ oz (3 Tbsp).

––––––– **Gibson** –––––––

See under *Martini.*

––––––– **Gilroy Cocktail** –––––––

1 oz (2 Tbsp) gin
1 oz (2 Tbsp) cherry brandy
½ oz (1 Tbsp) dry vermouth
2 tsp lemon juice
1–2 dashes bitters

Shake together with cracked ice and strain into chilled cocktail glass.

─────── **Gimlet** ───────

2 oz (4 Tbsp) gin
1 oz (2 Tbsp) Rose's lime juice
1 slice lime (optional)

Shake liquid ingredients with ice and strain into a chilled cocktail glass. Garnish with lime slice.

Variation: substitute fresh lime juice for Rose's and add ½ tsp sugar.

Vodka Gimlet: substitute vodka for the gin.

─────── **Gin & Bitters** ───────

2–3 oz (6 Tbsp) gin
3 dashes Angostura bitters

Put bitters into a cocktail glass and swirl the bitters to coat the inside of the glass. Shake out any excess and add the gin.

Variation: ice is not usually used in this drink but can be added if desired. Chilled gin can be used.

─────── **Gin & It** ───────

British slang for a sweet Martini.

2 oz (4 Tbsp) gin
1 oz (2 Tbsp) sweet vermouth

Place ingredients in a cocktail glass and stir. No ice is used.

(continued)

Variation: use equal parts of gin and vermouth [1½ oz (3 Tbsp) each]. Garnish with a maraschino cherry.

───────── **Gin & Sin** ─────────

1 oz (2 Tbsp) gin
1 oz (2 Tbsp) orange juice
1 oz (2 Tbsp) lemon juice
1 dash grenadine

Shake ingredients with ice and strain into a chilled cocktail glass.

───────── **Gin & Tonic** ─────────

3 oz (6 Tbsp) gin
4–6 oz cold tonic (quinine) water
slice or wedge of lemon or lime

Put 2 ice cubes in a highball glass, add gin, and fill glass with tonic water. Do not stir. Garnish with lemon or lime.

Vodka & Tonic: substitute vodka for gin.

───────── **Gin Buck** ─────────

2 oz (4 Tbsp) gin
juice of ½ lemon
chilled ginger ale

Pour gin and lemon juice over ice cubes in a chilled highball glass. Top with ginger ale.

Variation: substitute lime juice for lemon.

Gin Daisy

2 oz (4 Tbsp) gin
1 oz (2 Tbsp) lemon juice
½ tsp sugar
1 tsp raspberry syrup (or grenadine)
fresh fruit

Shake liquid ingredients with ice and strain into a chilled collins glass over ice cubes. Garnish with fresh fruit.

Gin Fizz

2 oz (4 Tbsp) gin
1 tsp sugar
1 oz (2 Tbsp) lemon juice
chilled club soda

Shake gin, sugar, and lemon juice with ice and strain into a chilled highball glass over ice cubes. Top with soda.

Sloe Gin Fizz: substitute sloe gin for the gin and use only ½ tsp sugar.

Gino's Kiwi Daiquiri

(serves 2)

4 oz (8 Tbsp) white rum
4 oz (8 Tbsp) water
2 oz (4 Tbsp) Galliano
1 kiwi fruit (peeled)
1 oz (2 Tbsp) sugar
juice of ½ lemon (or lime)
6–8 cubes ice (or 1 cup cracked ice)
2 slices of kiwi fruit

(continued)

Put ingredients, except kiwi slices, in a blender. Blend at high speed 20–30 seconds. Pour into 2 chilled highball glasses and garnish with kiwi slices.

—————— **Gin Rickey** ——————

2 oz (4 Tbsp) gin
juice of ½ lime
chilled club soda
maraschino cherry

Pour gin and lime into a chilled highball glass over ice cubes. Top with soda and stir gently. Garnish with maraschino cherry.

Sloe Gin Rickey: substitute sloe gin for the gin.

—————— **Gin Sangaree** ——————

See under *Sangaree.*

—————— **Gin Sling** ——————

See under *Sling.*

—————— **Gin Smash** ——————

See under *Brandy Smash.*

—————— **Gin Sour** ——————

See under *Whiskey Sour.*

—————— **Gin Stinger** ——————

See under *Stinger.*

——— **Gin Swizzle** ———

See *Swizzle*.

——— **Gin Toddy, Hot** ———

See under *Hot Toddy*.

——— **Ginza Fizz** ———

1½ oz (3 Tbsp) rye whiskey
½ oz (1 Tbsp) port
½ oz (1 Tbsp) fresh lemon juice
1 tsp sugar syrup
1 egg white
club soda
pineapple chunk

Shake first 5 ingredients together with 5 or 6 ice
cubes. Strain into chilled highball glass and top with
soda. Stir and garnish with pineapple chunk on toothpick or skewer.

——— **Glad Eye** ———

2 oz (4 Tbsp) Pernod or pastis
1 oz (2 Tbsp) peppermint liqueur

Stir ingredients with ice and strain into a chilled cocktail glass.

——— **Glögg** ———

(serves 10)

Sometimes called the Swedish national drink, and a
special Christmas drink throughout Scandinavia.

(continued)

2 qts dry red wine
1 pt sweet vermouth
15 whole cloves
2 cinnamon sticks
20 cardamom seeds (crushed)
2 oz (4 Tbsp) dried orange peel
1½ cups blanched almonds
1½ cups raisins
½ lb sugar lumps
1 cup aquavit

Put all ingredients, except sugar and aquavit, in a pan and boil slowly for 20 minutes, stirring occasionally. Place a rack on top of the pan and spread the sugar lumps on it. Warm the aquavit and thoroughly saturate the sugar. Ignite and let the sugar melt into the glögg mixture. Stir again. Serve in heated mugs or punch cups with a few almonds and raisins in each. Leftover glögg can be bottled and reheated.

–––––––– **Gloom Chaser** ––––––––

¾ oz (1½ Tbsp) Grand Marnier
¾ oz (1½ Tbsp) curaçao
¾ oz (1½ Tbsp) lemon juice
¾ oz (1½ Tbsp) grenadine
twist of orange peel (optional)

Shake liquid ingredients with ice and strain into a chilled cocktail glass. Garnish with orange peel.

–––––––– **Gloom Lifter** ––––––––

(serves 2)

4 oz (8 Tbsp) rye whiskey
juice of 1 lemon

1 tsp sugar
1 egg white

Shake ingredients vigorously with ice and strain into chilled cocktail glasses.

Variation: add 1 oz (2 Tbsp) brandy. Add 2 tsp raspberry syrup.

Gloom Raiser

2½ oz (5 Tbsp) gin
½ oz (1 Tbsp) dry vermouth
2 dashes Pernod
2 dashes grenadine

Stir ingredients with ice and strain into a chilled cocktail glass.

Variation: float Pernod on top of drink.

Godfather

2 oz (4 Tbsp) Scotch
1 oz (2 Tbsp) amaretto or almond liqueur

Pour ingredients into a chilled Old-Fashioned glass over ice cubes and stir gently.

Variation: substitute bourbon for Scotch.

Godmother

2 oz (4 Tbsp) vodka
1 oz (2 Tbsp) amaretto or almond liqueur

Pour ingredients into a chilled Old-Fashioned glass over ice cubes and stir gently.

——— Golden Cadillac ———

¾ oz (1½ Tbsp) Galliano
¾ oz (1½ Tbsp) white crème de cacao
¾ oz (1½ Tbsp) cream
⅓ cup crushed ice

Put ingredients into a blender and blend at low speed for 10 seconds. Pour into a chilled cocktail or champagne glass.

——— Golden Dawn ———

1½ oz (3 Tbsp) gin
¾ oz (1½ Tbsp) apricot brandy
¾ oz (1½ Tbsp) orange juice

Shake ingredients with ice and strain into a chilled cocktail glass or into an Old-Fashioned glass over ice cubes.

Variation: add ¾ oz (1½ Tbsp) apple brandy.

——— Golden Dream ———

1½ oz (3 Tbsp) Galliano
¾ oz (1½ Tbsp) Cointreau or triple sec
½ oz (1 Tbsp) orange juice
½ oz (1 Tbsp) cream

Shake ingredients with ice and strain into a chilled cocktail glass.

——— Golden Fizz ———

2 oz (4 Tbsp) gin
1 oz (2 Tbsp) lemon juice
¾ tsp sugar

1 whole egg
chilled club soda

Shake first 4 ingredients with ice and strain into a chilled collins or large wine glass. Top with soda.

——— **Golden Gate** ———

1 oz (2 Tbsp) light rum
½ oz (1 Tbsp) gin
½ oz (1 Tbsp) lemon juice
½ oz (1 Tbsp) white crème de cacao
pinch of ginger
slice of orange

Shake first 5 ingredients with ice and strain into a chilled Old-Fashioned glass over ice cubes. Garnish with orange slice.

Variations: use equal parts (¾ oz each), rum and gin. Substitute dark rum and dark crème de cacao for the light varieties.

——— **Golden Lemonade** ———

1 oz (2 Tbsp) orange-flavored brandy
1 egg yolk
1 oz (2 Tbsp) fresh lemon juice
2 tsp sugar syrup
club soda
orange slice
maraschino cherry

Place first 4 ingredients in shaker with 5 or 6 ice cubes. Cover and shake vigorously. Strain into chilled collins glass and top with soda. Stir and garnish with orange and cherry.

(continued)

Variation: substitute dry white wine or champagne for the soda.

Golden Slipper Cocktail

2 oz (4 Tbsp) apricot brandy
1 oz (2 Tbsp) yellow Chartreuse
1 egg yolk

Shake ingredients vigorously with ice and strain into a chilled cocktail glass.

Variation: stir brandy and Chartreuse with ice, strain into a chilled cocktail glass, and float egg yolk on top.

Golden Tang

1½ oz (3 Tbsp) vodka
¾ oz (1½ Tbsp) Strega
½ oz (1 Tbsp) banana liqueur
½ oz (1 Tbsp) orange juice

Shake ingredients with ice and strain into a chilled cocktail glass.

Golf Cocktail

2 oz (4 Tbsp) gin
1 oz (2 Tbsp) dry vermouth
2 dashes Angostura bitters

Stir ingredients with ice and strain into a chilled cocktail glass.

──────── **Granada** ────────

1 oz (2 Tbsp) dry sherry
1 oz (2 Tbsp) brandy
½ oz (1 Tbsp) orange curaçao
chilled tonic water
slice of orange

Shake sherry, brandy, and curaçao with ice and pour into a chilled highball glass. Top with tonic and garnish with orange slice.

──────── **Grand Passion** ────────

2 oz (4 Tbsp) gin
1 oz (2 Tbsp) passionfruit juice
1 dash Angostura bitters

Shake ingredients with ice and strain into a chilled cocktail glass.

Variations: add juice of ½ lemon. Substitute light rum or tequila for gin. Substitute peach bitters for Angostura.

──────── **Grand Royal Fizz** ────────

½ oz (1 Tbsp) fresh lemon juice
½ oz (1 Tbsp) orange juice
2 oz (4 Tbsp) gin
1 tsp sugar syrup
1 tsp Maraschino liqueur
1 egg white
chilled club soda

Add all ingredients but soda to shaker with 5 or 6 ice cubes. Cover and shake vigorously several times. Strain into chilled highball glass and top with soda. Stir gently.

(continued)

Variation: substitute 1 tablespoon heavy cream for egg white.

─────── **Grand Slam** ───────

1½ oz (3 Tbsp) Swedish punch
¾ oz (1½ Tbsp) sweet vermouth
¾ oz (1½ Tbsp) dry vermouth

Stir ingredients with ice and strain into a chilled cocktail glass.

─────── **Grapefruit Cocktail** ───────

2 oz (4 Tbsp) gin
1 oz (2 Tbsp) grapefruit juice

Shake ingredients with ice and strain into a chilled cocktail glass.

Variation: add 1 tsp Maraschino liqueur and garnish with a cherry.

─────── **Grapefruit Nog** ───────

1½ oz (3 Tbsp) brandy
4 oz (8 Tbsp) unsweetened grapefruit juice
1 oz (2 Tbsp) lemon juice
½ oz (1 Tbsp) honey
1 whole egg
½ cup crushed ice

Put ingredients in a blender and blend at low speed for 15–20 seconds. Pour into a chilled collins glass and add ice cubes.

Grappa Strega

1 oz (2 Tbsp) grappa
1 oz (2 Tbsp) Strega
1 tsp lemon juice
1 tsp orange juice
twist of lemon peel

Shake liquid ingredients with ice and strain into a chilled cocktail glass. Garnish with lemon peel.

Grasshopper Cocktail

1 oz (2 Tbsp) white crème de menthe
1 oz (2 Tbsp) green crème de menthe
1 oz (2 Tbsp) cream

Shake ingredients with ice and strain into a chilled cocktail glass.

Variations: garnish with finely grated chocolate. Substitute white crème de cacao for white crème de menthe.

Coffee Grasshopper: substitute 1 oz (2 Tbsp) coffee brandy for the green crème de menthe.

See also *Flying Grasshopper Cocktail.*

Greek Buck

1½ oz (3 Tbsp) Metaxa brandy
2 tsp lemon juice
chilled ginger ale
1 tsp Ouzo
slice of lemon (optional)

Shake Metaxa and lemon juice with ice. Strain into a chilled collins glass over ice cubes. Top with ginger

(continued)

ale and stir gently. Float Ouzo on top and garnish with lemòn if desired.

─────── **Greek Coffee** ───────

Not exactly the real thing, but a perfectly acceptable substitute.

6 oz hot coffee
1 oz (2 Tbsp) Metaxa brandy
½ oz (1 Tbsp) Kahlúa, Tia Maria,
or other coffee liqueur
1–1 oz (2 Tbsp) cream (optional)

In heavy glass mug pour in Kahlúa, followed by the Metaxa. Fill to desired level with the coffee. Top with cream, if desired.

─────── **Greenbriar** ───────

2 oz (4 Tbsp) dry sherry
1 oz (2 Tbsp) dry vermouth
1 dash Angostura or peach bitters
sprig of fresh mint

Stir liquid ingredients with ice and strain into a chilled cocktail glass or into an Old-Fashioned glass over ice cubes. Garnish with mint.

─────── **Green Devil** ───────

1½ oz (3 Tbsp) gin
2 tsp green crème de menthe
½ oz (1 Tbsp) lime juice
fresh mint leaves

Shake liquid ingredients with ice and strain into an Old-Fashioned glass over ice cubes. Garnish with mint.

--------- **Green Dragon Cocktail** ---------

1½ oz (3 Tbsp) gin
¾ oz (1½ Tbsp) kümmel
¾ oz (1½ Tbsp) green crème de menthe
½ oz (1 Tbsp) lemon juice
4 dashes orange or peach bitters

Shake ingredients with ice and strain into a chilled cocktail glass.

--------- **Green Lady** ---------

1½ oz (3 Tbsp) gin
½ oz (1 Tbsp) yellow Chartreuse
½ oz (1 Tbsp) green Chartreuse
½ oz (1 Tbsp) lime juice
twist of lime peel

Shake liquid ingredients with ice and strain into a chilled cocktail glass. Garnish with lime peel.

Variation: substitute lemon juice for lime and garnish with lemon peel.

--------- **Grog** ---------

1 slice lemon
4 whole cloves
1 tsp or 1 lump sugar
½ cinnamon stick
2 oz (4 Tbsp) Jamaican rum
3 oz (6 Tbsp) boiling water

(continued)

Stick cloves into lemon slice. Put lemon and other ingredients into heated mug or glass and stir to dissolve sugar.

See also *Navy Grog*.

———— Gypsy Life ————

2 oz (4 Tbsp) vodka
1 oz (2 Tbsp) Benedictine
1–2 dashes orange bitters

Shake ingredients with ice and strain into chilled cocktail glass.

H

———— Hair Raiser Cocktail ————

1½ oz (3 Tbsp) vodka
½ oz (1 Tbsp) Rock & Rye
juice of ½ lemon

Shake ingredients with ice and strain into a chilled cocktail glass.

Variation: substitute 1 oz (2 Tbsp) Dubonnet for Rock & Rye.

———— Happy Youth ————

1 oz (2 Tbsp) cherry brandy
3 oz (6 Tbsp) chilled orange juice
1 tsp sugar
chilled champagne
slice of orange

Pour ingredients, except champagne and orange slice, into a highball or large stemmed glass over ice cubes. Stir gently and top with champagne. Garnish with orange slice.

——— **Harvard Cocktail** ———

1½ oz (3 Tbsp) brandy
1½ oz (3 Tbsp) sweet vermouth
2 dashes Angostura bitters
1 dash sugar syrup
twist of lemon peel (optional)

Shake liquid ingredients with ice and strain into a chilled cocktail glass. Garnish with lemon peel.

Variation: use only ¾ oz (1½ Tbsp) vermouth. Add 1–2 tsp lemon juice.

——— **Harvard Cooler** ———

2 oz (4 Tbsp) applejack or apple brandy
1 tsp sugar
chilled club soda
twist of lemon peel

Dissolve sugar in brandy in a chilled collins glass. Add ice and top with soda. Stir gently and garnish with lemon peel.

Variation: add juice of ½ lemon.

——— **Harvey Wallbanger** ———

Simply a Screwdriver with a few dashes of Galliano, this drink has a colorful history. The story may or may not be true, but it was used successfully to promote the sale of Galliano, and the drink gained sud-

(continued)

den popularity in the 1960s. According to the story, a young California surfer named Harvey often consoled himself after losing a contest by consuming numerous Screwdrivers laced with Galliano. As he left the bar he would bang into the walls. Hence the name Harvey Wallbanger.

> 2 oz (4 Tbsp) vodka
> 4 oz (8 Tbsp) orange juice
> ½–1 oz (1–2 Tbsp) Galliano

Pour vodka and orange juice into a chilled collins glass over ice cubes and stir. Float Galliano on top.

Variation: shake vodka and orange juice with ice and strain into a chilled cocktail glass. Float Galliano.

———— Hasty Cocktail ————

> 1½ oz (3 Tbsp) gin
> ¾ oz (1½ Tbsp) dry vermouth
> ¼ tsp Pernod
> 3 dashes grenadine

Shake ingredients with ice and strain into a chilled cocktail glass.

———— Havana (Beach) Cocktail ————

> 1½ oz (3 Tbsp) light rum
> 1½ oz (3 Tbsp) pineapple juice
> ½ tsp lemon juice

Shake ingredients with ice and strain into a chilled cocktail glass.

Variation: eliminate the lemon juice and add 1 tsp sugar, ½ lime cut in pieces, and ½ cup crushed ice. Put ingredients in a blender and blend at medium speed for 15 seconds. Pour into a highball glass and top with chilled ginger ale. Garnish with a sliver of lime.

——————— **Hawaiian Cocktail** ———————

2 oz (4 Tbsp) gin
½ oz (1 Tbsp) Cointreau or triple sec
½ oz (1 Tbsp) pineapple juice

Shake ingredients with ice and strain into a chilled cocktail glass.

Variation: substitute orange juice for pineapple. Add 1 egg white.

——————— **Heavenly Express** ———————

1½ oz (3 Tbsp) brandy
½ oz (1 Tbsp) cherry brandy (kirsch)
½ oz (1 Tbsp) slivovitz

Pour ingredients in the order given into an Old-Fashioned glass filled with cracked ice. Stir gently.

——————— **Helen of Troy** ———————

1½ oz (3 Tbsp) vodka
1 oz (2 Tbsp) cherry brandy
1–2 dashes orange bitters

Place ingredients in shaker with 5 or 6 ice cubes and stir briefly. Strain into wineglass half filled with crushed ice.

—————— **Helen Twelvetrees** ——————

Apparently named for the famous screen beauty.

> 2 oz (4 Tbsp) Southern Comfort
> ½ oz (1 Tbsp) blackberry cordial
> 4–6 oz 7-Up or ginger ale
> sprig of mint

In a highball glass place 3 or 4 ice cubes and add ingredients in above order. Stir gently and garnish with sprig of mint. Serve with a long straw.

—————— **Hennessy Martini** ——————

Not gin or vodka but brandy, and surprisingly popular.

> 2 oz (4 Tbsp) Hennessy V.S. or other brandy
> squeeze of lemon juice
> zest of lemon peel

Combine liquid ingredients with 3 or 4 ice cubes and stir gently. Rub rim of chilled martini glass with lemon zest and add to glass. Pour in strained liquid.

—————— **Highball** ——————

See *Whiskey Highball.*

—————— **Highland Cooler** ——————

> 2 oz (4 Tbsp) Scotch
> 1 tsp sugar
> 2 oz (4 Tbsp) chilled club soda
> chilled ginger ale
> twist of lemon peel

Dissolve sugar in club soda in a chilled highball glass. Add ice cubes and Scotch. Top with ginger ale and stir gently.

Variation: add juice of ½ lemon.

Highland Fling Cocktail

2 oz (4 Tbsp) Scotch
1 oz (2 Tbsp) sweet vermouth
2–3 dashes orange bitters
green olive (optional)

Shake ingredients with ice and strain into chilled cocktail glass. Add a green olive, if desired.

Hole-In-One

2 oz (4 Tbsp) Scotch
1 oz (2 Tbsp) dry vermouth
2 dashes lemon juice
1 dash orange bitters

Shake ingredients with ice and strain into a chilled cocktail glass.

Hollywood Boulevard

2 oz (4 Tbsp) orange juice
1 oz (2 Tbsp) vodka
chilled white wine
sprig of mint
orange slice

To highball glass filled with cracked ice add orange juice and vodka and stir well. Top with wine and stir briefly. Garnish with mint and affix orange slice to rim of glass.

——— **Homestead Cocktail** ———

2 oz (4 Tbsp) gin
1 oz (2 Tbsp) sweet vermouth
slice of orange

Stir gin and vermouth with ice and strain into a chilled cocktail glass. Garnish with orange slice.

——— **Honeydew** ———

1½ oz (3 Tbsp) gin
1 dash Pernod
⅓ cup diced honeydew melon
¾ oz (1½ Tbsp) lemon juice
½ tsp sugar (optional)
½ oz (1 Tbsp) cream
½ cup crushed ice
chilled club soda

Put all ingredients, except soda, into a blender and blend at low speed for 20 seconds. Pour into a large chilled stemmed glass or highball glass over ice cubes. Top with soda.

Variation: eliminate the cream and top off with chilled champagne instead of soda.

——— **Honolulu Cocktail** ———

1½ oz (3 Tbsp) gin
1 dash Angostura bitters
½ tsp sugar
¼ tsp orange juice
¼ tsp lemon juice
¼ tsp pineapple juice

Shake ingredients with ice and strain into a chilled cocktail glass.

Hoopla

¾ oz (1½ Tbsp) brandy
¾ oz (1½ Tbsp) Cointreau or triple sec
¾ oz (1½ Tbsp) Lillet
¾ oz (1½ Tbsp) lemon juice

Shake ingredients with ice and strain into a large
chilled cocktail glass.

Hoot(s) Mon Cocktail

1½ oz (3 Tbsp) Scotch
¾ oz (1½ Tbsp) Lillet
¾ oz (1½ Tbsp) sweet vermouth
twist of lemon peel

Stir liquid ingredients with ice and strain into a chilled
cocktail glass. Garnish with lemon peel.

Variation: substitute 1 tsp Benedictine for Lillet.

Hop Toad

1½ oz (3 Tbsp) light rum
1½ oz (3 Tbsp) apricot brandy
2 tsp fresh lime juice

Shake all ingredients with cracked ice and strain into
chilled cocktail glass.

Hopscotch

1½ oz (3 Tbsp) Scotch whiskey
1 oz (2 Tbsp) sweet vermouth
½ tsp sugar syrup
1–2 dashes orange bitters
maraschino cherry (optional)

(continued)

Shake first 4 ingredients with cracked ice and strain into chilled cocktail glass. Add cherry, if desired.

Horse's Neck (With A Kick)

2 oz (4 Tbsp) rye or bourbon
peel of 1 lemon cut in a continuous spiral
chilled ginger ale

Put lemon peel in a chilled collins glass, allowing it to curl over the edge, and add ice cubes. Pour in whiskey and top with ginger ale. Stir gently.

Variation: substitute brandy for whiskey.

Hot Brick Toddy

1½ oz (3 Tbsp) rye whiskey
1 tsp butter
1 tsp brown or powdered sugar
dash of cinnamon
1 oz (2 Tbsp) hot water
4–6 oz boiling water

In heated whiskey glass dissolve butter, sugar, and cinnamon in hot water. Add whiskey and stir in boiling water to desired strength.

Hot Buttered Rum

1 lump sugar
½ cinnamon stick
2 cloves (optional)
slice of lemon
6 oz boiling water
½ oz (1 Tbsp) butter
2 oz (4 Tbsp) rum
nutmeg

Put sugar and spices, except nutmeg, in a heated mug and add boiling water. Add butter and rum and stir. Sprinkle with nutmeg.

Variations: add 1 tsp maple syrup.

Hot Rum Cow: substitute 8 oz hot milk for the boiling water.

———— **Hot Eggnog** ————

See under *Eggnog I.*

———— **Hot Mulled Wine** ————

See *Glögg, Mulled Wine.*

———— **Hot Rum Cow** ————

See under *Hot Buttered Rum.*

———— **Hot Spiced Wine (Vin Chaud)** ————

(serves 2)

1 pt Burgundy wine
1½–2 oz (2–3 Tbsp) sugar
5 whole cloves
stick of cinnamon
2 slices of lemon
2 dashes orange curaçao

Heat ingredients almost to a boiling point, stirring occasionally. Serve in heated wineglasses or mugs.

——— Hot Toddy ———

1 lump sugar
½ stick cinnamon
slice of lemon
3 whole cloves
2 oz (4 Tbsp) rye whiskey
4–6 oz boiling water
nutmeg

Dissolve sugar in boiling water in a heated mug. Add cinnamon, cloves, and rye and stir. Sprinkle with nutmeg.

Variations: eliminate cinnamon and cloves and simply mix together the rye, water, sugar, and lemon. Sprinkle with nutmeg.

Hot Gin Toddy: substitute gin for rye.

Hot Rum Toddy: substitute light rum for rye.

——— Hudson Bay ———

1 oz (2 Tbsp) gin
½ oz (1 Tbsp) cherry brandy
1 tsp 151-proof rum
½ oz (1 Tbsp) orange juice
1 tsp lime juice
slice of lime (optional)

Shake liquid ingredients with ice and strain into a chilled cocktail glass. Garnish with lime if desired.

——— Hula-Hula Cocktail ———

1½ oz (3 Tbsp) gin
¾ oz (1½ Tbsp) orange juice
½ tsp sugar

Shake ingredients with ice and strain into a chilled cocktail glass.

Variation: eliminate the sugar and add 2 dashes curaçao.

──────── **Hurricane** ────────

1 oz (2 Tbsp) dark rum
1 oz (2 Tbsp) light rum
juice of ½ lime
½ oz (1 Tbsp) passionfruit juice

Shake ingredients with ice and strain into a chilled cocktail glass.

Variation: shake 1½ oz (3 Tbsp) dark rum, 1½ oz (3 Tbsp) lemon juice, 2 oz (4 Tbsp) passionfruit juice, and 1 tsp sugar with ice. Strain into a chilled highball glass over ice cubes.

I

──────── **Ideal Cocktail** ────────

1½ oz (3 Tbsp) gin
1 oz (2 Tbsp) dry vermouth
2 dashes Maraschino liqueur
1 tsp grapefruit juice
maraschino cherry

Shake liquid ingredients with ice and strain into a chilled cocktail glass. Garnish with the cherry.

Variations: substitute lemon juice for grapefruit. Substitute sweet vermouth for dry.

——————— **Imperial Fizz** ———————

1½ oz (3 Tbsp) rye or bourbon
1 tsp sugar
juice of ½ lemon
chilled club soda

Shake ingredients, except soda, with ice and strain into a chilled highball glass. Top with soda.

Variation: add ½ oz (1 Tbsp) light rum. Substitute chilled champagne for soda.

——————— **Imperial (Martini) Cocktail** ———————

See under *Martini*.

——————— **Inca** ———————

¾ oz (1½ Tbsp) gin
¾ oz (1½ Tbsp) dry vermouth
¾ oz (1½ Tbsp) sweet vermouth
¾ oz (1½ Tbsp) dry sherry
1 dash Angostura or orange bitters
1 dash orgeat syrup

Stir ingredients with ice and strain into a chilled cocktail glass.

——————— **Income Tax Cocktail** ———————

1½ oz (3 Tbsp) gin
½ oz (1 Tbsp) dry vermouth
½ oz (1 Tbsp) sweet vermouth
1 dash Angostura bitters
juice of ¼ orange

Shake ingredients with ice and strain into a chilled cocktail glass.

———— **Ink Street** ————

1 oz (2 Tbsp) rye whiskey
1 oz (2 Tbsp) lemon juice
1 oz (2 Tbsp) orange juice

Shake ingredients with ice and strain into a chilled cocktail glass.

———— **Irish Blackthorn** ————

1½ oz (3 Tbsp) Irish whiskey
1 oz (2 Tbsp) dry vermouth
3 dashes Pernod
3 dashes Angostura bitters

Stir ingredients with ice and strain into a chilled Old-Fashioned glass over ice cubes.

See also *Blackthorn.*

———— **Irish Coffee** ————

1½ oz (3 Tbsp) Irish whiskey
1 tsp sugar (optional)
5 oz strong hot black coffee
whipped cream

Put sugar into a heated cup or stemmed goblet. Add whiskey and coffee and stir. Top with a dollop of whipped cream.

Variation: float heavy cream on top instead of whipped cream.

——— **Irish Cooler** ———

2 oz (4 Tbsp) Irish whiskey
chilled club soda
peel of ½ lemon cut in a continuous spiral

Pour whiskey into a chilled collins or highball glass over ice cubes. Fill with soda, stir gently, and garnish with lemon peel.

——— **Irish Shillelagh** ———

Packs the wallop of a shillelagh, but with an agreeable aftertaste.

2 oz (4 Tbsp) Irish whiskey
½ oz (1 Tbsp) light rum
½ oz (1 Tbsp) sloe gin
½ oz (1 Tbsp) fresh lemon juice
1 tsp sugar syrup
peach slice
maraschino cherry

Place first 5 ingredients in shaker with 5 or 6 ice cubes. Cover and shake vigorously. Strain into large Old-Fashioned glass half-filled with cracked ice. Garnish as desired and serve with short straw.

——— **Irish Whiskey Cream** ———

(serves 8)

1 cup heavy cream
1 can (14 oz) sweetened condensed milk
3 large eggs, lightly beaten
1 oz (2 Tbsp) chocolate syrup
½ tsp coconut extract
1 cup Irish whiskey

In bowl whisk together ingredients in the order given. Cover and refrigerate several hours or overnight. Serve in chilled punch cups or small Old-Fashioned glasses. Makes eight 4-oz servings.

J

Jack Frost

1 oz (2 Tbsp) rye whiskey
1 oz (2 Tbsp) dry sherry
1 oz (2 Tbsp) port
orange and lemon slices

Add ingredients to Old-Fashioned glass half-filled with cracked ice. Stir and garnish with orange and lemon slice. Serve with short straw.

Jack-In-The-Box Cocktail

1½ oz (3 Tbsp) apple brandy
1½ oz (3 Tbsp) pineapple juice
1 dash Angostura bitters

Shake ingredients with ice and strain into a chilled cocktail glass.

Jack Rose Cocktail

2 oz (4 Tbsp) Calvados or apple brandy
juice of ½ lime
2 dashes grenadine
lemon twist (optional)

Shake ingredients with ice and strain into a chilled cocktail glass. Garnish with lemon.

(continued)

Variation: substitute ¾ oz (1½ Tbsp) lemon juice for the lime juice.

——— Jade ———

1½ oz (3 Tbsp) dark rum
½ oz (1 Tbsp) green crème de menthe
½ oz (1 Tbsp) triple sec
½ oz (1 Tbsp) lime juice
1 tsp sugar
slice of lime

Shake first 5 ingredients with ice and strain into a chilled cocktail glass. Garnish with lime slice.

Variation: substitute light rum for dark.

——— Jamaica Glow ———

1½ oz (3 Tbsp) gin
½ oz (1 Tbsp) dark rum
½ oz (1 Tbsp) dry red wine
½ oz (1 Tbsp) orange juice

Shake ingredients with cracked ice and strain into chilled cocktail glass.

——— Jamaican Cocktail ———

1 oz (2 Tbsp) Jamaican rum
1 oz (2 Tbsp) Tia Maria or other coffee brandy
1 oz (2 Tbsp) lime juice
1 dash Angostura bitters (optional)

Shake ingredients with ice and strain into a chilled cocktail glass.

─────── **Jamaican Doubloon** ───────

1 oz (2 Tbsp) white or light rum
1 oz (2 Tbsp) dark Jamaican rum
1 oz (2 Tbsp) 151-proof rum
1 oz (2 Tbsp) orange juice
1 oz (2 Tbsp) grapefruit juice
1 tsp Pernod or Ricard
1 tsp orange curaçao
orange slice
maraschino cherry

In mixing glass with several ice cubes pour first 7 ingredients and stir to combine. Strain into highball glass half-filled with cracked ice and garnish with orange slice and cherry.

─────── **Jamaican Rumba** ───────

2 oz (4 Tbsp) dark Jamaican rum
1 oz (2 Tbsp) Tia Maria
2 or 3 dashes orange bitters
1 oz (2 Tbsp) cream

Shake all ingredients with ice. Strain into chilled wineglass.

─────── **Jamboree** ───────

2 oz (4 Tbsp) dark Jamaican rum
½ oz (1 Tbsp) peach brandy
½ oz (1 Tbsp) curaçao
2 tsp lime juice
1–2 dashes orange bitters
pineapple stick (optional)

Place first 5 ingredients in shaker, cover, and shake vigorously. Strain into highball glass three-quarters

(continued)

filled with cracked ice. Garnish with pineapple stick, if desired.

Japanese

2 oz (4 Tbsp) brandy
1 tsp orgeat syrup or almond extract
1½ tsp lime juice
1 dash Angostura bitters
twist of lemon peel

Shake liquid ingredients with ice and strain into a chilled cocktail glass. Garnish with lemon peel.

Java Cooler

2 oz (4 Tbsp) gin
½ oz (1 Tbsp) fresh lime juice
1–2 dashes bitters
tonic water

Place 4 or 5 ice cubes in a highball glass. Add gin, lime juice, and bitters and stir gently to combine. Top off with tonic water and stir again before serving.

Jewel Cocktail

1 oz (2 Tbsp) gin
1 oz (2 Tbsp) sweet vermouth
1 oz (2 Tbsp) green Chartreuse
1–2 dashes orange bitters
maraschino cherry

Shake first 4 ingredients with cracked ice and strain into chilled cocktail glass. Garnish with cherry.

--------- **Jockey Club Cocktail** ---------

2 oz (4 Tbsp) gin
2 dashes white crème de cacao
juice of ¼ lemon
1 dash Angostura or orange bitters

Shake ingredients with ice and strain into a chilled cocktail glass.

Variation: substitute crème de noyaux for the crème de cacao.

--------- **Jocose Julep** ---------

2½ oz (5 Tbsp) bourbon
½ oz (1 Tbsp) green crème de menthe
1 oz (2 Tbsp) lime juice
1 tsp sugar
5 mint leaves
chilled club soda
½ cup crushed ice
2 sprigs of mint

Put ingredients, except club soda and mint, into a blender and blend at low speed for 15 seconds. Pour into a thoroughly frosted collins glass or metal mug over ice cubes. Top with soda and garnish with mint sprigs.

--------- **John Collins** ---------

See under *Tom Collins*.

--------- **Joulouville** ---------

1 oz (2 Tbsp) gin
½ oz (1 Tbsp) apple brandy

(continued)

¼ oz sweet vermouth
½ oz (1 Tbsp) lemon juice
2 dashes grenadine

Shake ingredients with ice and strain into a chilled
cocktail glass.

———— **Judge Jr. Cocktail** ————

1 oz (2 Tbsp) gin
1 oz (2 Tbsp) light rum
1 oz (2 Tbsp) lemon juice
2 dashes grenadine
½ tsp sugar

Shake ingredients with ice and strain into a chilled
cocktail glass.

———— **Judgette Cocktail** ————

1 oz (2 Tbsp) gin
1 oz (2 Tbsp) peach brandy
1 oz (2 Tbsp) dry vermouth
3 dashes lime juice
maraschino cherry (optional)

Shake liquid ingredients with ice and strain into a
chilled cocktail glass. Garnish with the cherry.

———— **Julep** ————

See *Mint Julep*, etc.

K

Kahlúa Cocktail

2 oz (4 Tbsp) Kahlúa
2 dashes crème de noyaux
½ tsp cream

Fill a chilled Old-Fashioned glass ½ full of crushed ice.
Pour in Kahlúa and crème de noyaux and float cream
on top. Serve with a short straw.

Kamikaze

1 oz (2 Tbsp) vodka
1 oz (2 Tbsp) triple sec
1 oz (2 Tbsp) Rose's Lime Juice

Shake ingredients with ice. Serve over ice in an Old
Fashion glass. Garnish with lime.

Kangaroo Cocktail

1½ oz (3 Tbsp) vodka
¾ oz (1½ Tbsp) dry vermouth
twist of lemon peel

Stir vodka and vermouth with ice and strain into a
chilled cocktail glass or into an Old-Fashioned glass
over ice cubes. Garnish with lemon peel.

K. C. B. Cocktail

Sometimes called K.G.B., but the ingredients are the
same.

(continued)

2 oz (4 Tbsp) gin
½ oz (1 Tbsp) kümmel or kirsch
1 tsp apricot brandy
½ tsp lemon juice
twist of lemon

Shake first 4 ingredients with cracked ice and strain into chilled cocktail glass. Twist peel over glass to activate oils and drop in.

─────── **Kempinski Cocktail** ───────

(serves 2)

Probably originated at the Hotel Kempinski in Berlin.

1 oz (2 Tbsp) Bacardi rum
1 oz (2 Tbsp) Cointreau
2 oz (4 Tbsp) chilled grapefruit juice
maraschino cherries

Shake liquid ingredients with crushed ice and strain into chilled cocktail glasses. Garnish each with a cherry.

─────── **Kentucky Cocktail** ───────

1½ oz (3 Tbsp) bourbon
¾ oz (1½ Tbsp) pineapple

Shake ingredients with ice and strain into a chilled cocktail glass.

Variation: sugar-rim the glass by rubbing with lemon and dipping into sugar. Add ½ oz (1 Tbsp) lemon juice and 2 dashes Maraschino liqueur.

--------- **Kentucky Colonel Cocktail** ---------

1½ oz (3 Tbsp) bourbon
2 tsp Benedictine
twist of lemon peel (optional)

Stir liquid ingredient with ice and strain into a chilled cocktail glass or into an Old-Fashioned glass over ice cubes. Garnish with lemon peel.

--------- **Kerry Cooler** ---------

2 oz (4 Tbsp) Irish whiskey
1 oz (2 Tbsp) dry sherry
½ oz (1 Tbsp) orgeat syrup or almond extract
1 oz (2 Tbsp) lemon juice
chilled club soda
slice of lemon

Shake whiskey, sherry, orgeat, and lemon juice with ice. Strain into a chilled collins glass over ice cubes. Top with soda and garnish with lemon slice.

--------- **King Cole Cocktail** ---------

2 oz (4 Tbsp) bourbon
½ tsp sugar
1 slice orange
1 slice pineapple

Muddle sugar, orange, and pineapple in an Old-Fashioned glass. Add ice and bourbon and stir well.

--------- **Kingston** ---------

1 oz (2 Tbsp) Jamaican rum
1 oz (2 Tbsp) gin

(continued)

½ oz (1 Tbsp) lemon or lime juice
3 dashes grenadine

Shake ingredients with ice and strain into a chilled cocktail glass.

Variation: substitute curaçao for gin.

——————— **Kir Cocktail** ———————

Said to have been named after a former mayor of Dijon, France.

6 oz chilled dry white wine
½ oz (1 Tbsp) créme de cassis
twist of lemon peel

Pour wine and crème de cassis into a large chilled wineglass over ice cubes and stir. Garnish with lemon peel.

Kir Royale: substitute champagne for the white wine.

——————— **Klondike Cooler** ———————

2 oz (4 Tbsp) rye whiskey
peel of 1 orange cut in a continuous spiral
1 tsp sugar
chilled ginger ale or club soda

Dissolve sugar in a small amount of ginger ale in a chilled highball glass. Add orange peel, ice cubes, and rye. Top with ginger ale.

——————— **Knickerbocker Cocktail** ———————

1½ oz (3 Tbsp) gin
¾ oz dry vermouth

2 dashes sweet vermouth
twist of lemon peel

Stir liquid ingredients with ice and strain into a chilled cocktail glass. Garnish with lemon peel.

Knickerbocker Special Cocktail

2 oz (4 Tbsp) light rum
½ tsp triple sec
1 tsp raspberry syrup
1 tsp pineapple juice
1 tsp orange juice
1 tsp lemon or lime juice
small slice of fresh pineapple

Shake liquid ingredients vigorously with ice and strain into a chilled cocktail glass. Garnish with pineapple slice.

Knock-Out Cocktail

¾ oz (1½ Tbsp) gin
¾ oz (1½ Tbsp) Pernod
¾ oz (1½ Tbsp) dry vermouth
1 tsp white crème de menthe
sprig of fresh mint or a maraschino cherry

Stir liquid ingredients with ice and strain into a chilled cocktail glass. Garnish with mint or cherry.

Kretchma Cocktail

1 oz (2 Tbsp) vodka
1 oz (2 Tbsp) white crème de cacao
½ oz (1 Tbsp) lemon juice
1 dash grenadine

(continued)

Shake ingredients with ice and strain into a chilled cocktail glass.

——— **Kup's Indispensable Cocktail** ———

2 oz (4 Tbsp) gin
1 oz (2 Tbsp) sweet vermouth
1 oz (2 Tbsp) dry vermouth
1 dash Angostura bitters
twist of orange peel (optional)

Stir liquid ingredients with ice and strain into a chilled cocktail glass. Garnish with orange peel.

Variation: use only ½ oz (1 Tbsp) sweet vermouth.

L

——— **Ladies' Cocktail** ———

2 oz (4 Tbsp) bourbon
½ tsp Pernod
½ tsp anisette
2 dashes Angostura bitters
slice of fresh pineapple

Stir liquid ingredients with ice and strain into a chilled cocktail glass. Garnish with pineapple.

——— **Lady Be Good** ———

1½ oz (3 Tbsp) brandy
¾ oz (1½ Tbsp) white crème de menthe
¾ oz (1½ Tbsp) sweet vermouth

Shake ingredients with ice and strain into a chilled cocktail glass.

——— **Lady Finger** ———

1½ oz (3 Tbsp) gin
¾ oz (1½ Tbsp) kirsch
¾ oz (1½ Tbsp) cherry brandy

Shake ingredients with ice and strain into a chilled cocktail glass.

——— **Lady Macbeth** ———

2 oz (4 Tbsp) Scotch
1 tsp white curaçao
1 tsp amaretto
2 tsp lemon juice
1 tsp sugar
1–2 dashes orange bitters

Place ingredients in shaker with 5 or 6 ice cubes, cover, and shake vigorously several times. Strain into chilled cocktail glass.

——— **L'Aiglon** ———

2 tsp Mandarine Napoléon
(orange-flavored brandy)
cold champagne
maraschino cherry (optional)

In a chilled champagne flute pour the Mandarine Napoléon and fill the glass with champagne. Add cherry, if desired.

——— **La Jolla** ———

1½ oz (3 Tbsp) brandy
½ oz (1 Tbsp) banana liqueur

(continued)

2 tsp lemon juice
1 tsp orange juice

Sugar-rim a chilled cocktail glass by rubbing with
lemon and dipping into sugar. Shake ingredients with
ice and strain into the glass.

La Stupenda

Said to have been named for a famous opera star.

2 oz (4 Tbsp) vodka
½ oz (1 Tbsp) crème de framboise
1 oz (2 Tbsp) heavy cream

Place ingredients in shaker with 4 or 5 ice cubes,
cover, and shake vigorously several times. Strain into
chilled cocktail glass.

Lawhill Cocktail

1½ oz (3 Tbsp) rye whiskey
¾ oz (1½ Tbsp) dry vermouth
2 dashes Pernod
2 dashes Maraschino liqueur
1 dash Angostura bitters

Stir ingredients with ice and strain into a chilled cocktail glass.

Lazy Afternoon

dry white wine, chilled
½ oz (1 Tbsp) peach brandy
1 tsp anisette
1 tsp fresh lemon juice

In a highball glass filled with cracked ice pour brandy, anisette, and lemon juice. Stir briefly and top with wine. Serve with long straw.

--------- **Leave-It-To-Me Cocktail I** ---------

1 oz (2 Tbsp) gin
½ oz (1 Tbsp) apricot brandy
½ oz (1 Tbsp) dry vermouth
2 dashes lemon juice
1 dash grenadine

Shake ingredients with ice and strain into a chilled cocktail glass.

--------- **Leave-It-To-Me Cocktail II** ---------

2 oz (4 Tbsp) gin
1 tsp raspberry syrup
1 tsp lemon juice
1 dash grenadine
1 egg white (optional)

Shake ingredients vigorously with ice and strain into a chilled cocktail glass.

--------- **Leeward** ---------

1½ oz (3 Tbsp) light rum
½ oz (1 Tbsp) Calvados
½ oz (1 Tbsp) sweet vermouth
twist of lemon peel

Shake liquid ingredients with ice and strain into a chilled cocktail glass or into an Old-Fashioned glass over ice cubes. Garnish with lemon peel.

——————— **Liberty Cocktail** ———————

1½ oz (3 Tbsp) apple brandy
¾ oz (1½ Tbsp) light rum
1 dash sugar syrup

Stir ingredients with ice and strain into a chilled cocktail glass.

——————— **Lillet Cocktail** ———————

1½ oz (3 Tbsp) Lillet
¾ oz (1½ Tbsp) gin
twist of lemon peel

Stir gin and Lillet with ice and strain into a chilled cocktail glass. Garnish with peel.

Variation: add 1–2 dashes crème de noyaux.

——————— **Limey** ———————

1 oz (2 Tbsp) light rum
1 oz (2 Tbsp) lime liqueur
2 tsp triple sec
2 tsp lime juice
½ cup crushed ice
twist of lemon peel

Put first 5 ingredients into a blender and blend at low speed for 15 seconds. Pour into a large chilled wine or champagne glass. Garnish with lemon peel.

——————— **Linstead Cocktail** ———————

1 oz (2 Tbsp) Scotch
1 oz (2 Tbsp) pineapple juice
1 dash Pernod

½ tsp sugar
2 dashes lemon juice

Shake ingredients with ice and strain into a chilled cocktail glass.

Variation: substitute rye whiskey for Scotch.

——————— **Little Devil Cocktail** ———————

1 oz (2 Tbsp) gin
1 oz (2 Tbsp) light rum
¾ oz Cointreau or triple sec
juice of ¼ lemon

Shake ingredients with ice and strain into a chilled cocktail glass.

——————— **Little Princess Cocktail** ———————

1½ oz (3 Tbsp) light rum
1½ oz (3 Tbsp) sweet vermouth

Stir ingredients with ice and strain into a chilled cocktail glass.

——————— **Loch Lomond** ———————

2 oz (4 Tbsp) Scotch
1 tsp sugar
2–3 dashes Angostura bitters

Shake ingredients with ice and strain into a chilled cocktail glass.

——— London Buck ———

2 oz (4 Tbsp) gin
½ oz (1 Tbsp) lemon juice
ginger ale, chilled
thin slice lemon (optional) ·

In chilled highball glass filled with ice cubes pour gin and lemon juice. Top with ginger ale and float lemon slice, if desired.

——— London Special ———

cold champagne
lump of sugar
1–2 dashes orange bitters
strip of orange peel

Place sugar in bottom of chilled champagne glass and dash with bitters. Rub rim of glass with peel, twist to release oils, and add to glass. Fill with champagne, stir gently, and serve with small straw.

——— London Cocktail ———

2 oz (4 Tbsp) gin
2 dashes sugar syrup
2 dashes Maraschino liqueur
2 dashes orange bitters
twist of lemon peel

Stir liquid ingredients with ice and strain into a chilled cocktail glass. Garnish with lemon peel.

——— Long Island Iced Tea ———

½ oz (1 Tbsp) tequila
½ oz (1 Tbsp) rum

½ oz (1 Tbsp) vodka
½ oz (1 Tbsp) gin
½ oz (1 Tbsp) triple sec
1 oz (2 Tbsp) lemon juice
1 tsp sugar
4 oz (8 Tbsp) cola

Stir first 7 ingredients in highball glass over ice. Add cola and stir gently.

——————— **Long Shot** ———————

2 oz (4 Tbsp) blackberry brandy
½ oz (1 Tbsp) orange juice
1 tsp lemon juice
1–2 dashes orange bitters
chilled ginger ale

In highball glass filled with cracked ice pour first 4 ingredients. Top with ginger ale and stir gently.

Los Angeles Cocktail ———————

1½ oz (3 Tbsp) rye or bourbon
2 dashes sweet vermouth
1 tsp sugar
1 whole egg
juice of ½ lemon (optional)

Shake ingredients vigorously with ice and strain into a chilled cocktail glass or into an Old-Fashioned glass over ice cubes.

——————— **Lotus Land** ———————

2 oz (4 Tbsp) white rum
juice ½ lime
½ oz (1 Tbsp) crème de framboise
½ oz (1 Tbsp) cream

(continued)

Place all ingredients in shaker with several ice cubes. Cover and shake vigorously. Strain into chilled cocktail glass.

Love Cocktail

2 oz (4 Tbsp) sloe gin
2 dashes raspberry syrup
2 dashes lemon juice
1 egg white

Shake ingredients vigorously with ice and strain into a chilled cocktail glass.

Lover's Delight

1 oz (2 Tbsp) Cointreau
1 oz (2 Tbsp) brandy or cognac
1 oz (2 Tbsp) Forbidden Fruit

Shake ingredients with ice and strain into a chilled cocktail glass.

Loving Cup

(serves 2)

2 cups dry red wine
2 oz (4 Tbsp) peach brandy
1 oz (2 Tbsp) Cointreau or triple sec
½ oz (1 Tbsp) sugar
6 oz club soda
orange slices
mint sprigs

Fill 2-qt glass pitcher with ice cubes. Pour in liquors, sugar, soda, and orange slices. Stir several times and garnish pitcher with mint and orange slices.

M

----- **Madeira Mint Flip** -----

1½ oz (3 Tbsp) madeira
¾ oz (1½ Tbsp) chocolate mint liqueur
1 tsp sugar
1 whole egg
grated dark chocolate or nutmeg

Shake first 4 ingredients with ice and strain into a
chilled cocktail glass. Garnish with chocolate or nutmeg.

----- **Magna Carta** -----

1½ oz (3 Tbsp) well-chilled tequila
1 oz (2 Tbsp) well-chilled triple sec
champagne
lime juice
salt

Dip the rim of a chilled goblet in lime juice, then in
salt, shaking off excess. Pour in tequila and triple
sec, then fill with champagne and stir gently.

----- **Magnolia Cocktail** -----

1 egg white
1 oz (2 Tbsp) lemon juice
3 oz (6 Tbsp) gin
½ tsp grenadine
1 tsp cream

Place all ingredients in shaker with cracked ice. Cover and shake vigorously several times. Strain into
chilled cocktail glass.

———— Maiden's Blush Cocktail ————

1½ oz (3 Tbsp) gin
1 tsp Cointreau or triple sec
1 tsp grenadine
2 dashes lemon juice

Shake ingredients with ice and strain into a chilled cocktail glass.

———— Maiden's Prayer ————

1½ oz (3 Tbsp) gin
1½ oz (3 Tbsp) Cointreau or triple sec
½ oz (1 Tbsp) lemon juice

Shake ingredients with ice and strain into a chilled cocktail glass.

Variation: substitute orange juice for lemon.

———— Mai-Tai ————

Trader Vic claims to have invented this drink at his Oakland, California, restaurant in 1944. When he served it to a Tahitian friend, the comment was "Mai Tai—Roa Aé," which means "out of this world—the best" in Tahitian.

2 oz (4 Tbsp) dark Jamaican rum
½ oz (1 Tbsp) curaçao
½ oz (1 Tbsp) apricot brandy
juice of ½ lime
1 tsp grenadine
wedge of fresh pineapple
maraschino cherry
twist of lime peel

Shake liquid ingredients with ice and strain into a chilled collins or large Old-Fashioned glass over crushed ice. Garnish with pineapple, cherry, and lime peel.

Variation: substitute 1 oz (2 Tbsp) light and 1 oz (2 Tbsp) dark rum for the 2 oz (4 Tbsp) dark Jamaican rum.

——————— **Mamie Taylor** ———————

2 oz (4 Tbsp) Scotch
juice of ½ lime
chilled ginger ale

Pour Scotch and lime juice into a chilled collins glass over ice cubes. Top with ginger ale and stir.

——————— **Mañana** ———————

2 oz (4 Tbsp) golden rum
½ oz (1 Tbsp) apricot brandy
1 tsp lemon juice

Place ingredients in shaker with 4 or 5 ice cubes. Cover and shake vigorously several times. Strain into Old-Fashioned glass two-thirds full of cracked ice.

——————— **Mandeville** ———————

1½ oz (3 Tbsp) light rum
1½ oz (3 Tbsp) dark rum
1 tsp Pernod
¼ tsp grenadine
½ oz (1 Tbsp) lemon juice (optional)
½ oz (1 Tbsp) chilled cola

(continued)

Shake ingredients with ice and strain into a chilled Old-Fashioned glass over ice cubes.

——— Manhasset ———

1½ oz (3 Tbsp) rye whiskey
¼ oz dry vermouth
¼ oz sweet vermouth
½ oz (1 Tbsp) lemon juice
twist of lemon peel (optional)

Shake liquid ingredients with ice and strain into a chilled cocktail glass. Garnish with lemon peel, if desired.

——— Manhasset Mauler ———

2 oz (4 Tbsp) gin
1 oz (2 Tbsp) sloe gin
lemon zest

Place gins in shaker with 4 or 5 ice cubes, cover, and shake vigorously several times. Strain into chilled cocktail glass after rubbing the rim with lemon zest. Twist zest over drink to release oils and drop in.

——— Manhattan ———

The Manhattan, named for the New York City borough, is thought to have been invented (in New York City, of course) around 1890. The original version, which did not contain bitters or a garnish, was simply 2 parts rye to 1 part vermouth. Around 1919, gin was substituted for the whiskey and a new drink, the Bronx, was born. The Rob Roy is a Manhattan made with Scotch.

The standard Manhattan is sweet. For other types of Manhattans see variations below.

>2 oz (4 Tbsp) rye whiskey
>1 oz (2 Tbsp) sweet vermouth
>1 dash Angostura bitters
>maraschino cherry

Stir liquid ingredients with ice and strain into a chilled cocktail glass. Garnish with the cherry.

Variations: substitute bourbon for rye. Substitute orange bitters for Angostura.

Dry Manhattan: substitute dry vermouth for sweet.

French Manhattan: a Dry Manhattan with a dash of Cointreau.

Perfect Manhattan: use equal parts [½ oz (1 Tbsp) each] sweet and dry vermouth.

Scotch Manhattan: see *Rob Roy.*

Margarita

>1½ oz (3 Tbsp) tequila
>½ oz (1 Tbsp) Cointreau or triple sec
>juice of ½ lime

Salt-rim a chilled cocktail glass by rubbing the rim with lime and dipping into salt. Shake ingredients with ice and strain into the glass.

Frozen Margarita: in blender combine 1 oz (2 Tbsp) frozen limeade concentrate, ½ oz (1 Tbsp) triple sec, 1 oz (2 Tbsp) tequila, and ⅓ cup cracked ice and blend till smooth. Rub rim of chilled champagne glass with lime wedge and dip in salt to coat. Pour frappéed drink into glass.

──────   **Margarita Impériale**   ──────

1 oz (2 Tbsp) Mandarine Napoléon
(orange-flavored brandy)
1 oz (2 Tbsp) tequila
2 tsp fresh lemon juice
dash of curaçao

Fill Old-Fashioned glass with cracked ice. Add liquors
and juice and stir gently before serving.

──────   **Martini**   ──────

The exact origin of both the Martini and its name
are obscure. The cocktail seems to have appeared in
the United States in the 1860s, when it consisted of
2 parts gin to 1 part vermouth. It was attributed to a
bartender named Martinez, or may have been named
after a town of that name. Later, the name somehow
got linked with the Italian firm of Martini and Rossi,
vermouth manufacturers.

With the passage of time, the Martini has become
drier and drier; 6–1 is no longer considered dry;
10–1 (below) has become standard, and some fad-
dists perform such tricks as merely rinsing the glass
with vermouth before adding gin or dipping the ice
cubes in vermouth before placing them in the shaker with the gin. But when the ratio goes much beyond
10–1, there is little reason to use any vermouth at all
since its flavor is lost.

Here is the standard dry Martini, with the proportions 10 to 1. For other types of Martinis see variations below.

2½ oz (5 Tbsp) gin
¼ oz dry vermouth
twist of lemon peel or olive

Stir liquid ingredients with ice and strain into a chilled cocktail glass, the rim of which has been rubbed with the cut edge of the lemon peel. Garnish with lemon peel or olive.

Some Hints

1. Use nothing but the best liquor. Most confirmed Martini drinkers specify the gin when ordering in public. A cheap vermouth can ruin an otherwise fine Martini. This is particularly unnecessary since even the finest vermouth is not expensive.

2. Buy vermouth in small bottles unless you consume a lot of it. Once opened, vermouth gradually loses its flavor.

3. Pour the gin over the ice cubes for quicker chilling. Cracked or crushed ice will turn the Martini into a watery mush.

4. Stir the Martini to keep it clear. Shaking will turn it cloudy.

Variations: for a drier Martini, decrease the amount of vermouth; some individuals prefer only a drop or two, going so far as to add it with an eyedropper.

Blue Martini: see *Yale Cocktail.*

Boston Bullet: a Dry Martini garnished with an almond-stuffed olive.

Brandy Martini: see *Hennessy Martini.*

Fino Martini: 2 oz (4 Tbsp) gin, 1 tsp fino sherry, twist of lemon peel.

Gibson: a Dry Martini garnished with 2–3 cocktail onions.

(continued)

Imperial (Martini) Cocktail: 1½ oz (4 Tbsp) gin, 1½ oz (3 Tbsp) dry vermouth, 1 dash Angostura bitters, 2 dashes Maraschino liqueur. Garnish with maraschino cherry.

Martini-On-The-Rocks: strain ingredients into an Old-Fashioned glass over ice cubes.

Paisley Martini: 2 oz (4 Tbsp) gin, ¼ oz dry vermouth, and 1 tsp Scotch.

Perfect Martini: 1½ oz (3 Tbsp) gin, ½ oz (1 Tbsp) sweet vermouth, ½ oz (1 Tbsp) dry vermouth, twist of orange peel or an olive.

Rum Martini: substitute light rum for gin and add a dash of orange bitters.

Sweet Martini: 1 oz (2 Tbsp) gin, 1 oz (2 Tbsp) sweet vermouth, twist of orange peel or a cherry.

Tequini: substitute tequila for gin.

Vodka Martini: substitute vodka for gin.

─────── **Martinez Cocktail** ───────

1½ oz (3 Tbsp) gin
1 oz (2 Tbsp) dry vermouth
1 tsp curaçao
dash orange bitters
maraschino cherry

Place first 4 ingredients in mixing glass and stir several times to combine. Pour into chilled cocktail glass and garnish with cherry, if desired.

——— **Mary Garden Cocktail** ———

Perhaps invented by the famous opera diva, but at least a fitting tribute.

2 oz (4 Tbsp) Dubonnet
1 oz (2 Tbsp) dry vermouth

Shake ingredients with cracked ice and strain into chilled cocktail glass.

Variation: rub rim of glass with lemon peel before filling. Twist peel over drink to release oils and drop in.

——— **Mary Pickford** ———

1 oz (2 Tbsp) light rum
1 oz (2 Tbsp) pineapple juice
¼ oz tsp grenadine
1 or 2 dashes Maraschino liqueur (optional)

Shake ingredients with ice and strain into a chilled cocktail glass.

——— **Matador** ———

1 oz (2 Tbsp) tequila
2 oz (4 Tbsp) pineapple juice
juice of ½ lime

Shake ingredients with ice and strain into a chilled cocktail glass.

Frozen Matador: put ingredients, with ½ cup ice, into a blender and blend at low speed for 15 seconds. Pour into a chilled Old-Fashioned glass and garnish with a stick of fresh pineapple.

Matelot

Takes its name from the French word for "sailor."

2 oz (4 Tbsp) Pernod, Ricard, or pastis
½ oz (1 Tbsp) anisette
1–2 dashes bitters

In highball glass filled with ice cubes pour in the liquors and bitters. Stir to mix.

Matinee

(serves 2)

2 oz (4 Tbsp) gin
1 oz (2 Tbsp) Sambuca
1 egg white
4 dashes lime juice
1 oz (2 Tbsp) cream
nutmeg

Shake first 5 ingredients vigorously with ice and strain into chilled cocktail glasses. Sprinkle with nutmeg.

Maui Cocktail

2 oz (4 Tbsp) gin
1 oz (2 Tbsp) pineapple juice
½ oz (1 Tbsp) Cointreau

Place ingredients in shaker with 4 or 5 ice cubes. Cover and shake vigorously several times. Strain into chilled cocktail glass.

--------- **Maurice** ---------

1½ oz (3 Tbsp) gin
¾ oz (1½ Tbsp) sweet vermouth
¾ oz (1½ Tbsp) dry vermouth
juice of ¼ orange
1 dash Angostura bitters

Shake ingredients with ice and strain into a chilled cocktail glass.

--------- **Mayfair** ---------

spiral peel of half orange
1 cube sugar
1–2 dashes bitters
cold champagne or other sparkling wine

To chilled tulip champagne glass add sugar cube, orange peel, and bitters. Fill with champagne and stir gently.

--------- **Melon Ball** ---------

1 oz (2 Tbsp) vodka
½ oz (1 Tbsp) melon liqueur
3 oz (6 Tbsp) orange juice

Shake ingredients with ice. Strain into cocktail glass.

--------- **Melon Cocktail** ---------

2 oz (4 Tbsp) gin
1 tsp white Maraschino liqueur
½ tsp lemon juice
maraschino cherry

(continued)

Shake first 3 ingredients with cracked ice and strain into chilled cocktail glass. Garnish with cherry, if desired.

--------- **Merry Widow Cocktail I** ---------

1½ oz (3 Tbsp) sherry
1½ oz (3 Tbsp) sweet vermouth
twist of lemon peel

Stir liquid ingredients with ice and strain into a chilled cocktail glass. Garnish with lemon peel.

Variation: for a drier Merry Widow substitute Dubonnet for sherry and dry vermouth for the sweet.

--------- **Merry Widow Cocktail II** ---------

1½ oz (3 Tbsp) cherry brandy
1½ oz (3 Tbsp) Maraschino liqueur
maraschino cherry

Stir liquid ingredients with ice and strain into a chilled cocktail glass. Garnish with the cherry.

--------- **Merry Widow Fizz** ---------

2 oz (4 Tbsp) gin
juice of ½ orange
juice of ½ lemon
1 egg white
chilled club soda

Shake ingredients, except soda, vigorously with ice. Strain into a chilled highball or collins glass over ice cubes and top with soda.

Variation: substitute sloe gin or Dubonnet for gin.

--------- **Metropolitan** ---------

1½ oz (3 Tbsp) brandy
1½ oz (3 Tbsp) sweet vermouth
½ tsp sugar syrup
dash bitters
maraschino cherry

Shake with ice and strain into Old-Fashioned glass
half-filled with cracked ice. Garnish with cherry.

--------- **Miami** ---------

2 oz (4 Tbsp) light rum
1 oz (2 Tbsp) white crème de menthe
2 dashes lemon juice

Shake ingredients with ice and strain into a chilled
cocktail glass.

--------- **Miami Beach** ---------

2 oz (4 Tbsp) Scotch whiskey
2 oz (4 Tbsp) dry vermouth
2 oz (4 Tbsp) grapefruit juice

Pour into highball glass half-filled with cracked ice
and stir gently. Top off, if desired, with a little more
grapefruit juice before serving.

--------- **Mikado** ---------

2 oz (4 Tbsp) brandy
1 tsp crème de cacao
½ tsp crème de noyaux
½ tsp orgeat
1–2 dashes bitters

(continued)

Shake all ingredients with cracked ice and strain into chilled cocktail glass.

───────── **Milk Punch** ─────────

2 oz (4 Tbsp) rye whiskey
8 oz chilled milk
1 tsp sugar
nutmeg

Shake first 3 ingredients with ice and strain into a chilled cocktail glass. Sprinkle with nutmeg.

Variations: substitute brandy for rye or substitute 1 oz (2 Tbsp) brandy and 1 oz (2 Tbsp) rum for rye. A Milk Punch can also be served hot. Mix the sugar and liquor in a heated mug or glass and add hot milk. Sprinkle with nutmeg.

───────── **Millionaire Cocktail** ─────────

1½ oz (3 Tbsp) rye or bourbon
½ oz (1 Tbsp) curaçao
1 egg white
2 dashes grenadine

Shake ingredients vigorously with ice and strain into a chilled cocktail glass.

───────── **Million Dollar Cocktail** ─────────

1½ oz (3 Tbsp) gin
¾ oz (1½ Tbsp) sweet vermouth
1–2 tsp pineapple juice
1 tsp grenadine
1 egg white

Shake ingredients vigorously with ice and strain into a chilled cocktail glass.

─────── **Mimosa** ───────

4 oz (8 Tbsp) chilled champagne
4 oz (8 Tbsp) chilled orange juice

Pour ingredients into a chilled collins or balloon wine-glass over ice cubes and stir gently.

Variation: using equal parts of champagne and orange juice, pour ingredients into a chilled champagne glass but do not use ice.

See also *Cajun Mimosa.*

─────── **Mint Collins** ───────

2 oz (4 Tbsp) gin
5 sprigs of fresh mint
juice of ½ lemon
1 tsp sugar
chilled club soda
slice of lemon

In a chilled collins glass crush 4 mint leaves in the gin, lemon, and sugar. Add ice cubes and top with soda. Garnish with the remaining mint and lemon slice.

─────── **Mint Cooler** ───────

2 oz (4 Tbsp) Scotch
2–3 dashes white crème de menthe
chilled club soda
sprig of fresh mint

(continued)

Pour Scotch and crème de menthe into a chilled collins
or highball glass over ice cubes. Top with soda, stir
gently, and garnish with mint sprig.

───────── **Minted Brandy Ice** ─────────

(serves 6–8)

A rich dessert beverage.

6 oz brandy
4 oz (8 Tbsp) white crème de cacao
2 oz (4 Tbsp) white crème de menthe
1 qt vanilla ice cream
6–8 mint sprigs

Combine ingredients, except mint, in blender with 8–
10 ice cubes and blend until smooth. Serve in brandy
snifters or large Old-Fashioned glasses, garnished
with mint.

───────── **Mint Julep** ─────────

Although Mint Juleps are customarily associated with
Kentucky bourbon, the Mint Julep was an American
term for nearly 40 years before Kentucky bourbon
became popular. Juleps were originally nonalcoholic
minted fruited drinks.

2½ oz (5 Tbsp) bourbon
1 tsp sugar
2–3 dashes cold water or club soda
8 sprigs fresh mint
crushed or shaved ice

Muddle sugar, water, and 5 mint sprigs in a glass.
Pour into a thoroughly frosted collins glass or mug
and pack with ice. Add bourbon and mix (with a
chopping motion using a long-handled bar spoon).

Some variations suggest not stirring. Garnish with remaining mint and serve with a straw.

Some Hints

1. Clipping the ends of the mint used as a garnish will release the juices. If a less pronounced mint flavor is desired muddle only lightly.

2. A silver mug will frost better than a glass. If a glass is used it is best to use one with a handle to avoid a warm hand touching the surface of the glass. The finished drink can be additionally frosted by placing it in the refrigerator for an hour.

Variations: garnish with 1–2 slices of lemon. Float 2–3 drops of brandy or rum on top before serving.

See also *Creole Mint Julep.*

——— Mo Bay Special ———

"Mo Bay" is the nickname for Montego Bay, resort capital of Jamaica.

> 1½ oz (3 Tbsp) Jamaican rum
> 1 tsp lime juice
> ½ oz (1 Tbsp) pineapple juice
> 1 tsp grenadine

Shake all ingredients with 4 or 5 ice cubes and strain into Old-Fashioned glass filled with cracked ice.

——— Mocha Mint ———

> ¾ oz (1½ Tbsp) coffee brandy
> ¾ oz (1½ Tbsp) white crème de menthe
> ¾ oz (1½ Tbsp) white crème de cacao

(continued)

Shake ingredients with ice and strain into a chilled cocktail glass.

─────── **Modern Cocktail** ───────

2 oz (4 Tbsp) Scotch
½ tsp Jamaican rum
¼ tsp Pernod
½ tsp lemon juice
1 dash orange bitters
maraschino cherry

Shake liquid ingredients with ice and strain into a chilled cocktail glass. Garnish with the cherry.

─────── **Mojito** ───────

Its origin is unknown, but this drink is popular enough to be served at nearly every bar in the West Indies.

2 oz (4 Tbsp) light rum
1 tsp sugar
4–5 fresh mint leaves
1–2 dashes Angostura bitters

Shake ingredients with ice. Strain into a chilled cocktail glass or into a collins glass that has been packed with crushed ice.

Variation: add ½ lime, both the juice and the squeezed rind.

─────── **Monkey Gland** ───────

1½ oz (3 Tbsp) gin
1 oz (2 Tbsp) orange juice

2 dashes Benedictine
2 dashes grenadine

Stir or shake ingredients with ice. Strain into a chilled cocktail glass or into an Old-Fashioned glass over ice cubes.

Variation: substitute 1 oz (2 Tbsp) Pernod for the Benedictine and grenadine.

───────── **Montana** ─────────

2 oz (4 Tbsp) brandy
¾ oz (1½ Tbsp) port
¾ oz (1½ Tbsp) dry vermouth

Stir ingredients with ice and strain into a chilled Old-Fashioned glass over ice cubes.

Variation: add 2 dashes Angostura bitters and 2 dashes anisette.

───────── **Montmartre Cocktail** ─────────

1½ oz (3 Tbsp) gin
½ oz (1 Tbsp) sweet vermouth
½ oz (1 Tbsp) triple sec

Shake all ingredients with cracked ice and strain into chilled cocktail glass.

───────── **Moonlight** ─────────

2 oz (4 Tbsp) Calvados or apple brandy
juice of 1 lemon
1 tsp sugar

Shake ingredients with ice and strain into a chilled Old-Fashioned glass over ice cubes.

(continued)

Variation: strain into a chilled collins glass over ice cubes and top with chilled club soda.

———— **Morning Fizz** ————

(serves 2)

4 oz (8 Tbsp) rye whiskey
1 oz (2 Tbsp) Pernod
1 egg white
1 oz (2 Tbsp) lemon juice
2 tsp sugar
chilled club soda

Shake ingredients, except soda, vigorously with ice. Strain into chilled collins glasses over ice cubes. Top with soda and stir.

———— **Morning Glory** ————

2 oz (4 Tbsp) brandy
½ oz (1 Tbsp) curaçao
½ oz (1 Tbsp) lemon juice (optional)
2 dashes Pernod
2 dashes Angostura bitters
twist of lemon peel

Shake liquid ingredients with ice and strain into a chilled cocktail glass. Garnish with lemon peel.

Variation: strain into a collins glass over ice cubes and top with chilled club soda. Decrease brandy to 1 oz (2 Tbsp) and add 1 oz (2 Tbsp) rye whiskey.

———— **Morning Glory Fizz** ————

2 oz (4 Tbsp) Scotch
½ tsp Pernod

1 egg white
1 tsp sugar
1½ oz (3 Tbsp) lemon or lime juice
1 dash Angostura bitters (optional)
chilled club soda

Shake all ingredients, except soda, vigorously with ice and strain into a chilled highball or collins glass over ice cubes. Top with soda.

--------- **Morro** ---------

1 oz (2 Tbsp) gin
½ oz (1 Tbsp) dark rum
½ oz (1 Tbsp) lime juice
½ oz (1 Tbsp) pineapple juice
½ tsp sugar

Sugar-rim a chilled cocktail glass by rubbing the rim with lime and dipping into sugar. Shake ingredients with ice and strain into the glass.

--------- **Moscow Mule** ---------

3 oz (6 Tbsp) vodka
juice of ½ lime
chilled ginger beer
slice of lime

Pour lime juice and vodka into a chilled collins glass or beer mug over ice cubes. Fill with ginger beer and garnish with lime slice.

Variation: substitute ginger ale for ginger beer.

———— Mothers Milk ————

(serves 16–18)

1 qt vodka or gin
1 qt pineapple juice
1 qt grapefruit juice
thin slices of orange or lemon (optional)

Pour ingredients over a block of ice in a large punch bowl. Garnish with fruit slices if desired.

———— Mountain Cocktail ————

2 oz (4 Tbsp) rye whiskey
½ oz (1 Tbsp) dry vermouth
½ oz (1 Tbsp) sweet vermouth
½ oz (1 Tbsp) lemon juice
1 egg white

Shake ingredients vigorously with ice and strain into a chilled cocktail glass.

———— Mull ————

See *Mulled Wine, Glögg.*

———— Mulled Wine I ————

(serves 8)

2 fifths dry red wine
6 oz brandy
6 oz port
8 whole cloves
8 sticks cinnamon
peel of 1 orange cut in pieces
peel of 1 lemon cut in pieces

1 tsp nutmeg
1 oz (2 Tbsp) brown sugar

Combine ingredients in a large pan and bring almost
to a boil. Simmer 5 minutes. Serve in heated glasses
or mugs with a few spices and fruit peels in each.

See also *Glögg*.

Mulled Wine II

For 1 serving of mulled wine, the following is a simplified version.

5 oz dry red wine
1 tsp sugar
juice of ½ lemon
¼ tsp nutmeg
¼ tsp cinnamon
¼ tsp clove

Put ingredients into a metal mug. Hold a red-hot pok-
er in the mug until the liquid boils.

Murray Hill

2 oz (4 Tbsp) gin
2 tsp lime juice
½ tsp sugar syrup
½ oz (1 Tbsp) grenadine
club soda chilled
long-stemmed maraschino cherry

Shake first 4 ingredients with ice cubes. Strain into
collins glass filled with cracked ice. Top with soda
and stir. Garnish with cherry.

——— **Muskmelon** ———

1½ oz (3 Tbsp) light rum
¼ cup diced cantaloupe
½ oz (1 Tbsp) lime juice
½ oz (1 Tbsp) orange juice
½ tsp sugar (optional)
cube of cantaloupe

Put first 5 ingredients in a blender and blend at low speed for 15 seconds. Pour into a chilled Old-Fashioned glass over ice cubes. Garnish with the cantaloupe cube on a toothpick.

N

——— **Napobitter** ———

1 oz (2 Tbsp) Mandarine Napoléon
(orange-flavored brandy)
bitter lemon
thin slice lime (optional)

Fill Old-Fashioned glass with cracked ice. Pour in brandy and top off with the bitter lemon. Stir gently and garnish with lime slice, if desired.

——— **Napoleon Cocktail** ———

2 oz (4 Tbsp) gin
2 dashes curaçao
2 dashes Dubonnet
twist of lemon peel

Stir liquid ingredients with ice and strain into a chilled cocktail glass. Garnish with lemon peel.

——— **Navy Grog** ———

1 oz (2 Tbsp) light rum
1 oz (2 Tbsp) Jamaican rum
1 oz (2 Tbsp) demerara rum (86-proof)
juice of 1 lime
¾ oz (1½ Tbsp) grapefruit juice
¾ oz (1½ Tbsp) sugar syrup
rind of ½ lime
sprig of fresh mint

Shake ingredients, except lime rind and mint, with ice and strain into a chilled collins or highball glass over shaved ice. Garnish with lime rind and mint sprig and serve with a straw.

——— **Negroni** ———

1½ oz (3 Tbsp) gin
1½ oz (3 Tbsp) Campari
1½ oz (3 Tbsp) sweet vermouth
twist of lemon peel

Put 2–3 ice cubes in a large chilled Old-Fashioned glass or balloon wineglass. Add liquid ingredients and stir. Garnish with lemon peel.

Variation: stir liquid ingredients with ice and strain into a chilled cocktail glass. Garnish with lemon peel.

——— **Nevada Cocktail** ———

1½ oz (3 Tbsp) dark rum
1½ oz (3 Tbsp) grapefruit juice
½ oz (1 Tbsp) lime juice
1 tsp sugar
1 dash Angostura bitters (optional)

(continued)

Shake ingredients with ice and strain into a chilled cocktail glass.

——— Nevins ———

1½ oz (3 Tbsp) bourbon
¼ oz (½ Tbsp) apricot brandy
½ oz (1 Tbsp) grapefruit juice
¼ oz (½ Tbsp) lemon juice
1 dash Angostura bitters

Shake ingredients with ice and strain into a chilled cocktail glass.

Variation: sugar-rim the glass by rubbing with lemon and dipping into sugar.

——— New Orleans Buck ———

1½ oz (3 Tbsp) rum
½ oz (1 Tbsp) lime juice
½ oz (1 Tbsp) orange juice
chilled ginger ale
slice of lime

Shake first 3 ingredients with ice and strain into a chilled collins glass over ice cubes. Top with ginger ale and stir. Garnish with lime.

——— New Orleans Gin Fizz ———

2 oz (4 Tbsp) gin
juice of ½ lemon
juice of ½ lime
1 tsp sugar
1 egg white
½ oz (1 Tbsp) cream

chilled club soda
slice of lime or lemon

Shake first 6 ingredients with ice. Strain into a chilled highball or collins glass over ice cubes. Top with soda, stir, and garnish with lime or lemon.

New York(er) Cocktail

2 oz (4 Tbsp) rye or bourbon
juice of ½ lime
2 dashes grenadine
twist of orange peel

Shake liquid ingredients with ice and strain into a chilled cocktail glass. Garnish with orange peel.

New York Sour

2 oz (4 Tbsp) rye whiskey
juice of ½ lemon
1 tsp sugar
chilled dry red wine
small slice of lemon

Shake rye, lemon, and sugar with ice. Strain into a chilled sour glass and top with wine. Stir and garnish with lemon slice.

Night Cap

2 oz (4 Tbsp) brandy
1 whole egg
1 tsp sugar or ½ oz (1 Tbsp) honey
6 oz warm milk

Put brandy, egg, and sugar into a warmed mug. Add milk and stir.

(continued)

Variation: to serve cold, mix cold milk, egg, and sugar in a tall glass. Add brandy and stir.

——— Night Owl ———

2 oz (4 Tbsp) bourbon
½ oz (1 Tbsp) lemon juice
½ oz (1 Tbsp) triple sec
dash of bitters
chilled club soda

To highball glass filled with cracked ice add first 4 ingredients and stir gently. Top with soda and stir again.

——— Ninotchka ———

1½ oz (3 Tbsp) vodka
½ oz (1 Tbsp) white crème de cacao
½ oz (1 Tbsp) lemon juice

Shake ingredients with ice and strain into a chilled cocktail glass.

——— Nob Hill ———

2 oz (4 Tbsp) whiskey
1 oz (2 Tbsp) grapefruit juice
1 tsp honey

Shake ingredients with cracked ice and strain into chilled cocktail glass.

O

──────── **Ocho Rios** ────────

1½ oz (3 Tbsp) dark rum
1 oz (2 Tbsp) guava nectar or
½ cup diced guava
½ oz (1 Tbsp) lime juice
½ tsp sugar
½ oz (1 Tbsp) cream (optional)
⅓ cup crushed ice

Put ingredients in a blender and blend at low speed for 15 seconds. Pour into a chilled champagne glass.

──────── **Old Etonian** ────────

1½ oz (3 Tbsp) gin
1½ oz (3 Tbsp) Lillet
2 dashes orange bitters
2 dashes crème de noyaux
twist of orange peel

Stir liquid ingredients with ice and strain into a chilled cocktail glass. Garnish with orange peel.

──────── **Old-Fashioned** ────────

As in the case of numerous other cocktails, the origin of the Old-Fashioned is uncertain. Some say it was invented at the Pendennis Club, Louisville, Kentucky, in the late 1880s, the result of a bartender's being asked to make a "good old-fashioned cocktail." There are countless variations on this classic cocktail. Some "authorities" insist on sugar syrup instead of a cube; others may instruct the bartender to "hold the garbage," that is to eliminate the fruit.

(continued)

2 oz (4 Tbsp) rye or bourbon
½ cube sugar
1 dash Angostura bitter
1 tsp water
twist of lemon peel
maraschino cherry
1 slice lemon, lime, or orange

Muddle sugar and bitters in water in a chilled Old-Fashioned glass. Add whiskey slowly, while stirring. Add ice and garnish with the lemon peel and fruit.

Variations: add 1 dash curaçao. Soak fruit slices overnight in whiskey. Various liquors can be substitute for the whiskey (rum, Scotch, tequila, etc.), and the Old-Fashioned is then named after the liquor used (Rum Old-Fashioned).

——— Old Pal Cocktail ———

1 oz (2 Tbsp) rye whiskey
1 oz (2 Tbsp) Campari
1 oz (2 Tbsp) dry vermouth

Stir ingredients with ice and strain into a chilled cocktail glass.

Variation: for a sweeter drink, substitute sweet vermouth for the dry and grenadine for the Campari.

——— Olympic Cocktail ———

1 oz (2 Tbsp) brandy
1 oz (2 Tbsp) curaçao
1 oz (2 Tbsp) orange juice
twist of orange peel (optional)

Shake liquid ingredients with ice and strain into a chilled cocktail glass. Garnish with orange peel.

––––––– **Opal Cocktail** –––––––

1½ oz (3 Tbsp) gin
½ oz (1 Tbsp) Cointreau
½ oz (1 Tbsp) orange juice
½ tsp orange flower water
½ tsp sugar

Shake all ingredients with cracked ice and strain into chilled cocktail glass.

––––––– **Opening Cocktail** –––––––

2 oz (4 Tbsp) rye whiskey
1 oz (2 Tbsp) sweet vermouth
½ oz (1 Tbsp) grenadine

Shake ingredients with ice and strain into a chilled cocktail glass or into an Old-Fashioned glass over ice cubes.

––––––– **Opera Cocktail** –––––––

1½ oz (3 Tbsp) gin
½ oz (1 Tbsp) Dubonnet
1 tsp maraschino

Stir or shake ingredients with ice and strain into a chilled cocktail glass.

Variation: add 1 dash orange juice and garnish with a twist of orange peel.

––––––– **Orange Bloom** –––––––

1½ oz (3 Tbsp) gin
3 tsp Cointreau or triple sec
2 tsp sweet vermouth

(continued)

Shake ingredients with ice and strain into a chilled cocktail glass.

--------- **Orange Blossom Cocktail** ---------

2 oz (4 Tbsp) gin
1 oz (2 Tbsp) orange juice
¼ tsp sugar (optional)

Shake ingredients with ice and strain into a chilled cocktail glass.

Variation: add 2 tsp curaçao and 1 egg white and put in a blender at low speed for 15 seconds. Pour into a chilled sour or wine glass over ice cubes. Garnish with slice of orange.

--------- **Orange Buck** ---------

1½ oz (3 Tbsp) gin
1 oz (2 Tbsp) orange juice
½ oz (1 Tbsp) lemon or lime juice
chilled ginger ale
slice of lime (optional)

Shake gin and juices with ice. Strain into a chilled collins glass over ice cubes. Top with ginger ale and stir. Garnish with lime slice if desired.

--------- **Orange Fizz** ---------

2 oz (4 Tbsp) gin
2 tsp Cointreau or triple sec (optional)
1 tsp sugar
juice of ½ orange
juice of ½ lemon
chilled club soda
slice of orange

Shake first 5 ingredients with ice and strain into a chilled highball glass over ice cubes. Top with soda and garnish with orange slice.

────── **Orange Gin Cooler** ──────

2 oz (4 Tbsp) orange-flavored gin
½ oz (1 Tbsp) fresh lemon juice
½ oz (1 Tbsp) triple sec
chilled club soda
maraschino cherry

Shake together first 3 ingredients with 4 or 5 ice cubes. Strain into collins glass half-filled with cracked ice and top with soda. Stir briefly and garnish with cherry before serving.

────── **Orange Oasis** ──────

1½ oz (3 Tbsp) gin
½ oz (1 Tbsp) cherry brandy
1 oz (8 Tbsp) chilled orange juice
chilled ginger ale

Pour gin, brandy, and orange juice into a chilled highball glass over ice cubes. Top with ginger ale and stir.

────── **Orient Express** ──────

1 oz (2 Tbsp) gin
1 oz (2 Tbsp) bourbon
1 oz (2 Tbsp) brandy

In mixing glass stir ingredients with cracked ice and strain into chilled cocktail glass.

——————— **Ostend Fizz** ———————

¾ oz (1½ Tbsp) crème de cassis
¾ oz (1½ Tbsp) kirschwasser
chilled club soda

Shake crème de cassis and kirschwasser with ice.
Strain into a chilled collins or highball glass over ice
cubes and top with soda.

Variation: add ½ oz (1 Tbsp) lemon juice and 1 tsp
sugar and shake with other ingredients. Garnish with
slice of lemon.

P

——————— **Paddy Cocktail** ———————

1½ oz (3 Tbsp) Irish whiskey
1½ oz (3 Tbsp) sweet vermouth
1 dash Angostura bitters

Stir ingredients with ice and strain into a chilled cocktail glass.

——————— **Paisley Martini** ———————

See under *Martini.*

——————— **Pall Mall** ———————

1½ oz (3 Tbsp) gin
½ oz (1 Tbsp) dry vermouth
½ oz (1 Tbsp) sweet vermouth
1 tsp white crème de menthe
1 dash orange bitters (optional)

Stir ingredients with ice and strain into a chilled cocktail glass or into an Old-Fashioned glass over ice cubes.

─────── **Palm Beach Cooler** ───────

(serves 15)

2 bottles dry white wine
¼ cup sugar syrup
2 cups cubed pineapple
6 orange slices
6 lemon slices
block of ice
1 liter chilled club soda
mint sprigs

In large punch bowl with block of ice add first 5 ingredients and stir to combine. Just before serving pour soda over ice. Ladle into punch cups and garnish each with mint sprig.

─────── **Palmer Cocktail** ───────

2 oz (4 Tbsp) rye or bourbon
2 dashes lemon juice
1 dash Angostura bitters

Stir ingredients with ice and strain into a chilled cocktail glass.

─────── **Panama Cocktail** ───────

1 oz (2 Tbsp) rum
1 oz (2 Tbsp) crème de cacao
1 oz (2 Tbsp) cream

(continued)

Shake ingredients with ice and strain into a chilled cocktail glass.

Variation: substitute brandy for rum.

——— Panama Hattie ———

1½ oz (3 Tbsp) white rum
1 oz (2 Tbsp) banana liqueur
½ oz (1 Tbsp) curaçao
1 tsp lemon juice

Place all ingredients in blender with 1 cup cracked ice. Cover and blend at high speed 10 to 15 seconds. Pour into chilled wineglass.

——— Paradise Cocktail ———

1½ oz (3 Tbsp) gin
1 oz (2 Tbsp) apricot brandy
juice of ¼ orange
slice of orange (optional)

Shake liquid ingredients with ice and strain into a chilled cocktail glass. Garnish with orange slice.

——— Parisian ———

1 oz (2 Tbsp) gin
1 oz (2 Tbsp) dry vermouth
1 oz (2 Tbsp) crème de cassis

Shake ingredients with ice and strain into a chilled cocktail glass.

─────── **Park Avenue** ───────

2 oz (4 Tbsp) gin
1 oz (2 Tbsp) sweet vermouth
1 oz (2 Tbsp) pineapple juice
1–2 dashes curaçao (optional)

Shake ingredients with ice and strain into a large chilled cocktail glass or wineglass.

─────── **Park West** ───────

2 oz (4 Tbsp) gin
2 oz (4 Tbsp) pineapple juice
2 oz (4 Tbsp) grapefruit juice

Place ingredients in shaker with 5 or 6 ice cubes, cover, and shake briskly several times. Pour immediately into chilled highball glass.

Variation: substitute vodka for gin.

─────── **Peach Blossom** ───────

2 oz (4 Tbsp) gin
½ oz (1 Tbsp) peach brandy
1 tsp lemon juice
1 tsp sugar syrup
½ ripe peach

Put all ingredients in blender with ½ cup cracked ice. Blend 10–15 seconds at high speed till thoroughly puréed. Pour into chilled wineglass.

─────── **Peach Blow Fizz** ───────

2 oz (4 Tbsp) gin
½ oz (1 Tbsp) strawberry liqueur

(continued)

juice of ½ lemon
⅔ oz cream
1 tsp sugar
chilled club soda
2 fresh strawberries

Shake first 5 ingredients with ice. Strain into a chilled highball glass over ice cubes and top with soda. Garnish with strawberries.

───────── **Peach Buck** ─────────

1½ oz (3 Tbsp) vodka
½ oz (1 Tbsp) peach brandy
½ oz (1 Tbsp) lemon juice
ginger ale chilled

Place liquors and juice in shaker with 5 or 6 ice cubes, cover, and shake vigorously several times. Strain into highball glass three-quarters filled with cracked ice. Top with ginger ale and stir gently.

───────── **Peaches & Cream** ─────────

2 oz (4 Tbsp) golden rum
1 oz (2 Tbsp) peach brandy
½ oz (1 Tbsp) heavy cream

Place ingredients in shaker with 4 or 5 ice cubes. Cover and shake briskly several times. Strain into chilled sour glass.

───────── **Peach Fizz** ─────────

2 oz (4 Tbsp) cognac (brandy)
2 tsp peach brandy
2 tsp lemon juice

1½ tsp sugar syrup
1 tsp banana liqueur
cold champagne or sparkling wine
peach slice

In shaker with 4 or 5 ice cubes place first 5 ingredients. Cover and shake quickly 3 or 4 times. Strain immediately into chilled wineglass and top with champagne. Decorate glass with peach slice or add to drink.

Peach Sangaree

2 oz (4 Tbsp) peach brandy
chilled club soda
½ oz (1 Tbsp) port
grated nutmeg (optional)

In highball glass place 3 or 4 ice cubes and add brandy. Top with soda and stir. Carefully float port on top and, if desired, sprinkle lightly with nutmeg.

Pendennis Cocktail

From Louisville's famed Pendennis Club.

1½ oz (3 Tbsp) gin
½ oz (1 Tbsp) apricot brandy
½ oz (1 Tbsp) lime juice
1–2 dashes Peychaud's bitters

Add all ingredients to shaker with 4 or 5 ice cubes. Cover and shake vigorously several times. Strain into chilled cocktail glass.

Perfect Manhattan

See under *Manhattan*.

———— Perfect Martini ————

See under *Martini*.

———— Pernod Frappé ————

2½ oz (5 Tbsp) Pernod
½ oz (1 Tbsp) anisette (optional)
1 egg white
½ oz (1 Tbsp) cream

Shake ingredients vigorously with ice and strain into a chilled cocktail or wine glass.

———— Petite Fleur ————

1 oz (2 Tbsp) light rum
1 oz (2 Tbsp) Cointreau or triple sec
1 oz (2 Tbsp) grapefruit juice
twist of orange peel (optional)

Shake liquid ingredients with ice and strain into a chilled cocktail glass. Garnish with orange peel.

———— Philly Mainliner ————

2 oz (4 Tbsp) cognac (brandy)
1 oz (2 Tbsp) curaçao
dash anisette
stemmed maraschino cherry (optional)

Place liquors in shaker with ½ cup cracked ice. Cover and shake vigorously several times. Strain into chilled cocktail glass and garnish with cherry, if desired.

Phoebe Snow

1½ oz (3 Tbsp) Dubonnet
1½ oz (3 Tbsp) brandy
1–2 dashes Pernod

Place liquors in shaker with ½ cup cracked ice. Cover and shake briskly several times. Strain into Old-Fashioned glass two-thirds full of cracked ice.

Picador

3 oz (6 Tbsp) very dry sherry, chilled
½ oz (1 Tbsp) Cointreau
lemon zest

Add liquors to chilled sherry glass and stir gently. Twist zest over drink to release oils and add.

Piccadilly Cocktail

1½ oz (3 Tbsp) gin
¾ oz (1½ Tbsp) dry vermouth
1 dash Pernod
1 dash grenadine

Stir ingredients with ice and strain into a chilled cocktail glass.

Picon Cocktail

See *Amer Picon Cocktail.*

Pike's Peak

2 oz (4 Tbsp) gin
½ oz (1 Tbsp) lemon juice

(continued)

½ oz (1 Tbsp) white maraschino
1 egg white
whipped cream

Shake first 4 ingredients vigorously with ice cubes
and strain into chilled wine glass. Top with whipped
cream.

Pimm's Cup

3 oz (6 Tbsp) Pimm's No. 1
1 tsp Cointreau (optional)
1 tsp sugar
juice of 1 lime
6 oz chilled lemon soda or 7-Up
2 lengthwise peels of cucumber
sprig of fresh mint
slice of lemon

Dissolve sugar in lime juice in a large chilled mug or
highball glass. Add ice, Pimm's, and Cointreau. Top
with lemon soda and stir gently. Stand cucumber
peels upright in the glass and garnish with mint and
lemon slice.

Piña Colada

2½ oz (5 Tbsp) light rum
3 oz (6 Tbsp) pineapple juice or crushed
pineapple (canned)
2 oz (4 Tbsp) coconut cream
¾ cup crushed ice
2 pieces fresh pineapple for garnish

Put ingredients, except fresh pineapple pieces, in a
blender and blend at medium-high speed for 15 seconds. Pour into a chilled collins glass or stemmed
goblet. Garnish with fresh pineapple.

Variation: substitute tequila for rum.

See also *Banana Colada.*

──────── **Piña Fría** ────────

2 oz (4 Tbsp) light rum
2 oz (4 Tbsp) pineapple juice
½ oz (1 Tbsp) lemon juice
1 dash sugar syrup
2 slices fresh pineapple
½ cup crushed ice

Put ingredients into a blender and blend at medium speed for 10–15 seconds. Pour into a chilled stemmed goblet.

──────── **Pineapple Cooler** ────────

3 oz (6 Tbsp) chilled dry white wine
3 oz (6 Tbsp) pineapple juice
1 dash lemon juice
½ tsp sugar
peel of ½ lemon cut in a continuous spiral

Dissolve sugar in juice in a chilled collins glass or stemmed goblet. Add ice cubes and wine. Garnish with lemon peel.

──────── **Pineapple Fizz** ────────

2 oz (4 Tbsp) rum
1 tsp sugar
1 oz (2 Tbsp) pineapple juice
chilled club soda

(continued)

Shake rum, sugar, and juice with ice. Strain into a chilled collins glass over ice cubes and top with club soda.

Pine Valley Cocktail

juice of 1 lime
2 oz (4 Tbsp) gin
2 or 3 sprigs fresh mint
½ egg white (about 1 Tbsp)
½ tsp sugar

In shaker add all ingredients (first bruising the mint) along with several ice cubes. Cover and shake vigorously, then strain into chilled cocktail glass.

Pink Almond

1 oz (2 Tbsp) rye whiskey
½ oz (1 Tbsp) crème de noyaux
½ oz (1 Tbsp) orgeat
½ oz (1 Tbsp) kirsch
½ oz (1 Tbsp) lemon juice
slice of lemon

Shake liquid ingredients with ice and strain into a chilled Old-Fashioned glass over ice cubes. Garnish with lemon slice.

Pink Creole

1½ oz (3 Tbsp) light rum
½ oz (1 Tbsp) lime juice
1 tsp grenadine
1 tsp cream
1 black cherry soaked in rum

Shake liquid ingredients with ice and strain into a chilled cocktail glass. Garnish with black cherry.

─────── **Pink Gin** ───────

See *Gin & Bitters*.

─────── **Pink Lady Cocktail** ───────

2 oz (4 Tbsp) gin
1 tsp grenadine
1 tsp cream
1 egg white
1 tsp lemon juice (optional)

Shake ingredients vigorously with ice and strain into a chilled cocktail glass.

─────── **Pink Panther** ───────

2 oz (4 Tbsp) grain alcohol
4 oz (8 Tbsp) cranberry juice
2 or 3 ice cubes

Place 2 or 3 ice cubes in a chilled highball glass. Add alcohol, fill with cranberry juice, and stir.

Variation: place all ingredients, including ice cubes, in a blender and blend at high speed for 20–30 seconds. Pour into a chilled goblet.

─────── **Pink Rose** ───────

1½ oz (3 Tbsp) gin
1 tsp lemon juice
1 tsp heavy cream

(continued)

½ oz (1 Tbsp) egg white
½ tsp grenadine

Place all ingredients in shaker with 5 or 6 ice cubes.
Cover and shake vigorously. Strain into chilled cocktail glass or into Old-Fashioned glass filled with
crushed ice.

——————— **Pink Rose Fizz** ———————

2 oz (4 Tbsp) gin
½ oz (1 Tbsp) lemon juice
1 tsp grenadine
½ oz (1 Tbsp) heavy cream
1 egg white
1 tsp sugar syrup
chilled club soda

Place all ingredients but soda in shaker with 4 or 5
ice cubes. Cover and shake vigorously. Strain into
chilled highball glass. Top with soda and stir gently.

——————— **Pink Squirrel Cocktail** ———————

1 oz (2 Tbsp) créme de noyaux
1 oz (2 Tbsp) white crème de cacao
1 oz (2 Tbsp) light cream

Shake ingredients with ice and strain into a chilled
cocktail glass.

——————— **Pink Whiskers** ———————

1 oz (2 Tbsp) apricot brandy
½ oz (1 Tbsp) dry vermouth
1 oz (2 Tbsp) orange juice
1 tsp grenadine

2–3 dashes white crème de menthe
1 oz (2 Tbsp) port

Place all ingredients except port in shaker with ½ cup cracked ice. Shake vigorously several times and strain into Old-Fashioned glass filled halfway with cracked ice. Carefully float port on top.

——— **Pisco Punch** ———

2 oz (4 Tbsp) pisco brandy
1 tsp lemon or lime juice
1 tsp sugar
1 egg white
2–3 drops Angostura bitters

Shake ingredients, except bitters, with ice and strain into a chilled cocktail glass. Shake bitters on top.

Variation: sugar-rim the glass by rubbing with lemon or lime and dipping into sugar.

——— **Pisco Sour (Pisco Cooler)** ———

Although the addition of club soda actually makes this a cooler, it is commonly known as a sour.

2 oz (4 Tbsp) pisco brandy
½–¾ oz (1–1½ Tbsp) lemon juice
1 tsp sugar
2–3 dashes Angostura bitters
chilled club soda
slice of lemon

Stir first 4 ingredients with ice cubes in a chilled highball glass. Top with soda and garnish with lemon slice.

———— Plantation Cocktail ————

2 oz (4 Tbsp) bourbon
½ tsp crème de menthe
½ tsp sugar syrup
3 or 4 drops curaçao
dash bitters

Combine all ingredients in mixing glass. Pour over cracked ice in Old-Fashioned glass.

———— Plantation Punch ————

1½ oz (3 Tbsp) Southern Comfort
¾ oz (1½ Tbsp) lemon juice
2 dashes light rum
1 tsp sugar
chilled club soda
maraschino cherry
twist of orange peel

Mix first 4 ingredients in a large Old-Fashioned glass. Add ice cubes and top with soda. Garnish with cherry and orange peel.

———— Planter's Cocktail ————

1½ oz (3 Tbsp) light rum
¾ oz (1½ Tbsp) lemon juice
½ tsp sugar
¾ oz (1½ Tbsp) orange juice (optional)

Shake ingredients with ice and strain into a chilled cocktail glass.

——————— **Planter's Punch** ———————

3 oz (6 Tbsp) Jamaican rum
juice of 1 lime
1 tsp sugar
1 oz (2 Tbsp) chilled club soda
slices of orange and lime
maraschino cherry

Dissolve sugar in lime juice in a frosted collins glass. Add rum and fill with crushed ice. Top with soda, stir, and garnish with fruit.

Variation: add juice of ½ orange and top drink with 2 dashes triple sec.

——————— **Platinum Blonde** ———————

1 oz (2 Tbsp) light rum
1 oz (2 Tbsp) Cointreau
½ oz (1 Tbsp) cream

Shake ingredients with ice and strain into a chilled cocktail glass.

Variation: substitute Grand Marnier for Cointreau.

——————— **Poinsettia** ———————

1½ oz (3 Tbsp) cranberry juice, chilled
½ oz (1 Tbsp) apple brandy
cold champagne or other sparkling wine

To chilled champagne flute add ingredients in order given. Top off with champagne and stir briefly.

———— Pollyanna Cocktail ————

2 oz (4 Tbsp) gin
⅔ oz sweet vermouth
½ tsp grenadine
3 slices of orange
3 slices of pineapple

Muddle orange and pineapple slices. Add other ingredients and shake with ice. Strain into a chilled cocktail glass.

———— Polo Cocktail ————

1½ oz (3 Tbsp) gin
¾ oz (1½ Tbsp) orange juice
¾ oz (1½ Tbsp) lemon juice

Shake ingredients with ice and strain into a chilled cocktail glass.

Variation: substitute grapefruit juice for lemon juice.

———— Polonaise ————

1½ oz (3 Tbsp) brandy
½ oz (1 Tbsp) blackberry brandy
½ oz (1 Tbsp) dry sherry
2 dashes lemon juice
1 dash orange bitters (optional)

Shake ingredients with ice and strain into a chilled cocktail glass or into an Old-Fashioned glass over ice cubes.

Polynesia Cocktail

1½ oz (3 Tbsp) light rum
1½ oz (3 Tbsp) passionfruit juice
½ oz (1 Tbsp) lime juice
1 egg white
½ cup crushed ice

Put ingredients into a blender and blend at low speed for 10–15 seconds. Pour into a chilled champagne glass.

Pompano

1½ oz (3 Tbsp) gin
¾ oz (1½ Tbsp) dry vermouth
1½ oz (3 Tbsp) grapefruit juice
2 dashes orange bitters (optional)

Shake ingredients with ice and strain into a chilled cocktail glass.

Pope, The

See under *Bishop*.

Port In A Storm

3 oz (6 Tbsp) port
1 oz (2 Tbsp) brandy
½ oz (1 Tbsp) lemon juice
twist of lemon peel

Stir liquid ingredients with ice and pour into a wine-glass. Add more ice if necessary and garnish with lemon peel.

Variation: add 2 oz (4 Tbsp) dry red wine.

Port Wine Cocktail

2 oz (4 Tbsp) port
½ oz (1 Tbsp) brandy
twist of orange peel (optional)

Stir port and brandy with ice and strain into a chilled cocktail glass. Garnish with orange peel.

Port Wine Flip

4 oz (8 Tbsp) port
1 whole egg
1 tsp sugar
nutmeg

Shake ingredients, except nutmeg, vigorously with ice and strain into a chilled wine or flip glass. Sprinkle with nutmeg.

Variation: shake with cracked ice and pour into the glass. Add 2 tsp cream.

Port Wine Sangaree

2 oz (4 Tbsp) port
1 tsp sugar
chilled club soda
½ oz (1 Tbsp) brandy
slice of lemon
nutmeg

Dissolve sugar in port in a chilled highball glass. Add ice and top with soda. Float brandy on top. Garnish with lemon slice and sprinkle with nutmeg.

See also *Sangaree.*

———— **Pousse Café** ————

An after-dinner drink consisting of 2 or more liqueurs served in a tall cordial glass in separate layers. Carefully made, the drink can present a spectacular rainbow effect. The number of liqueurs combined usually varies from 2 to 7 and, since liqueurs vary in density, they should be poured heavy-to-light in ascending order of lightness. The best method of keeping them separate is to pour them slowly over the back of a spoon held inside the glass.

Listed below are several suggested variations of Pousse Cafés, but the combinations are almost limitless.

Variation 1:

> ½ oz (1 Tbsp) parfait d'amour
> ½ oz (1 Tbsp) crème Yvette

Variation 2:

> ¼ oz (½ Tbsp) orange curaçao
> ¼ oz (½ Tbsp) kirschwasser
> ¼ oz (½ Tbsp) cognac
> ¼ oz (½ Tbsp) green Chartreuse

Variation 3:

> ¼ oz (½ Tbsp) green crème de menthe
> ¼ oz (½ Tbsp) yellow Chartreuse
> ¼ oz (½ Tbsp) Peter Heering
> ¼ oz (½ Tbsp) cognac

Variation 4:

> ⅙ oz (1 tsp) grenadine
> ⅙ oz (1 tsp) yellow Chartreuse
> ⅙ oz (1 tsp) crème de cassis
> ⅙ oz (1 tsp) white crème de menthe
> ⅙ oz (1 tsp) green Chartreuse
> ⅙ oz (1 tsp) cognac

(continued)

Variation 5:

⅙ oz (1 tsp) grenadine
⅙ oz (1 tsp) dark crème de cacao
⅙ oz (1 tsp) Maraschino liqueur
⅙ oz (1 tsp) orange curaçao
⅙ oz (1 tsp) green crème de menthe
⅙ oz (1 tsp) parfait d'amour
⅙ oz (1 tsp) cognac

———— Prado ————

(serves 2)

3 oz (6 Tbsp) tequila
1½ oz (3 Tbsp) lime or lemon juice
1 oz (2 Tbsp) Maraschino liqueur
4 dashes grenadine
1 egg white
2 small slices of lemon
2 maraschino cherries

Shake first 5 ingredients with ice and strain into chilled sour glasses. Garnish with lemon slices and cherries.

———— Prairie Oyster Cocktail ————

1 egg yolk
1 oz (2 Tbsp) brandy
½ oz (1 Tbsp) wine vinegar
½ oz (1 Tbsp) Worcestershire sauce
1 tsp tomato catsup
dash of cayenne pepper

Shake all ingredients, except egg yolk and cayenne, with ice. Strain into a chilled Old-Fashioned glass. Add egg yolk, being careful not to break it, and sprinkle with cayenne. Swallow the drink in one gulp without breaking the yolk.

Variations: substitute 1½ oz (3 Tbsp) port for the brandy. Add a dash of bitters, celery salt, or Tabasco sauce.

Presbyterian

See under *Whiskey Highball.*

Pretty Penny

1½ oz (3 Tbsp) vodka
2 tsp crème yvette
1 tsp curaçao
1 egg white
dash bitters

Place all ingredients in shaker with 5 or 6 ice cubes. Cover and shake vigorously. Strain into chilled cocktail glass.

Prince Edward

1½ oz (3 Tbsp) Scotch
½ oz (1 Tbsp) dry vermouth
¼ oz (½ Tbsp) Drambuie
slice of orange

Shake liquid ingredients with ice and strain into a chilled Old-Fashioned glass over ice cubes. Garnish with orange slice.

Variation: substitute Lillet for vermouth.

———— **Princeton Cocktail** ————

2 oz (4 Tbsp) gin
1 oz (2 Tbsp) port
1–2 dashes orange bitters
twist of lemon peel

Stir liquid ingredients with ice and strain into a chilled cocktail glass. Garnish with lemon peel.

Variation: eliminate orange bitters, add juice of ½ lime, and substitute dry vermouth for the port.

———— **Puerto Apple** ————

1½ oz (3 Tbsp) applejack
¾ oz (1½ Tbsp) light rum
½ oz (1 Tbsp) lime juice
2 tsp orgeat
slice of lime

Shake liquid ingredients with ice and strain into a chilled Old-Fashioned glass over ice cubes. Garnish with lime slice.

———— **Purple Jesus** ————

1 oz (2 Tbsp) grain alcohol
4 oz (8 Tbsp) Concord grape juice

Put 2 or 3 ice cubes in a chilled highball glass. Pour in alcohol, fill with grape juice and stir.

Variation: substitute 2 oz (4 Tbsp) vodka for the grain alcohol.

Q

——— **Quaker's Cocktail** ———

1 oz (2 Tbsp) brandy
1 oz (2 Tbsp) light rum
½ oz (1 Tbsp) lemon juice
1½ tsp raspberry syrup
twist of lemon peel (optional)

Shake liquid ingredients with ice and strain into a
chilled cocktail glass. Garnish with lemon peel.

——— **Quarter Deck Cocktail** ———

2 oz (4 Tbsp) dark rum
1 oz (2 Tbsp) dry sherry
2 dashes lime juice

Stir ingredients with ice and strain into a chilled cock-
·tail glass.

Variation: substitute sweet sherry for dry.

——— **Quebec** ———

1½ oz (3 Tbsp) Canadian whiskey,
½ oz (1 Tbsp) dry vermouth
1 tsp Amer Picon
1 tsp Maraschino liqueur

Shake or stir ingredients with ice and strain into a
chilled cocktail glass.

Variation: sugar-rim the glass by rubbing with
lemon and dipping into sugar.

——————— ## Queen of Denmark ———————

1½ oz (3 Tbsp) Cherry Heering
½ oz (1 Tbsp) heavy cream

Pour liqueur into cordial glass. Carefully float cream
on top.

——————— ## Queen of Spades ———————

2 oz (4 Tbsp) dark Jamaican rum
1 oz (2 Tbsp) Tia Maria
1 oz (2 Tbsp) heavy cream

Blend with ½ cup cracked ice at high speed 10–15
seconds. Pour into chilled wine glass.

——————— ## Queens ———————

¾ oz (1½ Tbsp) gin
¾ oz (1½ Tbsp) dry vermouth
¾ oz (1½ Tbsp) sweet vermouth
¾ oz (1½ Tbsp) pineapple juice

Shake ingredients with ice and strain into a chilled
cocktail glass.

Variation: muddle a slice of fresh pineapple in place
of the pineapple juice.

——————— ## Quelle Vie ———————

Pronounced "kell vee," and as the French say, "What
a life!"

1½ oz (3 Tbsp) brandy
¾ oz (1½ Tbsp) kümmel

Stir ingredients with ice and strain into a chilled cocktail glass.

R

——— Racquet Club Cocktail ———

2 oz (4 Tbsp) gin
1 oz (2 Tbsp) dry vermouth
1 dash orange bitters

Stir ingredients with ice and strain into a chilled cocktail glass.

——— Rainbow Ridge ———

1 oz (2 Tbsp) apricot brandy
½ oz (1 Tbsp) cherry brandy
1 tsp fresh lemon juice
½ oz (1 Tbsp) heavy cream
½ ripe banana peeled and sliced

Place all ingredients into blender with ½ cup cracked ice. Blend at high speed for 10–15 seconds or until just puréed. Pour into chilled wine glass.

——— Ramos Gin Fizz I ———

2 oz (4 Tbsp) gin
2 oz (4 Tbsp) light cream or milk
1 egg white
juice of ½ lemon
1 tsp sugar
1 tsp orange-flower water

Shake ingredients with ice and strain into a chilled cocktail glass. Add ice cubes if desired.

——— Ramos Gin Fizz II ———

1½ oz (3 Tbsp) gin
1 oz (2 Tbsp) powdered sugar
juice of ½ lemon and ½ lime
½ tsp orange-flower water
1 egg white
1 oz (2 Tbsp) cream
crushed ice
club soda or seltzer

In bottom of cocktail shaker add all ingredients except soda, including ½ cup or more of crushed ice. Shake vigorously and strain into a chilled highball glass. Top with a jigger of club soda or seltzer.

——— Rancho Grande ———

2 oz (4 Tbsp) light rum
1 oz (2 Tbsp) dry sherry
½ oz (1 Tbsp) brandy
1 tsp curaçao

Pour all ingredients into an Old-Fashioned glass half-filled with cracked ice. Stir gently.

——— Raspberry Cream ———

2 oz (4 Tbsp) white rum
1 oz (2 Tbsp) Crème de Framboise
½ oz (1 Tbsp) cream
1–2 dashes orange bitters

Place ingredients in shaker with ice cubes. Cover and shake briskly several times. Strain into chilled cocktail glass.

——— **Red Apple** ———

1 oz (2 Tbsp) vodka
1 oz (2 Tbsp) apple juice
½ oz (1 Tbsp) lemon juice
2–3 dashes grenadine

Shake ingredients with ice and strain into a chilled cocktail glass.

——— **Red Cloud** ———

1½ oz (3 Tbsp) gin
½ oz (1 Tbsp) apricot brandy
½ oz (1 Tbsp) lemon juice
1 tsp grenadine
1 dash Angostura bitters (optional)

Shake ingredients with ice and strain into a chilled cocktail glass.

——— **Red-Eye Special** ———

Favored by some as a pick-me-up and by others as a morning-after remedy.

6 oz tomato juice
6 oz beer
1 tsp Worcestershire Sauce
1 tsp lemon juice
1–2 dashes Tabasco sauce

Combine all ingredients in a large glass with several ice cubes. Stir to mix.

——— **Red Lion** ———

1½ oz (3 Tbsp) Grand Marnier
¾ oz (1½ Tbsp) gin
1 oz (2 Tbsp) lemon juice
1 oz (2 Tbsp) orange juice
1 dash orange bitters (optional)
twist of orange peel

Shake liquid ingredients vigorously with ice and strain into a chilled cocktail glass. Garnish with orange peel.

——— **Renaissance Cocktail** ———

1½ oz (3 Tbsp) gin
1 oz (2 Tbsp) dry sherry
¾ oz (1½ Tbsp) cream
nutmeg

Shake liquid ingredients with ice and strain into a chilled cocktail glass. Sprinkle with nutmeg.

——— **Resolute Cocktail** ———

1½ oz (3 Tbsp) gin
¾ oz (1½ Tbsp) apricot brandy
½ oz (1 Tbsp) lemon juice

Stir or shake ingredients with ice and strain into a chilled cocktail glass.

——— **Rhine Wine Cup** ———

(serves 6–8)

1 bottle chilled Rhine wine
1 oz (2 Tbsp) brandy
1 oz (2 Tbsp) triple sec or curaçao

1 oz (2 Tbsp) Maraschino liqueur
8 oz chilled club soda
strips of cucumber peel and
sprigs of fresh mint

Mix brandy, triple sec, and maraschino and put into
a pitcher with ice cubes. Add wine and soda, stir, and
garnish with cucumber peels and mint. Serve in
chilled wineglasses.

—————— **Rhine Wine Punch** ——————

(serves 6–8)

2 qts chilled Rhine wine
1 qt chilled club soda
3 oz (6 Tbsp) brandy
3 oz (6 Tbsp) Cointreau or triple sec
1 cup strong tea
juice of 3 lemons
sliced fresh fruit
sprigs of fresh mint

Pour liquid ingredients into a punch bowl over a block
of ice and stir gently. Garnish with fruit and mint.

—————— **Rickey** ——————

See *Gin Rickey*.

—————— **Rittenhouse Special** ——————

Named for Philadelphia's famous square.

1½ oz (3 Tbsp) bourbon
1 oz (2 Tbsp) heavy cream
1 oz (2 Tbsp) brown crème de cacao

(continued)

Place all ingredients in shaker with 4 or 5 ice cubes. Cover and shake vigorously several times. Strain into chilled cocktail glass.

———— **Road Runner** ————

1½ oz (3 Tbsp) vodka
¾ oz (1½ Tbsp) amaretto
¾ oz (1½ Tbsp) coconut milk
nutmeg

Shake liquid ingredients with ice and strain into a chilled cocktail glass. Sprinkle with nutmeg.

Variations: sugar-rim the glass by rubbing with a slice of orange and dipping into sugar. The drink can also be made in a blender with ⅓ cup crushed ice (medium speed for 15 seconds) and poured into a chilled champagne or wine glass.

———— **Rob Roy** ————

Similar to a Manhattan but made with Scotch instead of rye, it is named after Rob Roy (Robert Macgregor), the Scottish Robin Hood.

2 oz (4 Tbsp) Scotch
1 oz (2 Tbsp) sweet vermouth
1 dash Angostura bitters
maraschino cherry

Stir liquid ingredients with ice and strain into a chilled cocktail glass. Garnish with the cherry.

Variations: substitute orange bitters for Angostura. Substitute a twist of orange peel for the cherry.

Dry Rob Roy: substitute dry vermouth for the sweet and garnish with a lemon twist instead of a cherry.

Perfect Rob Roy: equal parts (½ oz (1 Tbsp) each) of dry and sweet vermouth.

Rock & Rye Cooler

1½ oz (3 Tbsp) vodka
1 oz (2 Tbsp) Rock & Rye
½ oz (1 Tbsp) lime juice
chilled bitter lemon soda
slice of lime

Shake first 3 ingredients with ice. Strain into a chilled collins or highball glass over ice cubes. Top with lemon and garnish with lime slice.

Rolls Royce

1 oz (2 Tbsp) cognac
¾ oz (1½ Tbsp) Cointreau or triple sec
1 oz (2 Tbsp) orange juice

Shake ingredients with ice and strain into a chilled cocktail glass.

Roman Punch

2 oz (4 Tbsp) Jamaican rum
2 oz (4 Tbsp) brandy
1 oz (2 Tbsp) raspberry syrup
juice of 1 lemon

Mix ingredients in a chilled highball glass. Fill with shaved or crushed ice and stir.

(continued)

Variations: add 2 dashes curaçao or float port wine on top.

─────── **Rose Cocktail** ───────

1½ oz (3 Tbsp) gin
¾ oz (1½ Tbsp) cherry brandy
¾ oz (1½ Tbsp) dry vermouth
twist of orange peel (optional)
maraschino cherry (optional)

Stir liquid ingredients with ice and strain into a chilled cocktail glass. Garnish with orange peel and cherry.

Variation: substitute apricot brandy for cherry and add ½ tsp lemon juice. Shake with ice and strain into a sugar-rimmed cocktail glass. Do not garnish.

─────── **Rose Hall** ───────

Named in honor of the Jamaican landmark.

1½ oz (3 Tbsp) golden or dark Jamaican rum
½ oz (1 Tbsp) banana liqueur
1 oz (2 Tbsp) orange juice
1 tsp lime juice
thin slice of lime (optional)

Place half a cup of cracked ice in shaker. Add liquors and juices, cover, and shake vigorously several times. Strain into chilled cocktail glass, garnish with lime slice, if desired.

─────── **Roselyn Cocktail** ───────

1½ oz (3 Tbsp) gin
¾ oz (1½ Tbsp) dry vermouth

2 dashes grenadine
twist of lemon peel

Stir liquid ingredients with ice and strain into a chilled cocktail glass. Garnish with lemon peel.

Rosita

1½ oz (3 Tbsp) tequila
1 oz (2 Tbsp) Campari
½ oz (1 Tbsp) dry vermouth
½ oz (1 Tbsp) sweet vermouth
thin slice lemon

Fill large Old-Fashioned glass two-thirds with cracked ice. Add liquors and stir gently. Float lemon slice on top of drink.

Rough Rider

2 oz (4 Tbsp) whiskey
1 oz (2 Tbsp) apple brandy
½ oz (1 Tbsp) sloe gin
chilled club soda

Pour first 3 ingredients in highball glass filled with cracked ice. Top with soda and stir.

Royal Clover Club Cocktail

2 oz (4 Tbsp) gin
juice of ½ lemon or lime
½ oz (1 Tbsp) grenadine
1 egg yolk

Shake ingredients vigorously with ice and strain into a chilled cocktail or champagne glass.

———— Royal Cocktail ————

1½ oz (3 Tbsp) gin
juice of ½ lemon
1 whole egg
½ tsp sugar

Shake ingredients vigorously with ice and strain into a chilled cocktail glass.

———— Royal Gin Fizz ————

2 oz (4 Tbsp) gin
1 oz (2 Tbsp) lemon juice
1 whole egg
2 tsp sugar
chilled club soda
slice of lemon

Shake first 4 ingredients with ice. Strain into a chilled highball glass over ice cubes. Top with soda, stir, and garnish with lemon slice.

———— Royal Jamaican ————

1½ oz (3 Tbsp) Tia Maria
½ oz (1 Tbsp) heavy cream

Pour liqueur into cordial glass. Carefully float cream on top.

———— Royal Smile Cocktail ————

1½ oz (3 Tbsp) apple brandy
¾ oz (1½ Tbsp) gin
2 dashes lemon juice
2 dashes grenadine

Stir ingredients with ice and strain into a chilled cocktail glass.

——— **Rue de la Paix** ———

1 oz (2 Tbsp) brandy
1 oz (2 Tbsp) dry vermouth
½ tsp Pernod or Ricard
½ tsp Maraschino liqueur
½ tsp curaçao
1–2 dashes orange bitters
long-stemmed cherry

Shake first 6 ingredients with cracked ice and strain into chilled cocktail glass. Garnish with cherry.

——— **Rum Cola** ———

See *Cuba Libre.*

——— **Rum Collins** ———

See under *Tom Collins.*

——— **Rum Cow** ———

1½ oz (3 Tbsp) light rum
2 or 3 drops vanilla extract
1 dash nutmeg
1 dash Angostura bitters
8 oz chilled milk
1½ tsp sugar

Shake ingredients with ice and pour into a chilled highball glass.

———— **Rum Daisy** ————

2 oz (4 Tbsp) light rum
1½ tsp raspberry syrup
juice of ½ lemon
½ tsp sugar (optional)
fresh fruit for garnish

Shake ingredients, except fruit, with ice cubes or crushed ice and pour into an Old-Fashioned glass. Garnish with fruit and serve with a straw.

Variation: substitute grenadine for raspberry syrup. Pour into a highball glass and top with chilled club soda.

———— **Rum Dubonnet** ————

1½ oz (3 Tbsp) light rum
½ oz (1 Tbsp) Dubonnet
1 tsp lime juice
twist of lime peel

Shake liquid ingredients with ice and strain into a chilled cocktail glass. Garnish with lime peel.

———— **Rum Fix** ————

2 oz (4 Tbsp) light rum
juice of ½ lemon
1 tsp sugar
1 dash curaçao (optional)
slice of lemon

Stir liquid ingredients in a chilled highball glass and fill with crushed ice. Garnish with lemon slice and serve with a straw.

─────── **Rum Manhattan** ───────

See under *Manhattan*.

─────── **Rum Martini** ───────

See under *Martini*.

─────── **Rum Old-Fashioned** ───────

See under *Old-Fashioned*.

─────── **Rum Punch I** ───────

The mnemonic jingle for this is "one of sour, two of sweet, three of strong, and four of weak." The "parts," of course, can be tablespoons, cups, or whatever, and vary widely according to taste.

> 3 oz (6 Tbsp) dark rum
> 1 oz (2 Tbsp) lime juice
> 2 oz (4 Tbsp) brown sugar
> ½ cup crushed ice and/or
>   chilled water (optional)
> orange slice and/or maraschino cherry

Put ingredients in a blender and blend at medium speed for 10–15 seconds. Pour into a frosted collins glass and decorate with orange slice and/or maraschino cherry if desired.

─────── **Rum Punch II** ───────

(serves 25–30)

> 1 bottle Jamaican rum
> 4 oz (8 Tbsp) brandy
> 2 qts seltzer water

(continued)

1 pt lemon juice (approx. 16 lemons)
2 cups white wine
2 lemons thinly sliced
2½ cups sugar
block of ice

Mix sugar with water and stir till completely dissolved. Add other liquid ingredients and combine thoroughly. Pour over block of ice in large punch bowl and float lemon slices. Ladle into punch cups.

—————— **Rum Screwdriver** ——————

See under *Screwdriver.*

—————— **Rum Sour** ——————

See under *Whiskey Sour.*

—————— **Rum Swizzle** ——————

See under *Swizzle.*

—————— **Rum Toddy, Hot** ——————

See under *Hot Toddy.*

—————— **Russian Bear** ——————

See *White Russian.*

—————— **Russian Cocktail** ——————

¾ oz (1½ Tbsp) vodka
¾ oz (1½ Tbsp) gin
¾ oz (1½ Tbsp) white crème de cacao

Stir or shake ingredients with ice and strain into a chilled cocktail glass.

—————— **Rusty Nail** ——————

1½ oz (3 Tbsp) Scotch
1½ oz (3 Tbsp) Drambuie
twist of lemon peel (optional)

Pour Scotch and Drambuie into chilled Old-Fashioned glass over ice cubes. Stir gently and garnish with lemon peel.

Variations: stir liquid ingredients with ice and strain into a chilled cocktail glass. Instead of stirring, float Drambuie on top of the Scotch. Amount of Drambuie can be reduced to ¾ oz (1½ Tbsp).

S

—————— **Salty Dog** ——————

2 oz (4 Tbsp) gin
4 oz (8 Tbsp) grapefruit juice

Salt-rim a chilled collins or highball glass. Pour ingredients over ice cubes and stir.

Variations: use equal parts of gin and grapefruit juice.

Vodka Salty Dog: substitute vodka for the gin.

———— **Sangaree** ————

A forerunner of Sangría. In Colonial days it was a mixture of red wine, fruit and fruit juice, sugar, and spices.

2 oz (4 Tbsp) brandy
½ tsp sugar
1 tsp water
chilled club soda
1 tsp port
nutmeg

Dissolve sugar in water in a chilled Old-Fashioned glass. Add ice cubes and brandy. Top with soda and stir. Float port on top and sprinkle with nutmeg.

Variations: substitute flavored brandy, sherry, gin, or whiskey for the brandy, and the Sangaree is then named after the liquor used (Gin Sangaree).

See also *Port Wine Sangaree.*

———— **Sangría** ————

(serves 4–6)

1 qt dry red wine
1–2 oz (4 Tbsp) Spanish brandy (optional)
½ cup sugar
1 cup chilled water or club soda
juice of 1 orange
juice of 1 lemon
1 sliced orange
1 sliced lemon

Dissolve sugar in wine in a large pitcher. Add remaining ingredients and stir. Allow mixture to stand at room temperature for an hour before serving. Serve in large chilled wineglasses over ice cubes. Put pieces of lemon and orange in each glass.

See also *Santa Clara Sangría*.

─────── **Sangría Mexicali** ───────

(serves 12)

1 cup fresh orange juice
½ cup fresh lemon (or lime) juice
¼ cup superfine sugar
2 lemons (or limes) thinly sliced
2 oranges thinly sliced
1 bottle dry red (or white) wine
1 liter seltzer or club soda (chilled)
1½ oz (3 Tbsp) brandy
thin lemon slices for garnish (optional)

In large pitcher (or punch bowl) combine above ingredients, except garnish. Add 10–12 ice cubes. Pour or ladle into glasses or punch cups. Garnish each with lemon slice if desired. Makes approximately one dozen 6-oz servings.

─────── **Sangrita** ───────

(serves 4)

Variation on the above. A shot of tequila is downed and "chased" with the following:

½ cup tomato juice
½ cup fresh orange juice
¼ cup fresh lemon juice
dash or two of Tabasco, to taste
½ tsp salt
freshly ground pepper
½ tsp sugar

(continued)

In small pitcher combine the above and divide among 4 small glasses. This makes 4 servings but can easily be doubled and repeated as needed.

——— **Sanibel Cooler** ———

2 oz (4 Tbsp) gin
2 tsp fresh lime juice
1 tsp sugar syrup
1 tsp grenadine
chilled club soda

In collins glass filled with cracked ice add first 4 ingredients and stir. Top with soda and stir again before serving with long straw.

——— **San Juan** ———

1½ oz (3 Tbsp) light rum
1 oz (2 Tbsp) grapefruit juice
1 tsp coconut milk
2 tsp lime juice
⅓ cup crushed ice
2 tsp brandy

Put all ingredients, except brandy, into a blender and blend at low speed for 15 seconds. Pour into a chilled wine or champagne glass. Float brandy on top.

——— **San Sebastian** ———

1 oz (2 Tbsp) gin
¼ oz (½ Tbsp) light rum
¼ oz (½ Tbsp) triple sec
½ oz (1 Tbsp) grapefruit juice
½ oz (1 Tbsp) lemon juice

Shake ingredients with ice and strain into a chilled cocktail glass.

Santa Clara Sangría

(serves 16–18)

1 gal California zinfandel
1 cup lemon juice (approx. 4 large lemons)
½ cup sugar
½ cup brandy
2 oz (4 Tbsp) Strega
1 qt orange juice
1 qt club soda
thin slices of orange and lemon

Mix lemon juice and orange juice with sugar. Stir in brandy and Strega and pour over block of ice in large punch bowl (2-gal capacity). Add the wine and soda just before serving, stir gently, and float the fruit slices.

Santiago Cocktail

1½ oz (3 Tbsp) light rum
juice of 1 lime
2 dashes grenadine
½ tsp sugar

Shake ingredients with ice and strain into a chilled cocktail glass.

Variation: substitute 2 dashes curaçao for the grenadine.

—————— **Saratoga Cocktail** ——————

2 oz (4 Tbsp) brandy
2 dashes Angostura bitters
1 tsp pineapple juice
1 tsp lemon juice (optional)

Shake ingredients with ice and strain into a chilled cocktail glass.

—————— **Saturday Night Special** ——————

See *Mothers Milk.*

—————— **Saucy Sue Cocktail** ——————

2 oz (4 Tbsp) apple brandy
1 dash apricot brandy
1 dash Pernod
twist of orange peel (optional)

Stir ingredients with ice and strain into a chilled cocktail glass. Garnish with orange peel.

—————— **Sauternes Cup** ——————

(serves 6)

1 qt chilled Sauternes wine
3 oz (6 Tbsp) brandy
3 oz (6 Tbsp) Cointreau or triple sec
3 tsp sugar
6 oz chilled club soda
1 cup sliced fresh fruit (oranges, lemons,
grapefruit, strawberries, cucumber peel, etc.)

Mix ingredients in a large pitcher or punch bowl with ice cubes or a block of ice. Serve in chilled wineglasses or punch cups.

Variation: soak the fruit in the brandy and Cointreau for an hour before adding other ingredients.

——— **Savoy Hotel** ———

⅓ oz brandy
⅓ oz Benedictine
⅓ oz crème de cacao

Pour ingredients, in order given, into a Pousse-Café glass, being carefully that the layers do not mix.

——— **Saxon Cocktail** ———

2 oz (4 Tbsp) light rum
2 dashes grenadine
juice of ½ lime
twist of orange peel

Shake liquid ingredients with ice and strain into a chilled cocktail glass. Garnish with orange peel.

——— **Sazerac** ———

2 oz (4 Tbsp) rye whiskey
2 dashes Peychaud bitters
2 dashes Pernod
½ tsp sugar
twist of lemon peel

Dissolve sugar in whiskey in a chilled Old-Fashioned glass. Add ice cubes, Pernod, and bitters. Stir gently and garnish with lemon peel.

——— **Scarlett O'Hara** ———

2 oz (4 Tbsp) Southern Comfort
1 oz (2 Tbsp) cranberry juice
2 dashes lime juice

Shake ingredients with ice and strain into a chilled cocktail glass.

——— **Scorpion** ———

2 oz (4 Tbsp) light rum
1 oz (2 Tbsp) brandy
½ oz (1 Tbsp) orgeat
1½ oz (3 Tbsp) orange juice
1½ oz (3 Tbsp) lemon juice
½ cup crushed ice
slice of orange
sprig of fresh mint

Put first 6 ingredients in a blender and blend at low speed for 15 seconds. Pour into a chilled Old-Fashioned glass over ice cubes. Garnish with orange slice and mint.

——— **Scotch & Soda** ———

See *Whiskey Highball.*

——— **Scotch Collins** ———

See under *Tom Collins.*

-------- **Scotch Cooler** --------

2 oz (4 Tbsp) Scotch
3 dashes white crème de menthe
chilled club soda

Pour Scotch and crème de menthe into a chilled collins
or highball glass over ice cubes. Top with soda and
stir gently.

-------- **Scotch Holiday Sour** --------

(serves 2)

3 oz (6 Tbsp) Scotch
2 oz (4 Tbsp) cherry brandy
1 oz (2 Tbsp) sweet vermouth
2 oz (4 Tbsp) lemon juice
1 egg white (optional)
2 slices of lemon

Shake first 5 ingredients with ice and strain into a
chilled Old-Fashioned glass over ice cubes. Garnish
with lemon slices.

-------- **Scotch Manhattan** --------

See *Rob Roy*.

-------- **Scotch Mist** --------

2 oz (4 Tbsp) Scotch
twist of lemon peel

Pack a chilled Old-Fashioned glass with crushed ice.
Add Scotch and lemon twist. Serve with a short straw.

Bourbon Mist: substitute bourbon for Scotch.

Scotch Old-Fashioned

See under *Old-Fashioned*.

Scotch Solace

2½ oz (5 Tbsp) Scotch
½ oz (1 Tbsp) triple sec
½ oz (1 Tbsp) honey
4 oz (8 Tbsp) chilled milk
1 oz (2 Tbsp) cream
pinch of grated orange rind

Put Scotch, triple sec, and honey into a chilled high-ball glass and stir until honey is dissolved. Add milk, cream, orange rind, and ice cubes. Stir well.

Scotch Sour

See under *Whiskey Sour*.

Scotch Stinger

See under *Stinger*.

Scotch Symphony

2 oz (4 Tbsp) Scotch
1 oz (2 Tbsp) Drambuie
lemon zest

Place liquors in Old-Fashioned glass with 3 or 4 ice cubes. Twist zest over drink to release oils and drop in.

--------- **Screwdriver** ---------

The numerous theories as to the origin of this drink all revolve around its being first stirred with a screwdriver due to the lack of a proper stirring spoon. Who did the stirring and where it was done remain a mystery. The drink has been around for some time and continues to be one of the most popular vodka-based drinks in this country.

2 oz (4 Tbsp) vodka
chilled orange juice to taste

Pour vodka into a chilled Old-Fashioned or collins glass over ice cubes. Fill with orange juice and stir.

Variations: add 1 tsp lemon juice.

Rum Screwdriver: substitute rum for vodka.

See also *Creamy Screwdriver, Harvey Wallbanger.*

--------- **Sea Breeze** ---------

2 oz (4 Tbsp) vodka
3 oz (6 Tbsp) cranberry juice
3 oz (6 Tbsp) grapefruit or pineapple juice

Shake all ingredients and strain into highball glass over ice.

--------- **Sensation Cocktail** ---------

2 oz (4 Tbsp) gin
juice of ¼ lemon
2–3 dashes Maraschino liqueur
2 sprigs of fresh mint

(continued)

Shake liquid ingredients with ice and strain into a chilled cocktail glass. Garnish with mint.

—————— **September Morn Cocktail** ——————

1½ oz (3 Tbsp) light rum
juice of ½ lime
2–3 dashes grenadine
1 egg white

Shake ingredients vigorously with ice and strain into a chilled cocktail glass.

—————— **Seventh Heaven Cocktail** ——————

1½ oz (3 Tbsp) gin
½ oz (1 Tbsp) Maraschino liqueur
½ oz (1 Tbsp) grapefruit juice
sprig of fresh mint

Shake liquid ingredients with ice and strain into a chilled cocktail glass. Garnish with mint.

—————— **Sevilla Cocktail** ——————

1 oz (2 Tbsp) light rum
1 oz (2 Tbsp) port
1 whole egg
½ tsp sugar

Shake ingredients with ice and strain into a chilled cocktail or wine glass.

Variation: substitute dark rum for light and sweet vermouth for the port.

——— Sex On The Beach I ———

A name used for two different drinks. Try them both.

1 oz (2 Tbsp) vodka
1 oz (2 Tbsp) Peach Schnapps
3 oz (6 Tbsp) cranberry juice, chilled
3 oz (6 Tbsp) pineapple juice, or, optionally,
orange or grapefruit juice

Combine all ingredients in shaker with ice and shake vigorously. Strain into a chilled collins glass over ice.

——— Sex On The Beach II ———

1 oz (2 Tbsp) vodka
½ oz (1 Tbsp) Midori or other melon liqueur
½ oz (1 Tbsp) Chambord or
other raspberry liqueur
1 oz (2 Tbsp) cranberry juice
2 oz (4 Tbsp) pineapple juice

Combine all ingredients in shaker with ice and shake vigorously. Strain into a chilled collins glass over ice.

——— Shady Lady ———

1½ oz (3 Tbsp) tequila
1 oz (2 Tbsp) cranberry juice
½ oz (1 Tbsp) apple brandy
1 tsp fresh lime juice

Place ingredients in shaker with ½ cup cracked ice. Cover and shake vigorously several times. Pour into sour glass filled halfway with cracked ice. Serve with small straw.

────── **Shamrock Cocktail** ──────

1 oz (2 Tbsp) Irish whiskey
1 oz (2 Tbsp) dry vermouth
3 dashes green crème de menthe
stuffed green olive

Stir liquid ingredients with ice and strain into a chilled cocktail glass. Garnish with the olive.

Variation: add 3 dashes green Chartreuse.

────── **Shandy Gaff** ──────

4 oz (8 Tbsp) beer or ale
4 oz (8 Tbsp) ginger beer

Pour ingredients into a chilled collins or highball glass over ice cubes and stir gently.

Variation: substitute ginger ale for ginger beer.

────── **Shanghai Cocktail** ──────

1½ oz (3 Tbsp) dark rum
½ oz (1 Tbsp) Pernod
¾ oz (1½ Tbsp) lemon juice
½–1 tsp grenadine

Shake ingredients with ice and strain into a chilled cocktail glass.

────── **Shanghai Lady** ──────

1½ oz (3 Tbsp) golden rum
½ oz (1 Tbsp) Sambuca
2 tsp lemon juice
1–2 dashes bitters
orange zest

In shaker place liquors, juice, and bitters with 5 or 6 ice cubes. Cover and shake vigorously several times. Strain into chilled cocktail glass. Run zest through the flame of a match 2 or 3 times and add to drink.

Shark's Tooth

1½ oz (3 Tbsp) dark rum
¼ oz (½ Tbsp) sloe gin
¼ oz (½ Tbsp) sweet vermouth
¼ oz (½ Tbsp) lemon juice
¼ oz (½ Tbsp) passionfruit syrup
1 dash Angostura bitters
twist of orange peel
maraschino cherry

Shake liquid ingredients with ice and strain into a chilled cocktail glass. Garnish with orange peel and cherry.

Variations: sugar-rim the glass by rubbing with lemon and dipping into sugar. Substitute light rum for dark. Add ¼ oz cherry brandy.

Sharky Punch

1½ oz (3 Tbsp) Calvados or other apple brandy
½ oz (1 Tbsp) rye whiskey
1 tsp honey or sugar syrup
club soda

Place first 3 ingredients in shaker with ½ cup of cracked ice. Cover and shake vigorously several times. Strain into large Old-Fashioned glass half-filled with cracked ice. Top off with club soda and serve.

——— **Sherry Cobbler** ———

2 oz (4 Tbsp) sherry
2 oz (4 Tbsp) chilled water or club soda
1 tsp sugar
slices of fresh fruit (lemon, orange,
pineapple, etc.)

Dissolve sugar in water in a stemmed goblet. Fill glass ⅔ full of crushed ice, add sherry, and stir. Garnish with fruit and serve with a straw.

Variation: substitute ½ oz (1 Tbsp) orange juice for the water and add 1 oz (2 Tbsp) brandy.

——— **Sherry Eggnog** ———

2 oz (4 Tbsp) sherry
½ oz (1 Tbsp) brandy
1 tsp sugar
1 whole egg
chilled milk
nutmeg

Shake sherry, brandy, sugar, and egg vigorously with ice. Strain into a chilled collins glass and top with milk. Stir and sprinkle with nutmeg.

——— **Sherry Flip** ———

3 oz (6 Tbsp) medium dry sherry
1 whole egg
1 tsp sugar
nutmeg

Shake first 3 ingredients with ice and strain into a chilled wineglass over ice cubes. Sprinkle with nutmeg.

Variations: put ingredients in a blender with ½ cup crushed ice and blend at low speed for 15 seconds. Add 4 dashes crème de cacao or 2 tsp cream.

——— **Sherry Sangaree** ———

See under *Sangaree.*

——— **Shriner Cocktail** ———

1½ oz (3 Tbsp) sloe gin
1½ oz (3 Tbsp) brandy
2 dashes sugar syrup
2 dashes Angostura or Peychaud bitters
twist of lemon peel

Stir liquid ingredients with ice and strain into a chilled cocktail glass. Garnish with lemon peel.

——— **Sidecar** ———

Once an extremely popular drink, it is thought to have originated in Paris during World War I. The Sidecar makes an interesting after-dinner drink as well as a before-dinner cocktail. Go easy on the Cointreau or the drink will be sickly sweet.

2 oz (4 Tbsp) brandy
1 oz (2 Tbsp) Cointreau or triple sec
½ oz (1 Tbsp) lemon juice
twist of lemon peel (optional)

Shake liquid ingredients with ice and strain into a chilled cocktail glass. Garnish with lemon peel.

Variations: sugar-rim the glass by rubbing with lemon and dipping into sugar.

(continued)

Boston Sidecar: substitute lime juice for lemon and add ¾ oz light rum.

——————— **Silk Stocking** ———————

1½ oz (3 Tbsp) gin
½ oz (1 Tbsp) apple brandy
1 oz (2 Tbsp) orange juice

Place ingredients in shaker with 4 or 5 ice cubes. Cover and shake vigorously several times. Strain into wineglass half filled with cracked ice and serve with small straw.

——————— **Silver Arrow** ———————

2 oz (4 Tbsp) vodka
½ oz (1 Tbsp) crème de cassis
½ oz (1 Tbsp) cream

Place ingredients in shaker with ice cubes. Cover and shake vigorously several times. Strain into chilled cocktail glass.

——————— **Silver Bullet** ———————

1 oz (2 Tbsp) gin
1 oz (2 Tbsp) kümmel
¼ oz (½ Tbsp) lemon juice

Stir ingredients with ice and strain into a chilled cocktail glass.

——————— **Silver Cocktail** ———————

1 oz (2 Tbsp) gin
1 oz (2 Tbsp) dry vermouth

2 dashes orange bitters
½ tsp Maraschino liqueur
twist of lemon peel

Stir liquid ingredients with ice and strain into a chilled cocktail glass. Garnish with lemon peel.

--------- **Silver Fizz** ---------

2 oz (4 Tbsp) gin
1 oz (2 Tbsp) lemon juice
1 tsp sugar
1 egg white
2 oz (4 Tbsp) chilled club soda

Shake ingredients, except soda, with ice and strain into a chilled collins or wine glass over ice cubes. Top with soda.

--------- **Silver Jubilee** ---------

1½ oz (3 Tbsp) gin
1½ oz (3 Tbsp) banana liqueur
¾ oz (1½ Tbsp) cream
2–3 slices banana (optional)
slice of orange (optional)

Shake liquid ingredients with ice and strain into a chilled cocktail glass. Garnish with banana and orange if desired.

--------- **Silver King Cocktail** ---------

1½ oz (3 Tbsp) gin
juice of ½ lemon
½ tsp sugar
1 egg white
2 dashes orange bitters

(continued)

Shake ingredients with ice and strain into a chilled cocktail glass.

——————— **Silver Streak** ———————

1½ oz (3 Tbsp) gin
1½ oz (3 Tbsp) kümmel

Stir ingredients with ice and strain into a chilled cocktail glass.

——————— **Singapore Sling I** ———————

1½ oz (3 Tbsp) gin
½ oz (1 Tbsp) lemon juice
1 tsp grenadine
½ oz (1 Tbsp) cherry brandy
chilled club soda
slice of lemon or lime
maraschino cherry

Mix gin, lemon juice, and grenadine in a chilled highball or collins glass. Add crushed ice, top with soda, and stir. Float brandy on top, garnish with fruit, and serve with a straw.

——————— **Singapore Sling II** ———————

1½ oz (3 Tbsp) gin
½ oz (1 Tbsp) lemon juice
½ oz (1 Tbsp) lime juice
1 tsp grenadine
¼ oz (½ Tbsp) sloe gin
½ oz (1 Tbsp) crème de cassis
chilled club soda
½ oz (1 Tbsp) cherry brandy

slice of lemon or lime
maraschino cherry

Mix first 6 ingredients in a chilled highball glass. Add crushed ice, top with soda, and stir. Float brandy on top. Garnish with fruit and serve with a straw.

Variation: substitute ¼ oz (½ Tbsp) Benedictine and ¼ oz (½ Tbsp) brandy for the cherry brandy.

——— Sling ———

2 oz (4 Tbsp) gin
1 oz (2 Tbsp) cherry brandy
juice of ½ lemon
1 tsp sugar
1 tsp water
twist of lemon peel

Shake liquid ingredients with ice and strain into a chilled Old-Fashioned glass over ice cubes. Garnish with lemon peel.

Variations: strain into a chilled highball or collins glass over ice cubes and top with chilled water or club soda. Various liquors and brandies can be substituted for the gin and cherry brandy, and the Sling is then named after the liquor used (Gin Sling, Rum Sling, etc.).

See also *Singapore Sling.*

——— Sloe Gin Cocktail ———

2 oz (4 Tbsp) sloe gin
¼–½ oz (½–1 Tbsp) dry vermouth
1 dash orange bitters

(continued)

Stir ingredients with ice and strain into a chilled cocktail glass.

Variation: use ¼ oz (½ Tbsp) dry vermouth and add ½ oz (1 Tbsp) sweet vermouth.

———— **Sloe Gin Fizz** ————

See under *Gin Fizz*.

———— **Sloe Gin Rickey** ————

See under *Gin Rickey*.

———— **Sloe Tequila** ————

1 oz (2 Tbsp) tequila
½ oz (1 Tbsp) sloe gin
½ oz (1 Tbsp) lime juice
½ cup crushed ice
cucumber peel

Put first 4 ingredients into a blender and blend at low speed for 15 seconds. Pour into a chilled Old-Fashioned glass over ice cubes and garnish with cucumber peel.

———— **Sloe Vermouth** ————

1 oz (2 Tbsp) sloe gin
1 oz (2 Tbsp) dry vermouth
½ oz (1 Tbsp) lemon juice

Shake ingredients with ice and strain into a chilled cocktail glass.

——— Smash ———

See *Brandy Smash*.

——— Snowball Cocktail ———

1½ oz (3 Tbsp) gin
½ oz (1 Tbsp) anisette
½ oz (1 Tbsp) cream

Shake ingredients with ice and strain into a chilled cocktail glass.

Variation: add ½ oz (1 Tbsp) white crème de menthe.

——— Snowball Fizz ———

2 oz (4 Tbsp) grapefruit juice
1 oz (2 Tbsp) orange juice
1 tsp sugar
3 oz (6 Tbsp) gin
1 egg white

In shaker combine juices, sugar, and gin and stir till sugar is completely dissolved. Add egg white and several ice cubes. Cover and shake vigorously several times. Strain into chilled cocktail or wine glass.

——— Snowbird ———

2 oz (4 Tbsp) vodka
½ oz (1 Tbsp) Crème Yvette
1 oz (2 Tbsp) cream

Place ingredients in blender with 4 or 5 ice cubes. Cover and blend at high speed 15 or 20 seconds or

(continued)

until ice cubes are just puréed. Pour into chilled wine-glass.

─────── **Snowflake** ───────

2 oz (4 Tbsp) gin
½ oz (1 Tbsp) fresh lemon juice
1 tsp sugar syrup
1 tsp grenadine
1 egg white
½ oz (1 Tbsp) cream
club soda

Place all ingredients, except soda, in shaker with 6 or 8 ice cubes. Cover and shake vigorously. Strain into chilled highball glass and top with soda. Stir before serving.

─────── **Sombrero** ───────

1½ oz (3 Tbsp) coffee brandy
1 oz (2 Tbsp) cream

Shake ingredients with ice and strain into a chilled cocktail glass or into an Old-Fashioned glass over ice cubes.

Variation: pour brandy into an Old-Fashioned glass over ice cubes and float the cream on top.

─────── **Sophia** ───────

4 oz (8 Tbsp) dry white wine
1 oz (2 Tbsp) Strega
1 tsp fresh lime juice
thin slice lime

Add first 3 ingredients to wine glass filled halfway with cracked ice. Stir gently, float lime slice, and serve with small straw.

Sorrento

2 oz (4 Tbsp) gin
1 oz (2 Tbsp) Galliano
½ oz (1 Tbsp) fresh lemon juice
1 tsp orgeat or sugar syrup

Place ingredients in shaker with ½ cup cracked ice. Cover and shake vigorously several times. Strain into chilled cocktail glass.

Sour

See *Whiskey Sour.*

Southern Belle

2 oz (1 Tbsp) Southern Comfort
½ oz (1 Tbsp) crème de banane
1 tsp crème de cassis
½ oz (1 Tbsp) heavy cream

Place all ingredients in shaker with 5 or 6 ice cubes. Cover and shake vigorously. Strain into chilled wine-glass half-filled with cracked ice.

Southern Bride

1½ oz (3 Tbsp) gin
¾ oz (1½ Tbsp) grapefruit juice
2 dashes Maraschino liqueur

(continued)

Shake ingredients with ice and strain into a chilled cocktail glass.

Southern Gin Cocktail

2 oz (4 Tbsp) gin
2 dashes orange bitters
2 dashes triple sec
twist of lemon peel

Stir liquid ingredients with ice and strain into a chilled cocktail glass. Garnish with lemon peel.

Southern Peach

1 oz (2 Tbsp) Southern Comfort
1 oz (2 Tbsp) peach brandy
1 oz (2 Tbsp) cream
1 dash Angostura bitters (optional)
slice of fresh peach

Shake liquid ingredients with ice and strain into a chilled Old-Fashioned glass over ice cubes. Garnish with peach slice.

South-Side Cocktail

2 oz (4 Tbsp) gin
juice of ½ lemon
1 tsp sugar
2 sprigs of fresh mint

Shake first 3 ingredients with ice and strain into a chilled cocktail glass. Garnish with mint.

Soviet

1½ oz (3 Tbsp) vodka
½ oz (1 Tbsp) dry vermouth
½ oz (1 Tbsp) amontillado sherry
twist of lemon peel

Shake or stir liquid ingredients with ice and strain into a chilled Old-Fashioned glass over ice cubes. Garnish with lemon peel.

Spanish Town Cocktail

2 oz (4 Tbsp) light rum
2 dashes triple sec
nutmeg (optional)

Stir liquid ingredients with ice and strain into a chilled cocktail glass. Sprinkle with nutmeg.

Special Rough Cocktail

1½ oz (3 Tbsp) apple brandy
1½ oz (3 Tbsp) brandy
1 dash pernod

Stir ingredients with ice and strain into a chilled cocktail glass.

Spritzer Highball

3–4 oz (6–8 Tbsp) chilled dry white wine
peel of 1 lemon cut in a continuous spiral
chilled club soda

Put lemon peel into a large chilled wine or collins glass. Add ice cubes and wine. Top with soda.

————— **Star Cocktail** —————

1½ oz (3 Tbsp) apple brandy
1½ oz (3 Tbsp) sweet vermouth
1 dash Angostura or orange bitters
twist of lemon peel (optional)

Stir liquid ingredients with ice and strain into a chilled cocktail glass. Garnish with lemon peel.

————— **Star Daisy** —————

1½ oz (3 Tbsp) gin
1½ oz (3 Tbsp) apple brandy
2 tsp crème de framboise
½ oz (1 Tbsp) lemon juice
1 tsp sugar syrup

Shake all ingredients with 4 or 5 ice cubes and strain into large Old-Fashioned glass filled with cracked ice.

————— **Stars & Stripes** —————

⅓ oz Maraschino liqueur or grenadine
⅓ oz cream
⅓ oz blue curaçao

Pour, in order given, into a cordial glass.

See also *Pousse Café*.

————— **Stinger** —————

2¼ oz (4½ Tbsp) brandy
¾ oz (1½ Tbsp) white crème de menthe

Shake ingredients with ice and strain into a chilled cocktail glass or into an Old-Fashioned glass over ice cubes or crushed ice.

Variations: although the classic Stinger is always made with brandy, various liquors can be substituted, and the Stinger is then named after the liquor used (Scotch Stinger, etc.)

See also *White Spider*.

Stirrup Cup

1 oz (2 Tbsp) brandy
1 oz (2 Tbsp) cherry brandy
juice of ½ lemon
½ tsp sugar

Shake ingredients with ice and strain into a chilled Old-Fashioned glass over ice cubes.

Stone Fence

2 oz (4 Tbsp) Scotch
1–2 dashes Angostura bitters
chilled club soda or cider

Pour Scotch and bitters into a highball or collins glass over ice cubes. Top with soda or cider and stir.

Variation: substitute apple brandy for Scotch.

Strawberry Cream Cooler

1½ oz (3 Tbsp) gin
¼ cup frozen strawberries (thawed)
¾ oz (1½ Tbsp) lemon juice
1 oz (2 Tbsp) cream
1 tsp sugar
chilled club soda
1 fresh strawberry for garnish

(continued)

Put first 5 ingredients into a blender and blend at high speed for 10 seconds. Pour into a chilled wine or highball glass. Add a splash of soda and ice cubes and stir. Garnish with the strawberry.

———— **Strawberry Daiquiri** ————

See under *Daiquiri*.

———— **Strawberry Fizz** ————

2 oz (4 Tbsp) gin
6 strawberries
½ tsp sugar
juice of ½ lemon
chilled club soda

Crush 5 strawberries with the sugar and lemon juice in a chilled collins or highball glass. Add ice cubes and gin and top with soda. Stir gently and garnish with the remaining strawberry.

———— **Strega Flip** ————

1 oz (2 Tbsp) Strega
1 oz (2 Tbsp) brandy
2 tsp orange juice
1 tsp lemon juice
1 tsp sugar
1 whole egg
nutmeg

Shake first 6 ingredients vigorously with ice and strain into a large chilled cocktail glass. Sprinkle with nutmeg.

———— **Suissesse Cocktail** ————

2 oz (4 Tbsp) anisette
1 oz (2 Tbsp) Pernod
1 egg white

Shake ingredients vigorously with ice and strain into a chilled cocktail glass.

Variations: add a dash of lemon juice or heavy cream. Strain into a larger glass and add a splash of chilled club soda.

See also *Absinthe Suissesse*.

———— **Sunburst Cocktail** ————

1½ oz (3 Tbsp) apple brandy
½ oz (1 Tbsp) orange-flavored brandy
1–2 dashes orange bitters
cold champagne

In chilled wineglass add brandies and bitters. Top with champagne and stir briefly. Serve with short straw.

———— **Sunflower Cocktail** ————

1½ oz (3 Tbsp) light rum
½ oz (1 Tbsp) orange juice
1 tsp fresh lemon juice
½ oz (1 Tbsp) triple sec
2–3 dashes orange bitters
maraschino cherry

Place first 5 ingredients in shaker with 4 or 5 ice cubes. Cover and shake vigorously. Strain into chilled cocktail glass and garnish with cherry.

———— **Sure Shot** ————

2 oz (4 Tbsp) Scotch whiskey
2 tsp fresh lime juice
dash bitters
chilled club soda

Fill highball glass with ice cubes and add first 3 ingredients. Top off with soda and stir several times before serving.

———— **Sutton Place Cocktail** ————

1 oz (2 Tbsp) apricot brandy
1 oz (2 Tbsp) white crème de menthe
1 oz (2 Tbsp) Cointreau

Shake all ingredients with cracked ice and strain into chilled cocktail glass.

———— **Sweet Martini** ————

See under *Martini*.

———— **Sweet Patootie Cocktail** ————

1 oz (2 Tbsp) gin
½ oz (1 Tbsp) Cointreau or triple sec
½ oz (1 Tbsp) orange juice

Shake ingredients with ice and strain into a chilled cocktail glass.

———— **Swizzle** ————

Originally a drink of the West Indies, where it was stirred with a twig called a "swizzle stick."

2 oz (4 Tbsp) gin
juice of 1 lime
1 tsp sugar
1–2 dashes Angostura bitters
chilled club soda

Mix sugar, lime juice, and a small amount of soda in
a chilled collins glass. Fill ⅔ full of crushed or shaved
ice and stir. Add gin and bitters and top with soda. Stir
again and serve with a swizzle stick.

Variations: various liquors can be substituted for
the gin, and the swizzle is then named after the liquor
used (Scotch Swizzle, etc.).

Syllabub

(serves 6)

A festive favorite for well over 400 years.

2 cups dry white wine
½ cup powdered sugar
¼ cup fresh lemon juice
2 cups light cream
freshly grated nutmeg

Place wine, sugar, lemon juice, and cream in mixing
bowl and whisk until frothy. Spoon into 6-oz glasses and sprinkle with nutmeg before serving.

Sylvie

1½ oz (3 Tbsp) golden rum
½ oz (1 Tbsp) dry vermouth
2 oz (4 Tbsp) orange juice
1 tsp lemon juice
½ tsp orgeat

(continued)

Place ingredients in shaker with ½ cup cracked ice.
Cover and shake vigorously. Strain into chilled wineglass.

T

────── **Tahiti Club** ──────

2 oz (4 Tbsp) light rum
½ oz (1 Tbsp) lime juice
½ oz (1 Tbsp) lemon juice
½ oz (1 Tbsp) pineapple juice
2 dashes Maraschino liqueur
slice of lemon

Shake liquid ingredients with ice and strain into a
chilled Old-Fashioned glass over ice cubes. Garnish
with lemon slice.

────── **Tailspin** ──────

1 oz (2 Tbsp) gin
1 oz (2 Tbsp) sweet vermouth
1 oz (2 Tbsp) green Chartreuse
1–2 dashes orange bitters
twist of lemon (optional)

Shake together first 4 ingredients with 4 or 5 ice
cubes. Strain into wineglass half-filled with cracked
ice. Add twisted lemon peel if desired.

────── **Tango Cocktail** ──────

1½ oz (3 Tbsp) gin
¾ oz (1½ Tbsp) dry vermouth
¾ oz (1½ Tbsp) sweet vermouth

2 dashes curaçao
½ oz (1 Tbsp) orange juice

Shake ingredients with ice and strain into a chilled cocktail glass.

Variation: use equal parts of gin and sweet and dry vermouth (1 oz (2 Tbsp) of each).

Tarantella

2 oz (4 Tbsp) white rum
1 oz (2 Tbsp) Strega
lemon zest

Shake liquors with cracked ice and strain into chilled cocktail glass after rubbing rim with peel. Twist peel over glass to release oils and drop into drink.

Tea Punch

(serves 16–18)

1 qt cold strong black tea
1 fifth light rum
1 pt orange juice
1 pt lemon juice
sugar to taste
orange and lemon slices

Pour ingredients, except orange and lemon slices, into a punch bowl over a block of ice. Garnish with the fruit and serve in chilled punch cups.

Temptation Cocktail

1½ oz (3 Tbsp) rye or bourbon
½ tsp triple sec

(continued)

½ tsp Pernod
½ tsp Dubonnet
twist of lemon or orange peel

Shake liquid ingredients with ice and strain into a
chilled cocktail glass. Garnish with lemon or orange
peel.

–––––––– **Tempter Cocktail** ––––––––

1½ oz (3 Tbsp) ruby port wine
1½ oz (3 Tbsp) apricot brandy

Stir ingredients with ice and strain into a chilled cocktail glass.

–––––––– **Tequila Acapulco** ––––––––

See under *Acapulco*.

–––––––– **Tequila Collins** ––––––––

3 oz (6 Tbsp) tequila
1 tsp sugar
1½ oz (3 Tbsp) fresh lime juice
chilled seltzer or club soda
sprig of fresh mint (optional)

In highball glass place several ice cubes and add
tequila, sugar and lime juice. Top with seltzer and stir
gently. Garnish with mint.

–––––––– **Tequila Cooler** ––––––––

2 oz (4 Tbsp) tequila
juice of ½ lime
chilled tonic water

Pour tequila and lime juice into highball glass with 4 or 5 ice cubes. Top with tonic water and stir before serving.

Tequila Old-Fashioned

See under *Old-Fashioned.*

Tequila Punch

(serves 25–30)

1 qt tequila
6 bottles chilled dry white wine
½ cup sugar or to taste
6 cups sliced fresh fruit

Mix ingredients and let stand for an hour. Before serving pour into a large chilled punch bowl over a block of ice and stir. Serve in chilled punch cups or wineglasses.

Variation: add 1 fifth chilled champagne just before serving.

Tequila Solo

Traditional way of drinking tequila, that is "neat." There is a carefully prescribed ritual that should be followed, using these ingredients:

1½ oz (3 Tbsp) shot of tequila
salt
lime wedge

When ingredients are assembled, moisten the area between your left thumb and index finger with your tongue. Then sprinkle the area with salt. Take a bite

(continued)

of the lime wedge, lick the salt, and down the shot of tequila in one gulp. A second bite of lime is permissible. A chaser of cold beer is also sanctioned.

Variation: add a dash or two of Tabasco to the shot of tequila. If carefully done, a delicate rose is said to form in the glass. Proceed as above. This version is sometimes called a Desert Rose.

———— **Tequila Sour** ————

See under *Whiskey Sour.*

———— **Tequila Sunrise** ————

2 oz (4 Tbsp) tequila
4 oz (8 Tbsp) chilled orange juice
½–¾ oz (1–1½ Tbsp) grenadine

Pour tequila and then orange juice into a chilled collins or highball glass over ice cubes and stir gently. Add grenadine slowly.

Variation: stir tequila and orange juice with ice. Strain into a large chilled cocktail glass and add grenadine.

———— **Tequila Sunset** ————

Said to be a morning-after antidote to the preceding drinks.

1½ oz (3 Tbsp) orange juice
1½ oz (3 Tbsp) pineapple juice
1 oz (2 Tbsp) tequila
granulated sugar
lime peel

In a blender put 4–6 ice cubes and the liquids. Blend at high speed till ice cubes are just pureed. Serve in a chilled wineglass. Sugaring the rim first is entirely optional. Rub the rim with lime peel to make sugar adhere.

Tequini

See under *Martini*.

Thanksgiving Special Cocktail

1 oz (2 Tbsp) gin
1 oz (2 Tbsp) apricot brandy
1 oz (2 Tbsp) dry vermouth
1 dash lemon juice
maraschino cherry

Shake liquid ingredients with ice and strain into a chilled cocktail glass. Garnish with the cherry.

Third Degree Cocktail

1½ oz (3 Tbsp) gin
¾ oz dry vermouth
3–4 dashes Pernod

Stir ingredients with ice and strain into a chilled cocktail glass.

Third Rail Cocktail

1 oz (2 Tbsp) light rum
1 oz (2 Tbsp) brandy
1 oz (2 Tbsp) apple brandy
1–2 dashes Pernod

(continued)

Shake ingredients with ice and strain into a chilled cocktail glass.

───────── **Thistle Cocktail** ─────────

1½ oz (3 Tbsp) Scotch
1½ oz (3 Tbsp) sweet vermouth
2–3 dashes bitters

In mixing glass combine ingredients with several ice cubes. Stir well and strain into Old-Fashioned glass half-filled with cracked ice.

───────── **Three Miller Cocktail** ─────────

1½ oz (3 Tbsp) brandy
¾ oz (1½ Tbsp) light rum
1 dash lemon juice
1 tsp grenadine

Shake ingredients with ice and strain into a chilled cocktail glass.

───────── **Three Rum Punch** ─────────

½ oz (1 Tbsp) white rum
½ oz (1 Tbsp) golden rum
½ oz (1 Tbsp) dark rum
1 oz (2 Tbsp) pineapple juice
1 tsp fresh lime juice
½ oz (1 Tbsp) apricot brandy
club soda
orange slice (optional)

Place liquors and juices in shaker with several ice cubes. Cover and shake vigorously several times. Strain into highball glass half-filled with cracked ice and top off with club soda. Stir gently before serving. Garnish, if desired, with half an orange slice.

Variation: blend liquors and juices with ½ cup cracked ice. Pour into chilled highball glass and top off, if necessary, with a little soda. Stir before serving.

Three Stripes Cocktail

1½ oz (3 Tbsp) gin
¾ oz (1½ Tbsp) dry vermouth
¾ oz (1½ Tbsp) orange juice

Shake ingredients with ice and strain into a chilled cocktail glass.

Thunder Cocktail

2 oz (4 Tbsp) brandy
1 tsp sugar
1 egg yolk
1 pinch cayenne pepper

Shake ingredients with ice and strain into a chilled cocktail glass.

Tiger's Milk

(serves 15–20)

Perhaps so-named because of its deceptively attractive appearance.

1 qt pineapple juice
1 qt grapefruit juice
1 qt gin or vodka

(continued)

Pour ingredients over block of ice in punch bowl. Stir briefly and ladle into punch cups.

Tiger Tail

2 oz (4 Tbsp) Pernod
8 oz chilled orange juice
slice of lime

Pour liquid ingredients into a chilled highball glass over ice cubes. Garnish with lime slice.

Tipperary Cocktail

¾ oz (1½ Tbsp) Irish whiskey
¾ oz (1½ Tbsp) green Chartreuse
¾ oz (1½ Tbsp) sweet vermouth

Stir ingredients with ice and strain into a chilled cocktail glass.

T.N.T. Cocktail

1½ oz (3 Tbsp) rye whiskey
1½ oz (3 Tbsp) Pernod

Shake ingredients with ice and strain into a chilled cocktail glass.

Toasted Almond

1 oz (2 Tbsp) Kahlúa, Tia Maria, or
other coffee liqueur
½ oz (1 Tbsp) Amaretto
1 oz (2 Tbsp) heavy cream

Shake ingredients with ice and strain into chilled cocktail glass over ice cubes.

Tobago

1 oz (2 Tbsp) light rum
1 oz (2 Tbsp) gin
½ oz (1 Tbsp) lime juice
1 tsp guava syrup
½ cup crushed ice
twist of lemon peel

Put first 5 ingredients into a blender and blend at low speed for 15 seconds. Pour into a chilled Old-Fashioned glass over ice cubes and garnish with lemon peel.

Toddy

See *Hot Toddy*.

Tom-And-Jerry

⅓ cup milk
½ oz (1 Tbsp) butter
1 egg
1 tsp sugar
1 dash vanilla extract (optional)
1½ oz (3 Tbsp) dark rum
¾ oz (1½ Tbsp) brandy
nutmeg

Heat milk and butter together until hot. Beat egg yolk and egg white separately until frothy. Add the egg whites to the yolks and beat in the sugar and vanilla. Put into a heated mug, add milk and rum, and stir. Top with the brandy and sprinkle with nutmeg.

Variations: substitute hot water for milk. Add ¼ tsp allspice. Substitute bourbon for brandy.

———— **Tomate** ————

2 oz (4 Tbsp) Pernod
1 tsp grenadine
2–3 oz (6 Tbsp) chilled water

Pour into a chilled wineglass over ice cubes and stir.

———— **Tom Collins** ————

The Tom Collins originated in England in the late 19th century and was first made with sweetened Old Tom gin. A less popular collins, the John Collins, was made with Dutch gin. A John Collins, headwaiter at a London bar, is referred to in a rhyme published in 1892, and may be the source of the word "collins." Today a John Collins is made with whiskey and a Tom Collins is made with gin. They are among the most popular of "long, refreshing drinks."

2 oz (4 Tbsp) gin
juice of ½ lemon
1 tsp sugar
chilled club soda
slice of lemon or orange
maraschino cherry

Mix lemon juice and sugar in a chilled collins glass. Add ice cubes and gin. Top with soda and stir. Garnish with lemon or orange slice and cherry.

Variations: rum, vodka, Scotch, bourbon, rye, brandy, or applejack can be substituted for the gin, and the collins is then named after the liquor used (Rum Collins, etc.), except that it is called a John Collins if made with rye or bourbon.

Toreador

1½ oz (3 Tbsp) tequila
½ oz (1 Tbsp) crème de cacao
½ oz (1 Tbsp) cream
whipped cream
cocoa

Shake tequila, crème de cacao, and cream with ice and strain into a chilled cocktail glass. Top with a spoonful of whipped cream and sprinkle with cocoa.

Torridora Cocktail

1½ oz (3 Tbsp) light rum
½ oz (1 Tbsp) coffee brandy
¼ oz (½ Tbsp) cream
1 tsp 151-proof rum

Shake first 3 ingredients with ice and strain into a chilled cocktail glass. Float 151-proof rum on top.

Tovarich Cocktail

1½ oz (3 Tbsp) vodka
1 oz (2 Tbsp) kümmel
juice of ½ lime

Shake ingredients with ice and strain into a chilled cocktail glass.

Trade Winds

2 oz (4 Tbsp) rum
½ oz (1 Tbsp) lime juice
½ oz (1 Tbsp) sloe gin
1 tsp sugar

(continued)

⅓ cup crushed ice
black cherry

Put first 5 ingredients into a blender and blend at low speed for 15 seconds. Pour into a large chilled cocktail glass and garnish with the cherry.

Variation: substitute plum brandy for the sloe gin.

———— **Trilby Cocktail** ————

2 oz (4 Tbsp) bourbon
1 oz (2 Tbsp) sweet vermouth
2 dashes orange bitters

Stir ingredients with ice and strain into a chilled cocktail glass.

Variation: add 1–2 dashes Pernod and/or parfait d'amour.

———— **Trois Rivières** ————

1½ oz (3 Tbsp) Canadian whiskey
½ oz (1 Tbsp) Dubonnet
¼ oz (½ Tbsp) Cointreau or triple sec
twist of orange peel

Shake liquid ingredients with ice and strain into a chilled cocktail glass or into an Old-Fashioned glass over ice cubes. Garnish with orange peel.

———— **Tulip Cocktail** ————

1 oz (2 Tbsp) apple brandy
1 oz (2 Tbsp) sweet vermouth
½ oz (1 Tbsp) apricot brandy
½ oz (1 Tbsp) fresh lemon juice

Shake ingredients with cracked ice and strain into a chilled cocktail glass.

—————— **Turf Cocktail** ——————

1 oz (2 Tbsp) gin
1 oz (2 Tbsp) dry vermouth
2 dashes Pernod
¼ oz lemon juice (optional)
2 dashes Angostura bitters (optional)

Shake ingredients with ice and strain into a chilled cocktail glass or into an Old-Fashioned glass over ice cubes.

—————— **Tuxedo Cocktail** ——————

1½ oz (3 Tbsp) gin
1½ oz (3 Tbsp) dry vermouth
2 dashes Pernod
2 dashes Maraschino liqueur
2 dashes orange bitters
maraschino cherry

Stir ingredients with ice and strain into a chilled cocktail glass. Garnish with the cherry.

—————— **Twin Hills** ——————

2 oz (4 Tbsp) rye or bourbon
2 tsp Benedictine
1½ tsp lemon juice
1½ tsp lime juice
1 tsp sugar
slice of lime and lemon

(continued)

Shake first 5 ingredients with ice and strain into a chilled sour glass. Garnish with slices of lemon and lime.

─────── **Twin Six Cocktail** ───────

1½ oz (3 Tbsp) gin
¾ oz (1½ Tbsp) sweet vermouth
½ oz (1 Tbsp) orange juice
1 dash grenadine
1 egg white

Shake ingredients vigorously with ice and strain into a chilled cocktail glass.

─────── **Twister** ───────

2 oz (4 Tbsp) vodka
juice of ½ lime
7-Up, chilled
thin slice lime

In highball glass half-filled with cracked ice pour vodka and lime juice. Top with 7-Up and stir. Float lime slice before serving.

Variation: substitute club soda for 7-Up.

U

─────── **Ulanda Cocktail** ───────

2 oz (4 Tbsp) gin
1 oz (2 Tbsp) Cointreau or triple sec
1 dash Pernod

Stir ingredients with ice and strain into a chilled cocktail glass.

——— **Union Jack Cocktail** ———

1½ oz (3 Tbsp) gin
½ oz (1 Tbsp) crème Yvette

Stir or shake ingredients with ice and strain into a chilled cocktail glass.

V

——— **Valencia** ———

2 oz (4 Tbsp) apricot brandy
1 oz (2 Tbsp) orange juice
4 dashes orange bitters

Shake ingredients with ice and strain into a chilled cocktail glass.

Variation: stir ingredients with ice, strain into a chilled wineglass, and top with chilled champagne or sparkling wine.

——— **Vanderbilt Cocktail** ———

2 oz (4 Tbsp) brandy
1 oz (2 Tbsp) cherry brandy
2 dashes Angostura bitters
2 dashes sugar syrup

Stir ingredients with ice and strain into a chilled cocktail glass.

Variation: use equal parts of brandy and cherry brandy.

———— Velvet Hammer ————

1½ oz (3 Tbsp) vodka
1 oz (2 Tbsp) crème de cacao
½ oz (1 Tbsp) cream

Shake ingredients with ice and strain into a chilled cocktail glass.

Variations: substitute Strega for vodka. Substitute 1 oz (2 Tbsp) brandy for vodka and add 1 oz (2 Tbsp) Cointreau or triple sec.

———— Verboten ————

1½ oz (3 Tbsp) gin
½ oz (1 Tbsp) Forbidden Fruit
½ oz (1 Tbsp) lemon juice
½ oz (1 Tbsp) orange juice
brandied cherry

Shake liquid ingredients with ice and strain into a chilled cocktail glass. Garnish with the cherry.

———— Vermouth Cassis ————

2 oz (4 Tbsp) dry vermouth
1 oz (2 Tbsp) crème de cassis
chilled club soda
twist of lemon peel (optional)

Stir vermouth and crème de cassis with ice cubes in a chilled highball or large wine glass. Top with soda and stir gently. Garnish with lemon peel.

─────── **Vermouth Cocktail** ───────

1½ oz (3 Tbsp) dry vermouth
1½ oz (3 Tbsp) sweet vermouth
2 dashes Angostura or orange bitters
maraschino cherry

Stir liquid ingredients with ice and strain into a chilled cocktail glass. Garnish with the cherry.

Variation: use only dry or sweet vermouth instead of both.

─────── **Via Veneto** ───────

(serves 2)

3½ oz (7 Tbsp) brandy
1 oz (2 Tbsp) sambuca
4 tsp lemon juice
2 tsp sugar syrup
1 egg white

Shake ingredients vigorously with ice and strain into chilled cocktail glasses or into Old-Fashioned glasses over ice cubes.

─────── **Victor** ───────

1½ oz (3 Tbsp) gin
1 oz (2 Tbsp) brandy
½ oz (1 Tbsp) sweet vermouth

Shake ingredients with ice and strain into a chilled cocktail glass.

─────── **Vin Chaud** ───────

See *Hot Spiced Wine.*

──────── **Virgin Cocktail** ────────

1 oz (2 Tbsp) gin
1 oz (2 Tbsp) white crème de menthe
1 oz (2 Tbsp) Forbidden Fruit

Shake ingredients with ice and strain into a chilled cocktail glass.

──────── **Virgin's Kiss** ────────

1½ oz (3 Tbsp) peach brandy
½ oz (1 Tbsp) amaretto
1–2 dashes orange bitters
½ oz (1 Tbsp) heavy cream

Place all ingredients in shaker with 5 or 6 ice cubes. Cover and shake vigorously. Strain into chilled cocktail glass.

──────── **Vodka & Tonic** ────────

See under *Gin & Tonic.*

──────── **Vodka Collins** ────────

See under *Tom Collins.*

──────── **Vodka Cooler** ────────

2 oz (4 Tbsp) vodka
½ tsp sugar
chilled club soda
peel of 1 lemon cut in a continuous spiral

Dissolve sugar in a little soda in a chilled collins or highball glass. Add crushed ice and vodka and top with club soda. Garnish with the lemon peel.

Vodka Daisy

2 oz (4 Tbsp) vodka
½ oz (1 Tbsp) fresh lemon juice
1 tsp sugar syrup
1 tsp grenadine
garnish of orange or lemon slice

Shake first 4 ingredients together with cracked ice and strain into collins glass filled with ice cubes. Garnish with fruit slice.

Vodka Gimlet

See under *Gimlet*.

Vodka Martini

See under *Martini*.

Vodka Sling

See under *Sling*.

Vodka Stinger

See under *Stinger*.

Volga Boatman

2 oz (4 Tbsp) vodka
1 tsp kirsch
1½ oz (3 Tbsp) chilled orange juice

Shake ingredients with ice and strain into a chilled cocktail glass.

(continued)

Variation: substitute cherry brandy for kirsch and use equal parts [1 oz (2 Tbsp) each] of the 3 ingredients.

W

Wallaby

1 oz (2 Tbsp) peach brandy
1 oz (2 Tbsp) Dubonnet
1 tsp lime juice
½ tsp red Maraschino liqueur

Place ingredients in shaker with several ice cubes. Shake well and strain into chilled cocktail glass.

Wallis Blue Cocktail

1 oz (2 Tbsp) gin
1 oz (2 Tbsp) blue curaçao
juice of 1 lime

Sugar-rim a chilled Old-Fashioned glass by rubbing with lime and dipping into sugar. Shake ingredients with ice and pour into the glass over ice cubes.

Wall Streeter

2 oz (4 Tbsp) gin
½ oz (1 Tbsp) white crème de menthe
2 tsp lemon juice
cold champagne

Shake first 3 ingredients with cracked ice and strain into chilled wine or champagne glass. Top with champagne.

--------- **Ward Eight** ---------

2 oz (4 Tbsp) rye whiskey
juice of ½ lemon
1 tsp sugar
½–1 tsp grenadine
slices of fresh fruit

Shake first 4 ingredients with ice and strain into a
large chilled wineglass over cracked ice. Garnish with
fruit and serve with a straw.

--------- **Warsaw Cocktail** ---------

1½ oz (3 Tbsp) vodka
½ oz (1 Tbsp) blackberry vodka
½ oz (1 Tbsp) dry vermouth
1 dash lemon juice
twist of lemon peel

Shake liquid ingredients with ice and strain into a
chilled cocktail glass. Garnish with lemon peel.

--------- **Washington Cocktail** ---------

1½ oz (3 Tbsp) dry vermouth
¾ oz (1½ Tbsp) brandy
2 dashes Angostura bitters
2 dashes sugar syrup

Stir ingredients with ice and strain into a chilled cocktail glass.

——— **Wassail Bowl** ———

(serves 8–10)

6 12-oz bottles of beer
1 cup sweet sherry
¼ lb sugar
1½ tsp nutmeg
1 dash ginger
slices of lemon

Heat the sherry and 1 bottle of beer but do not boil.
Add sugar and spices and stir until dissolved. Add
remaining beer and stir again. Let mixture stand at
room temperature for 2–3 hours. Pour into a punch
bowl, garnish with lemon slices, and serve in punch
cups.

Variation: garnish with several apples that have
been baked with sugar and spices.

——— **Waterbury Cocktail** ———

1½ oz (3 Tbsp) brandy
juice of ½ lime
½ tsp grenadine
½ tsp sugar
1 egg white

Shake ingredients vigorously with ice and strain into
a chilled cocktail glass.

Variation: sugar-rim the glass by rubbing with
lime and dipping into sugar.

——— **Watermelon Cooler** ———

½ cup diced watermelon (seeds removed)
2 oz (4 Tbsp) vodka

2–3 dashes grenadine
½ cup crushed ice
slice of lime or sprig of fresh mint

Put first 4 ingredients into a blender and blend at low speed until smooth. Pour into a chilled collins glass and garnish with lime or mint.

Variations: add ½ oz (1 Tbsp) lime juice and 1 tsp sugar. Substitute light rum for the vodka.

--------- **Watermelon Punch** ---------

(serves 28)

1 large watermelon
2 qts lemonade
1 qt vodka
2 cups melon balls
large container of crushed ice

Slice top third off the watermelon. Scoop out 2 cups of balls and set aside. Scoop out remaining meat and reserve. Refrigerate shell and balls. Press reserved watermelon meat through a colander or cheesecloth to obtain 2 cups juice. Combine juice, lemonade, and vodka and chill several hours. To serve, place watermelon shell in bed of crushed ice. Add vodka mixture and melon balls. Fill punch cups half-full of crushed ice and ladle in punch. Makes about 28 4-oz servings.

--------- **Webster Cocktail** ---------

1½ oz (3 Tbsp) gin
¾ oz (1½ Tbsp) dry vermouth
½ oz (1 Tbsp) apricot brandy
juice of ½ lime

(continued)

Shake ingredients with ice and strain into a chilled cocktail glass.

-------- **Wedding Belle Cocktail** --------

1 oz (2 Tbsp) gin
1 oz (2 Tbsp) Dubonnet
½ oz (1 Tbsp) cherry brandy
½ oz (1 Tbsp) orange juice

Shake ingredients with ice and strain into a chilled cocktail glass.

-------- **Wembly Cocktail** --------

1½ oz (3 Tbsp) gin
¾ oz (1½ Tbsp) dry vermouth
2 dashes apple brandy

Stir ingredients with ice and strain into a chilled cocktail glass.

Variation: add a dash of apricot brandy.

-------- **Western Rose** --------

1 oz (2 Tbsp) gin
½ oz (1 Tbsp) apricot brandy
½ oz (1 Tbsp) dry vermouth
1 dash lemon juice

Shake ingredients with ice and strain into a chilled cocktail glass.

--------- **Whip Cocktail** ---------

¾ oz (1½ Tbsp) brandy
¾ oz (1½ Tbsp) Pernod
¾ oz (1½ Tbsp) dry vermouth
¾ oz (1½ Tbsp) triple sec or orange curaçao
twist of orange peel

Stir or shake liquid ingredients with ice and strain
into a chilled cocktail glass. Garnish with orange peel.

--------- **Whiskey Cobbler** ---------

2 oz (4 Tbsp) bourbon
½ tsp sugar syrup
½ oz (1 Tbsp) orange juice
chilled club soda

Mix together syrup and juice and pour into highball
glass filled with cracked ice. Add bourbon and top
with soda. Stir gently and serve with pair of straws.

--------- **Whiskey Cocktail** ---------

2 oz (4 Tbsp) rye or bourbon
1–2 dashes Angostura bitters
1 tsp sugar syrup
maraschino cherry

Stir liquid ingredients with ice and strain into a chilled
cocktail glass. Garnish with the cherry.

Variation: substitute Scotch for the rye, eliminate
the sugar syrup, and add ½ oz (1 Tbsp) orange curaçao.

———— Whiskey Collins ————

See under *Tom Collins*.

———— Whiskey Flip ————

2 oz (4 Tbsp) rye or bourbon
1 whole egg
1 tsp sugar
nutmeg

Shake first 3 ingredients vigorously with ice and strain into a chilled cocktail glass. Sprinkle with nutmeg.

Variation: add 2 tsp cream.

———— Whiskey Frost ————

1½ oz (3 Tbsp) whiskey
1½ oz (3 Tbsp) medium sherry
1½ oz (3 Tbsp) port
½ tsp sugar syrup
lemon slice

In mixing glass stir liquors and syrup with several ice cubes. Strain into large Old-Fashioned glass filled with cracked ice. Garnish rim with lemon slice.

———— Whiskey Highball ————

Though this type of drink has been a longtime favorite, the term "highball" didn't become popular until the 1890s, when it referred to a mixture of Scotch and soda. "Ball" was a slang term for glass, and a *high*ball was a tall glass.

2 oz (4 Tbsp) rye, Scotch, or bourbon
chilled ginger ale or club soda
twist of lemon peel (optional)

Pour whiskey into a chilled highball glass over ice
cubes. Fill with ginger ale or soda and stir gently.
Garnish with lemon peel.

Presbyterian: use bourbon whiskey and half ginger ale and half club soda.

——— **Whiskey Sangaree** ———

See under *Sangaree.*

——— **Whiskey Sling** ———

See under *Sling.*

——— **Whiskey Smash** ———

See under *Smash.*

——— **Whiskey Sour** ———

The Whiskey Sour is one of the first of all the sours
and has gained such popularity that a specially
shaped glass has been named for it. It is also one of
the most basic of the classic drinks, containing only
whiskey, lemon, and sugar. It can be served with or
without ice but is most popular "up" (no ice). The
garnishes are also optional. Sours first became popular in the 1860s, when they were made with brandy.
The Whiskey Sour was introduced in 1891.

2 oz (4 Tbsp) rye whiskey
½–¾ oz (1–1½ Tbsp) lemon juice

(continued)

1 tsp sugar
maraschino cherry
slice of lemon or orange

Shake first 3 ingredients with ice and strain into a chilled sour glass. Garnish with the fruit.

Variations: various liquors can be substituted for the rye (rum, Scotch, bourbon, tequila, gin, or flavored brandies), and the sour is named for the liquor used (Rum Sour, Amaretto Sour, etc.).

———— **Whiskey Toddy, Hot** ————

See *Hot Toddy.*

———— **White Cloud** ————

1½ oz (3 Tbsp) Sambuca
club soda
lime slice or wedge (optional)

Put 2 or 3 ice cubes in a highball glass. Pour in Sambuca and fill with soda. Stir and garnish with lime.

———— **White Lady Cocktail** ————

2 oz (4 Tbsp) gin
¾ oz (1½ Tbsp) Cointreau
¾ oz (1½ Tbsp) lemon juice

Shake ingredients with ice and strain into a chilled cocktail glass.

Variation: add 1 egg white and shake vigorously.

--------- **White Lily** ---------

1 oz (2 Tbsp) gin
1 oz (2 Tbsp) rum
1 oz (2 Tbsp) triple sec
½ tsp anisette

Shake with cracked ice and strain into chilled cocktail or champagne glass.

--------- **White Lion Cocktail** ---------

1½ oz (3 Tbsp) light rum
juice of ½ lemon
1 tsp sugar
2 dashes Angostura bitters
2 dashes grenadine

Shake ingredients with ice and strain into a chilled cocktail glass.

Variation: substitute dark rum for the light. Substitute raspberry syrup for the grenadine.

--------- **White Rose Cocktail** ---------

1 oz (2 Tbsp) gin
½ oz (1 Tbsp) orange juice
½ oz (1 Tbsp) lime juice
1 tsp sugar
1 egg white

Shake ingredients vigorously with ice and strain into a chilled cocktail glass.

—————— **White Russian (Russian Bear)** ——————

2 oz (4 Tbsp) vodka
1 oz (2 Tbsp) white crème de cacao
2 tsp cream

Shake ingredients with ice and strain into a chilled cocktail glass.

—————— **White Spider** ——————

2 oz (4 Tbsp) vodka
1 oz (2 Tbsp) white crème de menthe

Stir ingredients with ice and strain into a chilled cocktail glass.

—————— **White Velvet** ——————

1½ oz (3 Tbsp) vodka
1 oz (2 Tbsp) white crème de menthe
½ oz (1 Tbsp) heavy cream
1–2 dashes orange bitters

Shake all ingredients briskly with several ice cubes and strain into chilled cocktail glass.

—————— **Why Not?** ——————

1 oz (2 Tbsp) gin
¾ oz (1½ Tbsp) apricot brandy
¾ oz (1½ Tbsp) dry vermouth
1 dash lemon juice

Shake ingredients with ice and strain into a chilled cocktail glass.

--------- **Widow's Dream Cocktail** ---------

1½ oz (3 Tbsp) Benedictine
1 whole egg
2 tsp cream

Shake ingredients with ice and strain into a chilled cocktail glass.

Variation: shake only the Benedictine and the egg and float the cream on top.

--------- **Widow's Kiss Cocktail** ---------

1½ oz (3 Tbsp) Calvados or other apple brandy
½ oz (1 Tbsp) yellow Chartreuse
½ oz (1 Tbsp) Benedictine
dash of bitters

Place all ingredients in shaker with 4 or 5 ice cubes. Cover and shake vigorously. Strain into chilled cocktail glass.

--------- **Wild Irish Rose** ---------

2 oz (4 Tbsp) Irish whiskey
½ oz (1 Tbsp) grenadine
juice of ½ lime
chilled club soda

Shake whiskey, grenadine, and lime juice with ice. Strain into a chilled highball glass over ice cubes and top with soda.

--------- **Will Rogers** ---------

1½ oz (3 Tbsp) gin
¾ oz (1½ Tbsp) dry vermouth

(continued)

¾ oz (1½ Tbsp) orange juice
2 dashes triple sec

Shake ingredients with ice and strain into a chilled cocktail glass.

——— **Woodstock** ———

1½ oz (3 Tbsp) gin
1 oz (2 Tbsp) lemon juice
2 tsp maple syrup
1 dash orange bitters

Shake ingredients vigorously with ice and strain into a chilled cocktail glass.

X

——— **Xanthia Cocktail** ———

1 oz (2 Tbsp) gin
1 oz (2 Tbsp) cherry brandy
1 oz (2 Tbsp) yellow Chartreuse

Stir ingredients with ice and strain into a chilled cocktail glass.

——— **Xeres Cocktail** ———

The name probably derives from the ancient name of Jerez, Spain, a city noted for its fine sherry.

2 oz (4 Tbsp) dry sherry
2 dashes orange bitters
2 dashes peach bitters

Stir ingredients with ice and strain into a chilled cocktail glass.

—————— **XYZ Cocktail** ——————

1½ oz (3 Tbsp) dark rum
¾ oz (1½ Tbsp) triple sec
¾ oz (1½ Tbsp) lemon juice

Shake ingredients with ice and strain into a chilled cocktail glass.

Y

—————— **Yacht Club Punch** ——————

2 oz (4 Tbsp) light rum
3 dashes Pernod
1 oz (2 Tbsp) lemon juice
½ oz (1 Tbsp) grenadine
chilled club soda
slices of fresh fruit

Shake rum, Pernod, lemon juice, and grenadine with ice and strain into a chilled collins or highball glass over shaved ice. Top with soda and garnish with fruit.

—————— **Yale Cocktail** ——————

1½ oz (3 Tbsp) gin
½ oz (1 Tbsp) dry vermouth
2 dashes orange bitters
2 dashes blue curaçao

Stir ingredients with ice and strain into a chilled cocktail glass.

Variation: substitute a dash of sugar syrup and a dash of maraschino for the curaçao.

——— **Yankee Clipper** ———

(serves 16–18)

2 qts rye whiskey
1 pt dark rum
½ cup sugar
4 qts water
1 lemon thinly sliced

Dissolve sugar in rum. Pour all ingredients over block of ice in large punch bowl and stir gently. Garnish with lemon slices.

Variation: substitute pineapple juice and/or soda water for 1 or 2 qts of the water.

——— **Yellow Bird** ———

2 oz (4 Tbsp) golden rum
½ oz (1 Tbsp) Cointreau
½ oz (1 Tbsp) Galliano
2 tsp lime juice

Place ingredients in blender with ½ cup cracked ice and blend at high speed 10–15 seconds, or just till ice is puréed. Pour into chilled sour glass and serve at once.

——— **Yellow Fingers** ———

1 oz (2 Tbsp) gin
1 oz (2 Tbsp) blackberry brandy
½ oz (1 Tbsp) banana liqueur
½ oz (1 Tbsp) cream

Shake ingredients with ice and strain into a chilled cocktail glass.

——— **Yellow Parrot Cocktail** ———

1 oz (2 Tbsp) yellow Chartreuse
1 oz (2 Tbsp) apricot brandy
1 oz (2 Tbsp) Pernod

Shake ingredients with ice and strain into a chilled cocktail glass.

Z

——— **Zaza Cocktail** ———

1½ oz (3 Tbsp) Dubonnet
¾ oz (1½ Tbsp) gin
1 dash orange bitters (optional)
twist of orange peel

Stir liquid ingredients with ice and strain into a chilled cocktail glass.

Variation: use 1½ oz (3 Tbsp) gin and ¾ oz (1½ Tbsp) Dubonnet.

——— **Zombie** ———

2 oz (4 Tbsp) light rum
1 oz (2 Tbsp) dark rum
½ oz (1 Tbsp) apricot brandy
juice of 1 lime
1 oz (2 Tbsp) pineapple juice
1 oz (2 Tbsp) passionfruit juice
1 tsp sugar
½ cup crushed ice
½ oz (1 Tbsp) 151-proof rum
slice of fresh pineapple and orange
maraschino cherry

(continued)

Put first 8 ingredients into a blender and blend at low speed until smooth. Pour into a chilled highball glass and float 151-proof rum on top. Garnish with fruit.

Variation: add a dash of Pernod or grenadine.

NONALCOHOLIC BEVERAGES

Recipes for some popular nonalcoholic "drinks" are given below. In addition, remember that most of the collinses, coolers, fizzes, eggnogs, etc., in the body of the book can be made without liquor.

———— Appleade ————

2 large apples, diced
2 cups boiling water
1 tsp sugar
slices of apple

Pour water over the apple pieces and add sugar. Strain and allow to cool. Pour into a highball glass over ice cubes and garnish with apple slices.

———— Bloody Shame (Virgin Mary) ————

6 oz tomato juice
½ oz (1 Tbsp) lemon juice
2 dashes Worcestershire sauce
2–3 drops Tabasco sauce
dash of celery salt
½ tsp sugar (optional)
salt and pepper to taste
stalk of celery

Shake first 4 ingredients with ice and strain into a large chilled wineglass. Sprinkle with salt, celery salt, and pepper. Garnish with celery stalk.

Variations: serve with ice cubes or at room temperature. Substitute Clamato juice for tomato.

Cherry Zest

1 cup orange juice
1 or 2 tsp maraschino cherry juice
½ orange slice
maraschino cherry

Pour liquids over ice cubes in chilled glass and stir.
Garnish with orange slice and cherry.

Cinderella

1 oz (2 Tbsp) lemon juice
1 oz (2 Tbsp) pineapple juice
1 oz (2 Tbsp) orange juice
1 dash grenadine
chilled club soda
slice of fresh pineapple

Shake juices with ice and pour into a chilled collins
or highball glass. Top with soda, add grenadine, and
garnish with pineapple.

Himbeersaft

1½ oz (3 Tbsp) raspberry syrup
chilled club soda
sprig of fresh mint

Pour raspberry syrup over crushed ice in a chilled
highball glass. Fill with soda and stir. Garnish with
mint and serve with a straw.

Johnny Julep

1½ oz (3 Tbsp) lemon juice
1 tsp sugar syrup
1–2 dashes Angostura bitters

ginger ale
maraschino cherry

Combine lemon juice, syrup, and bitters with cracked ice in a chilled highball glass. Fill with ginger ale and garnish with maraschino cherry.

Lemonade

juice of 1 lemon
2 tsp sugar
chilled water
slice of lemon
maraschino cherry

Mix lemon juice and sugar in a chilled collins glass. Add ice cubes and water and stir. Garnish with lemon slice and cherry.

Variation: add 1 egg yolk and shake.

Limeade

juice of 3 limes
3–4 tsp sugar
chilled water
wedge of lime
maraschino cherry

Mix lime juice and sugar in a chilled collins glass. Add ice cubes and water and stir. Garnish with lime wedge and cherry.

Pussyfoot

1 oz (2 Tbsp) lemon juice
1 oz (2 Tbsp) orange juice
1 oz (2 Tbsp) lime juice (optional)

(continued)

2 dashes grenadine
1 egg yolk
maraschino cherry

Shake first 5 ingredients with cracked ice and pour into a chilled wineglass. Garnish with the cherry.

——— Shirley Temple (Roy Rogers) ———

Primarily a children's drink, though some adults might like one, too. What you call it depends on whether it's being served to a girl or a boy.

chilled ginger ale
2 dashes grenadine
maraschino cherry
slice of orange

Put ice cubes into a chilled collins glass. Fill with ginger ale and add grenadine. Garnish with orange slice and cherry.

Variation: substitute 7-Up for ginger ale. If it's for a boy, you can also call it a Gene Autry or a Gordie Howe.

——— Spiced Cider ———

(serves 6–8)

1 qt cider
2 oz (4 Tbsp) brown sugar
4 whole cloves
cinnamon sticks (optional) or
powdered cinnamon

In a large saucepan, combine cider, sugar, and cloves and bring to the boil. Cool and refrigerate overnight or for several hours. Reheat before serving. Pour into coffee mugs and garnish each with a cinnamon stick or add a dash of powdered cinnamon.

——————— **Sunday School Punch** ———————

(serves 40)

A sprightly taste and enough for everybody.

juice of 12 lemons and 6 oranges
1 qt water
46-oz can pineapple juice
4 qts grape juice
sugar syrup to taste
3 qts ginger ale
crushed ice

In a 3 or 4 gallon container combine juices, water, and sugar syrup. When ready to serve, add ginger ale and stir. Ladle into glasses containing crushed ice. Makes about forty 8-oz servings.

——————— **Texas Sunshine** ———————

(serves 12–24)

A variation on old-fashioned lemonade.

1½ cups sugar
2½ cups water
juice of 6 lemons
juice of 2 oranges
juice of 2 limes
1 cup fresh mint leaves
2–3 qts club soda or water

Combine sugar and water in saucepan and bring to boil. Remove from heat and cool. Combine fruit juices and mint leaves and pour sugar syrup over the mix-

(continued)

ture. Let stand 1 or 2 hours, then strain and refrigerate. To serve, combine concentrate with 2 quarts water or club soda in punch bowl containing block of ice. Ladle into punch cups or water glasses.

──── Virgin Manhattan ────

"Virgin" as a prefix for any drink indicates that it contains no liquor.

¼ cup cranberry juice
¼ cup orange juice
½ tsp maraschino cherry juice
¼ tsp lemon juice
1–2 dashes orange bitters

Shake with ice, strain, and serve in a chilled cocktail glass. Or serve on the rocks in an Old-Fashioned glass. Garnish with maraschino cherry.

──── Virgin Mary ────

See *Bloody Shame.*

TYPES OF DRINKS

To facilitate the locating of a particular drink, many of the more popular recipes have been grouped together by their general type. The drinks listed under these general headings will be found in alphabetical order in the main body of this book.

Cobblers
Bourbon Cobbler
Brandy Cobbler
Champagne Cobbler
Cherry Cobbler
Claret Cobbler
Sherry Cobbler
Whiskey Cobbler

Coffees
Amaretto Café
Black Maria
Café Brûlot
Café Kirsch
Café Royale
Irish Coffee

Collinses
Apricot Anise Collins
Mint Collins
Tequila Collins
Tom Collins

Coolers
Applejack Cooler
Apricot Cooler
Blush Wine Cooler
Boston Cooler

Champagne Cooler
Cherry Brandy Cooler
Country Club Cooler
Harvard Cooler
Highland Cooler
Irish Cooler
Java Cooler
Kerry Cooler
Klondike Cooler
Mint Cooler
Orange Gin Cooler
Palm Beach Cooler
Rock & Rye Cooler
Sanibel Cooler
Tequila Cooler

Daisies
Gin Daisy
Rum Daisy
Star Daisy
Vodka Daisy

Eggnogs
Bourbon Eggnog
General Harrison's
  Eggnog

Fixes
Brandy Fix
Rum Fix

Fizzes
Alabama Fizz
All-American Fizz
Apple Blow Fizz
Apricot Fizz
Brandy Fizz
Buck Fizz
Cherry Fizz
Danish Gin Fizz
Derby Fizz
Dubonnet Fizz
Fraise Fizz
Gin Fizz
Ginza Fizz
Golden Fizz
Grand Royal Fizz
Imperial Fizz
Merry Widow Fizz
Morning Fizz
Morning Glory Fizz
New Orleans Gin Fizz
Orange Fizz
Ostend Fizz
Peach Fizz
Peach Blow Fizz
Pink Rose Fizz
Ramos Gin Fizz
Royal Gin Fizz
Silver Fizz
Snowball Fizz
Strawberry Fizz

Flips
Brandy Flip
Coffee Flip
Madeira Mint Flip
Port Wine Flip
Sherry Flip
Strega Flip
Whiskey Flip

Highballs
Bermuda Highball
Cablegram Highball
Cuba Libre
Gin & Tonic
Horse's Neck
Mamie Taylor
Spritzer Highball
Stone Fence
Whiskey Highball

Juleps
Brandy Smash
Champagne Julep
Creole Mint Julep
Jocose Julep
Mint Julep

Punches
Applejack Punch
Artillery Punch
Bacio Punch
Bellini Punch
Bombay Punch
Brandied Cranberry
  Punch
Brandy Punch
Brandy Milk Punch
Brandy Shrub

Cajun Party Punch
Cardinal Punch
Champagne Punch
Champagne Sherbert
  Punch
Cider Cup
Cold Duck
Cranberry Punch
Creole Champagne
  Punch
Fish House Punch
Glögg
Hot Spiced Wine
  (Vin Chaud)
Mothers Milk
Mulled Wine
Rum Punch I & II
Santa Clara Sangría
Sauternes Cup
Stirrup Cup
Sunday School Punch
Tea Punch
Tequila Punch
Texas Sunshine
Three Rum Punch
Tiger's Milk
Wassail Bowl
Watermelon Punch
Yacht Club Punch
Yankee Clipper

Rickeys
Gin Rickey
Sloe Gin Rickey

Slings
Brandy Sling
Gin Sling
Singapore Sling
Sling (Classic)

Sours
Apricot Sour
Boston Sour
Firemen's Sour
Frisco Sour
New York Sour
Whiskey Sour

Swizzles
Barbados Rum Swizzle
Gin Swizzle

Toddies
Hot Brick Toddy
Hot Gin Toddy
Hot Rum Toddy
Hot (Whiskey) Toddy

GLOSSARY

Absinthe
Illegal in the U.S. since 1912 because it was found to cause permanent mental deterioration, it may still be consumed legally in some countries, including Spain. In addition to wormwood, absinthe is made from star anise, licorice, and other aromatics. Too potent to be drunk straight, it is usually diluted with water, which changes its yellowish green color to milky white. Absinthe substitutes include anisette and Pernod.

Advocaat
A Dutch liqueur made with brandy, egg yolks, and sugar. It is similar in flavor to eggnog.

Ale
Similar to beer but with a more bitter, "heavier" taste, and a slightly higher alcohol content. See page 23.

Almond Syrup
See *Orgeat.*

Amaretto
An almond-flavored Italian liqueur made from apricots.

Amer Picon
A French brand of bitters that derives much of its flavor from gentian root and oranges. It is often served with water or club soda and ice.

Angostura Bitters
Made in Trinidad from a rum-spirit base, it has a bright-red color and is flavored with the bitter gentian root. Bitters are closely related to liqueurs, and a dash

357

or two are often added to a cocktail for zest. Angostura is the most popular brand of bitters.

Anisette
A French brand of licorice-flavored liqueur made from anise seed.

Apéritif
A drink taken before a meal to stimulate the appetite. See page 15.

Apple Brandy
See *Applejack; Calvados.*

Applejack
An apple brandy distilled from apple cider in New England and eastern Canada. It has a lighter flavor and aroma than Calvados.

Apricot Brandy
An unsweetened brandy made from the juice of apricots.

Apry
An apricot liqueur made by the Marie Brizard company.

Aquavit
Popular in the Scandinavian countries, it is similar to vodka. It is a high-proof neutral spirit made from grain or potatoes. Usually served chilled in small glasses, it is produced either unflavored or flavored with caraway, dill, or coriander.

Armagnac
Produced in the Armagnac region of France, it is one of the world's most popular brandies. Unlike Cognac,

which is double-distilled, Armagnac is distilled only once and gains much of its flavor through aging.

Beer
Most likely the first alcoholic beverage known to man, beer is produced by fermenting and aging a mash of malted cereal grain and hops. The wide variety of beers (lager, ale, stout, porter, malt, bock, and Pilsner) is due to variations in the fermenting process and alterations in the proportions of cereal and hops ingredients. See page 23.

Benedictine
An amber-colored French liqueur, it was invented in 1510 by Benedictine monks at the Abbey Fécamp. The carefully guarded secret recipe, which has a cognac base, contains at least 30 different aromatic plants. Benedictine is still manufactured at Fécamp, but no longer by the religious order.

Bitters
Closely related to liqueurs, bitters are neutral spirits flavored with roots, herbs, and fruits, particularly gentian and orange. The most popular brand is Angostura bitters.

Bourbon
An American whiskey (produced largely in Kentucky), it is distilled from a fermented mash of grain that must contain at least 51% corn. Aged in charred white oak barrels for at least two and up to four years, it is distinguished from rye whiskey by its high proportion of corn. *Straight* bourbon is generally fuller in flavor and body than *blended* bourbon, which is bourbon that has been blended with other whiskey or a neutral spirit.

Branch Water
Plain water, distinguished from soda water, mineral water, or the like.

Brandy
A distillation of the fermented juice of grapes or other fruits. Although made all over the world, the chief producers are France and the United States. When a fruit other than grapes is used, the type of fruit is used in the name of the brandy (apple brandy, cherry brandy, etc.). The best-known brandy is Cognac.

Byrrh (bir)
A French apéritif made from a red-wine base. It is dry and has a slight quinine and orange flavor.

Calisay
A mixture of herbs and quinine, this liqueur is a specialty of Catalonia, Spain. The recipe is said to have originated in Bohemia.

Calvados
An apple brandy made in the Normandy region of France. Considered the world's finest apple distillate, it is aged in oak for three to ten years before being blended and bottled.

Campari
A brilliant-red, dry Italian apéritif in the bitters category. It is commonly served on the rocks with club soda.

Canadian Whisky
Whisky made only from cereal grains, usually with large amounts of corn and some barley and rye. Canadian whisky is similar to American but lighter in body. The Hiram Walker Co. and Seagram are two of the largest Canadian distilleries.

Cassis (kă sēs')
A black-currant-flavored nonalcoholic syrup.

Champagne
A dry white wine that has been subjected to a second fermentation (in the bottle) to make it heavily carbonated and effervescent.

Chartreuse
An herbal liqueur made by Carthusian monks at Voiron, France. Green Chartreuse (110 proof) is the original recipe, dating from 1605 and containing 130 different herbs; yellow Chartreuse (80 proof) is honey-flavored and contains fewer herbs.

Cherry Brandy
A liqueur made from brandy flavored with cherries and produced in various countries throughout the world. The best known is Peter Heering, made in Denmark. Cherry brandy also refers to brandy distilled from cherries, such as kirsch. The best known is Cherry Heering, made in Denmark.

Cider
The pressed juice of apples. Hard cider is fermented and sometimes carbonated. Sweet cider is unfermented.

Cinzano
The name of an Italian manufacturer of vermouths.

Cobbler
A tall drink made with liquor or wine, fruit juice or soda, and a large quantity of crushed ice and usually garnished with fresh fruit. For an example, see *Sherry Cobbler.*

Coffee Brandy
An aromatic liqueur flavored by coffee beans. The flavors of the various coffee brandies are as distinctive as the various types of coffee beans. Two of the most popular coffee brandies are Kahlúa and Tia Maria.

Cognac
Brandy that comes from the area around the town of Cognac in southwestern France. Considered the most elegant of all brandies, it is distilled twice in pot stills and is always blended. Among the most popular brands of Cognac are Courvoisier, Hennessy, Bisquit, Rémy Martin, and Martell. Cognac labels carry initials: *V.S.*—Very Special (aged about five years); *V.S.O.P.*—Very Superior Old Pale (10–15 years); *V.O.*—Very Old (aged slightly longer than *V.S.O.P.*; it has a soft, woody flavor); *X.O.*—Extra Old; and *X.X.O.*—Extra Extra Old, which are very expensive and rare, having been aged as long as 50 years. The word "Napoleon" on the label means only that the Cognac has been aged at least five years and is considered a premium blend.

Cointreau (kwän'trō)
Probably the best-known brand of triple sec, it is a clear, orange-flavored liqueur.

Collins
A tall drink in which any liquor can be used along with lemon or lime juice and sugar. It is topped with club soda. For an example, see *Tom Collins,* the most popular collins drink.

Cooler
A tall drink made with a large quantity of crushed ice or ice cubes. Various liquors or wine can be used, along with a flavoring, and it is usually topped with

a carbonated beverage. A cooler is generally garnished with the peel of a fruit cut in one continuous spiral. For an example, see *Pineapple Cooler.*

Cordial
A synonym for liqueur. A cordial is usually sold under the name of its particular flavor (blackberry cordial, mint cordial, etc.).

Crème de Banane
A bright-yellow, sweet liqueur with a cream base and banana flavor.

Crème de Cacao
A chocolate-flavored French liqueur. It is a blend of cacao beans and vanilla flavoring and is available in white and dark brown.

Crème de Cassis
A sweet, black-currant-flavored liqueur from the Burgundy region of France.

Crème de Fraise
A strawberry-flavored liqueur.

Crème de Framboise
A raspberry-flavored liqueur.

Crème de Menthe
A sweet, mint-flavored liqueur, available in either clear or bright green. The clear, or white, is preferred when combining with other liquors.

Crème de Noyaux (nwä yō′)
An almond-flavored liqueur sometimes made with peach or apricot pits.

Crème Yvette (ē vet')
A very sweet violet-flavored liqueur made in the United States.

Cup
A type of drink containing wine or liquor, soda, fruit juices, etc., usually served from a pitcher to 4–6 guests. For an example, see *Champagne Cup*.

Curaçao (kōōr' ə sou)
An orange-flavored liqueur made from the peel of small, bitter oranges that grow in the Netherlands Antilles. It comes in a variety of colors including white, blue, green, and dark orange.

Daisy
A daisy is served over ice cubes and is made with a liquor, raspberry syrup (or grenadine), and fruit juice. For an example, see *Gin Daisy*.

Drambuie
A Scotch-based herbal liqueur made from Highland malt whisky, heather honey, and herbs.

Dubonnet
An aromatic French apéritif that is a blend of sweet red wine and quinine. There is also a dry blond version of Dubonnet manufactured in the United States.

Fernet-Branca
A very bitter herbal Italian apéritif.

Fix
A tall drink similar to a cobbler, in which sugar, water, and lemon juice are added to a liquor. For an example, see *Brandy Fix*.

Fizz
A tall drink in which a liquor, fruit juice, and sugar
are shaken together and strained into a glass over
ice cubes. It is topped with club soda. For an example, see *Gin Fizz.*

Flip
Similar to eggnog, a flip is a combination of liquor,
egg, and sugar shaken vigorously with ice and
strained into a stemmed glass. For an example, see
Sherry Flip.

Forbidden Fruit
A brandy-based American liqueur flavored with
grapefruit, orange, and honey.

Fraise (frez)
A nonalcoholic strawberry syrup.

Framboise (främ bwäz')
A nonalcoholic raspberry syrup.

Frappé
A short drink in which a liquor is poured into an Old-
Fashioned glass over shaved or crushed ice. It is
served with a short straw. For an example, see *Crème
de Menthe Frappé.*

Galliano
A honey-sweet, Italian liqueur that is bright yellow
in color and flavored with herbs.

Gin
Invented in the Netherlands in the 17th century, gin
is made from distilled fermented grains, chiefly rye but
also corn, barley, and oats, and is usually flavored
with juniper berries. Gin does not require aging and
can be drunk immediately, but some *London dry*

gins are aged, and the aging process gives them a pale golden color. All gins are dry, but there are distinctive characteristics about the three basic types. *London dry gin,* made principally in the United States, is the best known of all gins and is usually distilled from a mash composed mostly of corn. In addition to juniper berries, other botanicals are also added in varying proportions (caraway, cassis bark, angelica, licorice roots, etc.), and these flavorings account for the differences among the various brands. *Genever gin* is a Dutch gin with a strong malty aroma and is more heavily flavored with juniper than London dry. It is not aged, which accounts for its lack of color, and because of its strong aroma is usually drunk straight instead of being mixed in a cocktail. *Plymouth gin*, made solely in Plymouth, England, is somewhat sweeter than London gins, and its juniper flavor ranks midway between the other two types of gin. (The name "gin" is an anglicized and abbreviated form of *jenever*, one of the terms that the Dutch used for gin. The Dutch term is an altered form of the French *genièvre*, meaning juniper.)

Glögg (glōōg)
A Swedish hot punch.

Gomme Syrup
See *Sugar Syrup*.

Grain Alcohol
A nearly pure, colorless alcohol, usually about 180 proof. Also called pure grain alcohol.

Grand Marnier
A high-quality French liqueur with a Cognac base and orange flavor.

Grappa
The Italian name for a strong, pungent brandy that
is distilled from the pulp that remains after grapes
have been pressed and the juice drained off. Grappa
that has not been aged is extremely fiery; it mellows
slightly with age.

Grenadine
A sweet, nonalcoholic red syrup flavored with pome-
granate juice.

Highball
A long drink of whiskey or other liquor (approximately 2 oz) poured into a tall glass over 2 or 3 ice
cubes and topped with chilled soda water, branch
water, etc. For an example, see *Whiskey Highball*.

Irish Whiskey
Usually blended with any number of whiskeys from
other distillations to ensure smoothness and consistency of taste, Irish whiskey is distilled from a grain
mixture that is low in malted barley. It is cured over
charcoal to avoid the heavy flavor found in Scotch
whiskey.

Julep
A tall, mint-flavored drink served in a well-frosted
glass, often made of silver, pewter, or other metal. It
can be made with a variety of liquors, but bourbon
is traditional. For an example, see *Mint Julep*.

Kahlúa
A strong, sweet, coffee-based liqueur from Mexico. It
is not as dry or light as Tia Maria, which is made
from Jamaican coffee.

Kirsch (Kirschwasser)
A clear, cherry-flavored brandy made in the border region of France, West Germany, and Switzerland.

Kümmel
An herbal liqueur flavored with caraway.

Lillet (lē lā´)
A light, medium-dry, vermouth-type apéritif with a slight orange flavor, produced in France. The most common type is white, but there is also a sweeter red variety.

Liqueur
The term tends to be used interchangeably with *cordial* and refers to an alcoholic beverage (usually between 35 and 60 proof) produced by combining a distilled spirit with a strong flavoring, most often a sweetener. Liqueurs are also referred to as fruit brandies. Among the most popular liqueurs are those flavored with strawberries, oranges, and almonds, as well as various combinations containing chocolate, coffee, or mint. See also page 16.

Madeira
A wine fortified with brandy (added during the fermentation process) that is made on the island of Madeira off the northwestern coast of Africa. It is relatively sweet and is usually drunk as an apéritif or dessert wine.

Maraschino
A sweet, aromatic, cherry-flavored liqueur made primarily in Italy. It is available in either clear or dark red.

Metaxa
A strong, aromatic Greek brandy.

Mull
A warm drink, usually made in quantity, that contains wine, sugar, spices, and sometimes brandy. For an example, see *Mulled Wine*.

Orange Bitters
A dry, orange-flavored essence often used as a flavoring for cocktails.

Orange-Flower Water
A diluted preparation based on the oil of orange blossoms, used as a flavoring.

Orgeat (or zhä')
An almond-flavored, nonalcoholic syrup.

Ouzo (oo' zō)
An absinthe substitute made in Greece. It turns milky white when mixed with water or ice. Ouzo is drier than some absinthe substitutes.

Parfait d'Amour
A sweet, citrus liqueur flavored with essence of violets. It is usually purple in color.

Passionfruit
A sweet, citrus liqueur made in the Hawaiian Islands from the passionfruit. It has a peachlike flavor.

Pastis
An absinthe substitute, this liqueur has a more pronounced licorice flavor than Pernod.

Peppermint Schnapps
A mint-flavored liqueur similar to crème de menthe, but lighter and less sweet.

Pernod
An anise-flavored apéritif, it was the first absinthe
substitute and was named after Henri-Louis Pernod,
the first manufacturer of absinthe. It takes on a milky
appearance when mixed with water.

Peter Heering
See under *Cherry Brandy*.

Peychaud Bitters (pā shō')
A bitter apéritif, made in New Orleans and used to
flavor cocktails.

Pimm's No. 1
A cordiallike preparation having a gin base, the basic ingredient of the standard Pimm's Cup. Other
Pimm's have a base of whiskey (No. 2), rum (No.
3), or brandy (No. 4).

Port
A ruby-red, fortified Portuguese wine that is now also
manufactured elsewhere in the world. There are a
number of different brands and types, including a
white port. Brandy is added to the wine during the
fermentation process, and the wine is then aged in
casks or bottles. If aged less than 12 years it is called
ruby port; after 12 years of aging the wine is considered *tawny port*; after 15 to 20 years it is considered *vintage port*.

Puff
A drink of milk and liquor. For an example, see
Brandy Puff.

Punch
A drink that can easily be made in quantity to serve
large groups of people. Typically it contains liquor
(brandy, rum, vodka, etc.), fruit juice, and soda or

ginger ale. A recipe usually serves 8–12 persons, making it a simple matter to double or triple the recipe for large numbers. For an example, see *Champagne Sherbet Punch*.

Punt e Mes
A reddish-brown, yermouth-type Italian apéritif with sweet orange flavor.

Rickey
A tall drink consisting of liquor (traditionally gin but often rum, vodka, or sloe gin) and lime juice topped off with club soda. For an example, see *Gin Rickey*.

Rock & Rye
A citrus fruit liqueur made by steeping fruits in rye whiskey and sweetening with rock candy.

Rum
First manufactured in the West Indies in the early 17th century, rum is made from the distilled juice of sugar cane or, more commonly, from distilled molasses, a byproduct of sugar refining. Although it is now manufactured in many parts of the world, the chief producers are still in the West Indies. There are basically two kinds of rum: light and dark. *Light rum*, which is light-bodied and usually dry, comes mainly from Puerto Rico, Cuba, and the Virgin Islands. *Dark Rum*, which is heavier and full-bodied, is made mainly in Jamaica, Barbados, and Guyana. Variations within the two basic types are the result of the quality of the ingredients and the methods of fermentation, distillation, and aging. All rum is colorless when first distilled, and those that are aged for only a year are often artificially colored with caramel. Even the better rums that are aged in oak casks for up to 20 years (during which time they acquire some of their color) are sometimes subjected to artificial coloring.

Rye

Probably the first grain whiskey distilled in the United States, rye dates from the arrival of Scottish and Irish immigrants in Pennsylvania. It is distilled from a mash grain that contains at least 51% rye, filled out with barleys, corn, and oats. After fermentation the rectified (redistilled) spirit is barreled in charred white oak. Rye is almost always blended (combining the products of several distillations) for consistency of flavor and a wider appeal. However, there are a few brands of straight that have a devoted following.

Sake

Commonly referred to as "rice wine," this traditional alcoholic beverage of Japan is not a true wine because a raw material other than grapes is used. Sake is fermented from a mixture of rice and malted barley, and because the fermented beverage is colorless or amber-colored and slightly sweet, it resembles a wine in both taste and appearance.

Sambuca

An Italian liqueur flavored with anise. It is often served flamed with three or four coffee beans floating on the top.

Sangaree and Sangría

Sangaree is an older version of sangría. In Colonial days it was a mixture of red wine, fruit and fruit juice, sugar, and spices. For the basic recipes, see *Sangaree, Sangría*.

Scotch

Considered by many to be the finest whiskey in the world, it is produced only in Scotland. Distilled from fermented cereal grains, virtually all commercially available Scotches are *blends* of several different types and distillations. A high proportion of grain whisky from a patent still is blended with a quantity of full-flavored malt whisky. Scotch *malt whisky* has a unique smoky quality due primarily to the peat that is used to dry the malted barley.

Sherry
A fortified wine that originated in Spain, it is the product of fermented palomino grapes to which brandy is added during the fermentation process. Sherry comes in three varieties: *dry* (fino), *medium dry* (oloroso), and *sweet* (amoroso). The drier varieties are light in color and are usually drunk as apéritifs. Sweet sherry is darker, includes the heavily sweetened oloroso, or *cream*, varieties, and is generally drunk as a dessert wine.

Shrub
A drink of brandy, sherry, etc., in which fruit and often fruit juice have been steeped, often for several days.

Sling
A drink of liquor, sweetened and flavored with cherry brandy, grenadine, sloe gin, etc., with both lemon or lime juice and peel, and often stretched with club soda. For an example, see *Sling*.

Slivovitz
A rich, spicy, plum brandy made in Yugoslavia.

Sloe Gin
Not a gin, but a gin-based fruit liqueur flavored with sloes, the berries of the blackthorn.

Smash
A small-size julep served in an Old-Fashioned glass, usually containing brandy, gin, or whiskey. For an example, see *Brandy Smash*.

Sour
A classic mixed drink combining liquor, fruit juice, and sugar. For an example, see *Whiskey Sour*.

Southern Comfort
A whiskey-based American liqueur flavored with peaches. It was first made in New Orleans in the mid-1870s.

Stinger
A drink of brandy, rum, vodka, etc., flavored with white crème de menthe. For an example, see *Stinger*.

Strega
A sweet, spicy Italian liqueur similar to yellow Chartreuse and containing over 70 herbs.

Sugar Syrup
A syrup of sugar dissolved in boiling water.

Swedish Punch
A rum-based, spicy liqueur that is a traditional Swedish drink. It is sometimes mixed with hot water and drunk as a punch. Others prefer to drink it straight as a liqueur.

Tequila
The national alcoholic beverage of Mexico, it is a clear spirit distilled from the fermented mash of some species of the agave plant, usually maguey. A strong liquor, it is often drunk straight preceded by a taste of salt and followed by a taste of lemon or lime.

Tia Maria
A Jamaican liqueur made from fermented sugar cane and flavored with coffee. A little lighter and drier than Kahlúa, it has a slight hint of chocolate.

Toddy
A favorite bedtime drink or cold remedy, it consists primarily of a jigger or two of liquor (whiskey, rum, brandy, etc.) in a glass of hot water, sweetened, and often spiced with nutmeg or cinnamon or flavored with lemon peel. For an example, see *Hot Toddy*.

Triple Sec
A clear, orange-flavored liqueur, it is a type of curaçao. Cointreau is the best-known brand of triple sec.

Vermouth
An herbal wine fortified with brandy. Usually thought of in connection with a Martini cocktail, it is also used as an apéritif. *French* vermouth is light gold in color and has a dry, nutty flavor. *Italian* vermouth is dark red in color and has a sweet, syrupy flavor. Traditionally French vermouth is dry and Italian vermouth is sweet, however both countries produce the two varieties. *Bianco* vermouth, a compromise, is both white and sweet.

Vodka
The traditional alcoholic beverage of Russia, Poland, and the Baltic states, it is distilled from a variety of agricultural products (most often rye, corn, barley, wheat, potatoes, and, less frequently, sugar beets). The base from which vodka is made is not especially important because it is first distilled at or above 190 proof, which is almost pure alcohol This liquid is reduced to a marketable strength by the addition of distilled water. The most neutral of spirits, vodka does not have a distinctive aroma or a taste other than fiery hot. It is consequently popular as an ingredient in mixed drinks because it does not change the taste of the other ingredients (orange juice, tomato juice, etc.).

Whiskey

The distilled spirits of rye, corn, or other grain, usually containing about 40% alcohol (80 proof). In general, when a customer asks merely for "whiskey," the bartender will understand it to mean rye whiskey (blended type). "Whiskey" is the preferred spelling of the product distilled in the United States and Ireland. "Whisky" is the preferred spelling of the product distilled in Scotland and Canada.

Wine

The fermented juice of grapes, a favorite beverage of mankind for more than 6,000 years. As grape fermentation processes are relatively uniform, the particular character of a distinct wine depends primarily on the grape variety, the composition of the soil and the weather conditions where the grapes are grown, and the time of harvest. To produce *white* wine the grape skins are separated from the juice immediately after crushing; in the making of *rosé* wine the skins are usually allowed to soak in the juice for a day or two; in the production of *red* wine the skins are allowed to remain in the juice for two or three weeks during the fermentation process. All wines are then aged in wood before bottling, and aging continues in the bottle. Although not true wines, the fermented juices of other fruits are designated as wines and bear the name of their basic raw material (apple wine, plum wine, etc.).